CW00673772

THE FINAL CHOICE

THE FINAL CHOICE

DEATH OR TRANSCENDENCE?

by

MICHAEL GROSSO

www.whitecrowbooks.com

The Final Choice
Death or Transcendence?

Copyright © 2017 by Michael Grosso. All rights reserved.

Published and printed in the United States of America and the United Kingdom
by White Crow Books; an imprint of White Crow Productions Ltd.

The right of Michael Grosso to be identified as the author of this work has been
asserted by him in accordance with the Copyright, Design and Patents act 1988.

No part of this book may be reproduced, copied or used in any form
or manner whatsoever without written permission, except in the
case of brief quotations in reviews and critical articles.

For information, contact White Crow Books
at 3 Hova Villas, Hove, BN3 3DH United Kingdom,
or e-mail to info@whitecrowbooks.com.

Cover Designed by Butterflyeffect
Interior design by Velin@Perseus-Design.com

Paperback ISBN 978-1-78677-029-5
eBook   ISBN 978-1-78677-030-1

Non Fiction / Body, Mind & Spirit / Death & Dying / Philosophy

www.whitecrowbooks.com

Disclaimer: White Crow Productions Ltd. and its directors, employees, distributors,
retailers, wholesalers and assignees disclaim any liability or responsibility for
the author's statements, words, ideas, criticisms or observations. White Crow
Productions Ltd. assumes no responsibility for errors, inaccuracies, or omissions.

PRAISE FOR
THE FINAL CHOICE

In this well-documented, well-written book, Michael Grosso concludes that materialist science fails to grasp the fundamental nature of mind, or the importance of recent consciousness research on the immortal, transpersonal dimension of mind. His thesis: We urgently need a major transformation in human consciousness to change the way we live, and to survive as human on our endangered planet.

~ PIM VAN LOMMEL, CARDIOLOGIST, NDE-RESEARCHER,
AUTHOR OF *CONSCIOUSNESS BEYOND LIFE*

The Final Choice is nothing less than a mythopoetic manifesto. This book reads like a supranatural detective story, as we follow him from the ancient Greek philosophers to modern psi researchers, in search of evidence that might "jolt the collective unconscious into new forms of awareness." His research helps us envision a kind of new Manhattan Project, one that would unleash our deepest human potentials. The ominous sounding final choice turns out to be the most optimistic choice of all, which is to believe not in the demons of finality but in the angels of transcendence.

~ PHIL COUSINEAU, AUTHOR OF *DEADLINES: A RHAPSODY OF THE THEME OF FAMOUS LAST WORDS, THE ART OF PILGRIMAGE,* AND *THE ACCIDENTAL APHORIST*

"*THE FINAL CHOICE* offers the reader a myth as well as a logic for our time. Michael Grosso's concepts are original, thoughtful and provocative, presenting an alternative to the nuclear death dance which currently threatens our existence."

—STANLEY KRIPPNER, PH.D.,
PROFESSOR OF PSYCHOLOGY, SAYBROOK INSTITUTE

"Michael Grosso's book offers us an inspired—and inspiring—vision of the possibilities of human consciousness for planetary transformation as a direct response to the nuclear peril of our time. His message of hope is one that deserves to resound throughout the world—if we wish to preserve our world."

—Kenneth Ring, Ph.D.,
Author of *HEADING TOWARD OMEGA*

"Michael Grosso guides us on a rich intellectual and spiritual journey of transformation into deep inner space and proposes that the very 'threat of thermonuclear war is a spur to the evolution of human consciousness.' An impressive work with an argument for seeking our own power in the interface between life and death."

—Carmi Harari, Executive Director,
The Humanistic Psychology Center of New York

Behind each of us is an overwhelming charge able to bear down every resistance and clear the most formidable obstacles, perhaps even death.

—Henri Bergson, *Creative Evolution*

CONTENTS

PREFACE TO THE 2017 EDITION

I am grateful to Jon Beecher of White Crow Books for the chance to see my first book (1985) back in print, revised and updated. A great deal about the near-death experience and related forms of data have been added to our store of knowledge since that time.

One advance among researchers today is the growing chorus of voices willing to argue what is rank heresy to folks who call themselves *physicalists*: the belief that we are not just irreducibly mental beings but participants in the life of one great mind.

Among the educated classes today, this is not a popular piece of metaphysics. Nevertheless, more than ever I'm inclined to stand by this view. The concept goes back to the French philosopher, Henri Bergson, and much further back to the Upanishads.

More influential for me, however, have been sporadic paranormal experiences of my own, ranging from precognition to being physically attacked by a ghost in a haunted house.[1] In light of my own experiences, I am naturally more receptive to other people's initially queer-sounding stories.

The aim of this book is to show that in light of a large but academically ignored body of data, it is possible to create a new, fact-based mythology of transcendence.

What I mean by this is fairly precise. I underscore two aspects of transcendence: the survival of consciousness after death and, no less momentous, the idea of an extended *trans*personal mind. Pim Van Lommel calls it "endless consciousness" or following the Upanishads, Irwin Schroedinger referred to the *one mind*. Later, Larry Dossey coined the phrase "nonlocal mind" and has described in detail how we can make sense of being part of the one mind in his book of that title.[2]

This specific dual sense of transcendence is the core idea of the book. One key datum is the near-death experience, the discovery of a group of American scientists in the mid-1970s, perhaps the most important psychological phenomenon of the 20th century, as shocking and counter-intuitive as quantum mechanics and in a way comparable in potential to the "good news" associated with reports of the resurrection of Jesus—except that now we have millions of repetitions of the near-death experience (NDE), and can study and analyze it with the tools of science and other intellectual disciplines. The NDE experientially provides access to a greater mental, indeed *spiritual* sphere of being.

I wrote the *Final Choice* before Mikhail Gorbachev assumed power and instituted *glasnost* (openness) and *perestroika* (removal of barriers) in the Soviet Union. It was a period of acute awareness of the threat of nuclear war and, as it was carefully explained, the end of life on Earth—except maybe for the cockroaches.

The predicament of the great powers being able to arrange for mutually assured destruction (known as MAD), prompted me to wonder about the scope of human consciousness. Is our poor consciousness up to dealing with what we have created?

I looked around at our fear-and-greed driven world and thought that maybe something like the near-death experience could be the template for the needed transformation.

I found it helpful as a model for speculating on what might happen to consciousness in the event of a near or actual global disaster.

The question I kept asking: Are we approaching a time when events of such enormous proportions may jolt the collective consciousness into new forms of awareness, perhaps a more vivid sense of human solidarity?

As to my aim in this book: Evidence exists of an array of extended human capacities—intellectual, moral, aesthetic, mystical, and superphysical. In the interests of life at large, we need to focus on the skills and rich potentials that human beings possess and think of ways of mobilizing their creative uses. The times seem ripe for a new Manhattan Project about harnessing our neglected human potentials.

There are times of crisis and transition when breakthroughs to a larger frame of reference, a newer take on reality itself, can slip into focus, become viable, even inevitable. The discontents of civilization are finding their voices. Instability is magnified by information and communication technologies operating 24/7. Whatever the dynamic, it's being accelerated. The vaguest whisper of a thought can flash across the world at the speed of light.

We live in a strange time. Our fellows have unleashed destructive forces infinitely disproportionate to the moral IQ of the species. Nine nations on earth possess about 15 thousand nuclear weapons, most belonging to the United States and Russia. Such power in the employ of small groups of men or women of dubious mental and moral capacity is an unsettling thought.

Regarding the title of this book; it's rhetorical and meant to underscore the drama of the choices at stake today. In reality, there are no final choices. As long as we are conscious beings we are free to keep making new and hopefully better choices.

This book is a hybrid: part philosophical critique, part empirical review of human potential, and part exercise of active imagination.

INTRODUCTION

A MYTH OF LIFE BEYOND DEATH

Beneath the ceaseless changes of history, death remains a changeless fact of life. The fact is constant; the meaning varies from culture to culture and from age to age. We are at present living through a twilight of worldviews, and nobody quite has the answers, in spite of science, to the perennial questions and great mysteries of life and death.

Whether we see it as life's black hole or the gateway to another world, death remains the supreme mystery. The old stories have lost their hold on the minds of the educated classes, the old healing fictions that placed us in a universe with a plan and a way beyond the miseries of ordinary life. Part of the plan, we should note, was the assumption of an afterlife.

But as we know, the mythologies spawned by ancient tribal religions cannot stand up to the cosmology of modern science. Whole vocabularies and concepts like God, angel, immortality, soul, heaven, hell, ecstasy, prayer, miracle, sacred, and so on, have become automatically suspect. As a result of the enormous success of material science, such locutions are nowadays regarded as archaic, retrograde, and superstitious. This is more than an academic concern. It is, in fact, highly practical; for whole swathes of human experience end up being put down and relegated to metaphysical ghettoes.

But there are signs of discontent with the materialism of the ruling classes in many places. This book is born of that discontent. Resistance is evident in various ways ranging from the political to the spiritual. In this book, the resistance is philosophical: the aim being to gather materials for forging a new mythology of transcendence.

Myths are the maps we make to guide our gropings in a world riddled with uncertainties. Because we think, we reach beyond ourselves with difficult questions. We like the comforts of mundane life, but have inklings of cutting loose, of travelling toward parts unknown.

The medieval philosophers understood the need for the transcendent. All desires, they claimed—even the shady and disreputable ones—gravitate toward a source of ultimate satisfaction. We may pause in the evening at the inn; but by morning are back on the trail. Wisdom, they said, was to aim for this ultimate peak experience, to stay en route toward the ultimate encounter.

Born space travellers, our myths are the star crafts we use to explore the edge of reality. Inevitably, the great myths have been dying since the birth of modern science. Science has detailed maps of the atom, the human body, the earth, the forms of life, the stars, galaxies, black holes, and on and on. But it lacks even a rough map of the complex multiverse of mental life. Continents remain unknown and unexplored; huge sprawling terrains of meaning stand unseen and uncomprehended.

Yet this isn't quite fair. We have been given an implicit map, an unspoken myth, of what lies beyond by our highly successful, highly influential scientific materialists. Call it a one-dimensional myth that exalts the will to power and ends with the core image of nothingness waiting to swallow us up in the last act.

The steps by which we inherit the now dominant stripped-down worldview are well known. It's a familiar tale. Copernicus shattered our man-centered vanity by proving a sun-centered cosmology. The old Western myth of death, in Dante's *Divine Comedy*, had Earth as the center of the universe. The afterlife myths were tied to a discredited cosmology, and that seemed to doom them.

But every loss can lead to some gain. After the fall of the old mythologies, the wicked of the world could roam free from disquieting thoughts of hellfire. You may now pursue your earthly adventure unruffled by thoughts of posthumous justice. In their day, enlightened folk hailed the passing of the old hells as progress. Final causes became otiose, the world became a clockwork mechanism.

In Dante's now quaint universe, the motive force behind the stars was love; the end of the human adventure was consummate joy. In modern cosmology, love was knocked off its cosmic perch, then degraded to a dubious emotion with mixed after-effects.

Modern behaviorism carries on the reduction: banishing human consciousness *in toto*, along with soul, mind and spirit to the limbo of the meaningless. The old belief that human consciousness survived bodily death becomes increasingly near dead and nine-tenths buried. But the decimation goes on. Belief in the reality of mind was condemned as the error of ages. No question about it, science has opened up mind-boggling vistas of outer and micro-physical reality; but in the intoxication of discovery, the mysteries of inner space have been forgotten and their exploration reduced to nothing in the mainstream.

Copernicus, Galileo, Darwin, Freud, Watson and other masters notwithstanding, we are still perplexed before the mystery of life and the mystery of death. The subject seems unfairly to be ignored and even despised. What's lacking is a picture of the world that we can live with, a picture to guide us through a dangerous world with what used to be called wisdom, which is something different from information. Reductive science smothers us with machines and information, but is useless when it comes to matters of the heart or questions of the soul.

As for soul or *psyche*, I have learned much from depth psychologist, C.G. Jung (1875-1961) and psychical researcher, F. W. H. Myers (1843-1901). Jung brought to light the *transpersonal* dimension of mind, and believed that the health of the soul depended on contact with that deeper part of oneself. Myers used the term *evolutive* to mark the ecstatic-expansive propensities of consciousness, which also depended on creative "uprushes" from the "subliminal self."

Traditional societies instinctively evolved methods of engaging the subliminal or transpersonal part of ourselves. But a funny thing happened in the course of history. Scientific rationalism, as it evolved in Western history, cut us off from the deeper dimensions of reality, stripped the psyche down to the bare, solitary ego, leaving it to face existence and the specter of mortality. Death is demythologized and existence becomes meaningless. At the same time, some mythologies of death and the afterlife are retained and used by moral psychopaths to justify acts of shocking inhumanity.

The dominant scientific worldview does nothing for the manqué notion of spiritual reality. But the unpalatable truth is that it offers little of real material promise, real material joy, except for the rich and powerful minorities. Materialism as a philosophy works well for technocrats, capitalists, hedge-fund manipulators, and in general for the rich and powerful.

What's at stake is not an academic matter. To revise our existential mythology and renew our vision of what it means to be human is no small thing. A new mythology of transcendence touches on the deepest needs of human being.

The Russian sociologist, Pitirim Sorokin, wrote in the 1920s that the West was a disintegrating sensate culture on the threshold of becoming a new "ideational"[3] culture. In effect, he foretold the near-death experience of our sensate civilization. A dangerous transition, we will need to enlist the aid of a new conception of spiritual reality. Key is to move beyond one-sided parochialism toward a creative synthesis of science *and* religion, art *and* technology, reason *and* intuition, personal *and* social, masculine *and* feminine.

But instead of conjunction now, we have a world wrestling with disjunction. Divisions are magnified. There is talk of a new cold war. Arming the world with increasingly destructive military technologies is accelerating. Meanwhile, climate catastrophe is gaining on us. An abundance of facts and much very obvious testimony prove it is for real, and by no means a hoax invented by the Chinese.

Oh those pesky facts, like Antarctica melting and 2016 being the hottest year on record. 97 percent of climatologists believe the climate is warming up because of human activity, due to CO_2 saturating the Earth's atmosphere. Since 1950 the level of carbon dioxide has been steadily rising beyond a baseline that had persisted for 400,000 thousand years of terrestrial history. We are approaching a point where sudden, potentially irreversible changes will cause massive disruptions of societies and ecosystems. If nothing is done about it, climate change will destroy civilization. No wonder the scientists keep pushing the hands of the Doomsday Clock toward midnight.

Two historical vectors are converging: thanks to the scientific sabotage of traditional religion, people are at an all-time low as far as inner resources for coping with disaster and mortality. At the same time, scientific ingenuity, serving the ambitions of state and capitalism, has created the most diabolical weapons of mass destruction in world history. The combined risks are real and not likely to diminish, especially in light of growing economic instabilities everywhere. The world is increasingly on edge and getting crowded. As a species we need to wake up and unite in an effort to change ourselves and save the world.

The Quixotic Hope of this Book

Here is my guiding intuition. I aim to draw a picture of the greater mind, which, after Aldous Huxley, I sometimes call *Mind at Large*. In the scientific mainstream, just to posit a personal mind is suspect; in my view we have to move much further. There is, in fact, evidence for the reality of a greater mind (boundaries unknown), in which each of us may be thought to participate. Both argument and empirical data justify the working assumption that our individual selves are grounded in an extended sphere of mental life.

I draw on consciousness research, data from history, medicine, anthropology, mysticism, and psychical research to explore the concept of an expanded mental life. I will for short use the letter *psi* (first letter of the Greek word *psyche*) to denote the entire spectrum of paranormal phenomena, extrasensory perception and psychokinesis. I mean to use this material to address the need to enrich a new healing mythology of life and death.

Part 1 covers the Crisis.

In this Introduction we are setting the stage, reminding ourselves that the time has come to create a new story or reinvent the old ones.

Chapter 1 looks at the credentials and underpinning of the story we want to tell. This will involve reference to matters of fact often neglected by mainstream scientists and theologians. These raw often strange givens form the bedrock of further speculation and experimental potential.

Chapter 2 reminds us that other times and cultures are more forthright in dealing with taboo subjects such as death. In a culture based on the denial of death, we will, however, look back at some classic "death-crafts" such as Plato's in the *Phaedo* and the Tibetan Bardo Thodol that so inspired Carl Jung.

Chapter 3, "Repressing Immortality" details the resistance to expanded conceptions of consciousness.

Part 2 covers the Potential to respond.

Chapters 4 and 5 are about out-of-body experiences (OBEs) and near-death epiphanies (OBEs), controversial insofar as they transcend the remit of neuroscience. In these widely reported strands of human experience, we have some building blocks for a post-materialist myth of extended human capacity.

Chapter 6, "The Cosmic Detective Story" offers some general remarks and some case histories, bearing on the postmortem fate of our interior life. The extent of our mental outreach is unknown, but people have experiences that seem to point to different zones, layers, dimensions of consciousness. The most dramatic "zone" would reach into another—the "next" world.

In Chapter 7 we come to the core idea of an archetype of death and enlightenment (ADE). This is meant to suggest the wider hypothesis of a collective psychism that links breakdown to breakthrough. Evidence for this lies in mystical experience, ancient mystery rites, visionary and high dream life, and other phenomena. This chapter draws on the archetypal psychology of C. G. Jung. Jung's work is about special images and imagination, and relates to Vico's philosophy of imagination as the driving force of history.

Part 3 covers the Transformation.

Chapter 8 takes us into the endgame of our inquiry. A global near-death experience? That is the question. It may be hard to wrap our heads around it, but we have entered an age when public intellectuals like Noam Chomsky are discussing the real and present danger of the total collapse and destruction of the world-system, and even the end of most higher forms of life on Earth. We look at the issues here and ponder the question of what might happen to human consciousness, as it faces off against these mounting, unprecedented dangers.

Chapter 9 is a response to Chapter 8. It sketches a phenomenology of what I'm simply calling helping visions. Reported throughout history, they cover a wide range of experiences: St. Paul en route to Damascus, the voices of Joan of Arc, helpful apparitions of the dead, benign hallucinations of the mad, and so on. The point is to describe what appears like a higher-order intelligence built into the deep structure of the human mind. We perhaps under-utilize this subliminal resource, although people do attempt to utilize it through prayer.

Chapter 10 continues to focus on types of visionary experience that suggest the presence of benevolent agencies at large: Near-death experiences, NDEs; unidentified flying objects and visitors, UFOs; and visions of the Blessed Virgin Mary, sometimes referred to as BVMs. Something seems to be coming from outside the parameters of normal existence, apparently on a mission to expedite human enlightenment and transformation.

In Chapter 11 we explore the idea of creative truth. In building a new, more human and democratic civilization, scientific, quantitative truth is not enough. The facts and technological wonders of science are spiritually inert and passive. What we do with our material science is not something we can decide based on material science. For this we need the creative truths of the moral, aesthetic, and spiritual imagination. The inconvenience is that Science has undermined the very idea of spiritual truth.

In the Coda, we call for an awakening of this mysterious creative spirit, which resists the alliance of heartless materialism and inhuman power.

Part One: The Crisis

I

SKETCH OF A SCIENCE OF TRANSCENDENCE

It is true that advance is partly the gathering of details into assigned patterns. This is the safe advance of dogmatic spirits, fearful of folly. But history discloses another type of progress, namely the introduction of novelty of pattern into conceptual experience. There is a new vision of the great Beyond.

—ALFRED NORTH WHITEHEAD

The Riddle of the Sphinx

The curious center of experience I call myself—will it cease and come to nothing with the death of my body? Or will it flicker on and even know a greater life? Does our center of awareness persist, contract, or widen perhaps as Plato and Bergson thought; grow more dull or more brilliant; divide by fission into a plurality or fuse in new ways with other centers of consciousness?

The survival problem raises the riddle of the Sphinx, the riddle of what it is to be a person, treated by analytic philosophers as a puzzle about personal identity, and by the rishis of the Hindu Upanishads as an experiment in the pursuit of higher consciousness. The modern scientific answer to the riddle is well known:

A human being is a physical object, unique in many remarkable ways, but essentially a complex machine. The language of mind, soul and spirit is treated as a hold-over from folklore. And to say that human consciousness survives bodily death is treated as barely thinkable. I as a person can no more be separated from my body, it is said, than roundness can be separated from the penny in my pocket.

But the evidence of psychical research—especially the more challenging survival data—clashes with this orthodox answer to the riddle. There are too many facts that contradict the prevailing one-dimensional view of the Self.

The Origins of Psi Science

The English origins of psychical research in 1882 were linked to a quest for evidence of life after death. Along the way the researchers discovered many things about the depth and complexity of the subliminal self—before Freud's work. Frederic Myers, for instance, wrote in his great work, *Human Personality and Its Survival of Bodily Death*:

> The 'conscious Self' of each of us, as we call it,—the empirical, the supraliminal Self, as I should prefer to say—does not comprise the whole of the consciousness or of the faculty within us. There exists a more comprehensive consciousness, a profounder faculty, which for the most part remains potential only so far as regards the life on earth, but from which the consciousness and faculty of earth-life are mere selections, and which reasserts itself in its plenitude after the liberating change of death.[4]

Myers called this "more comprehensive consciousness" the subliminal Self— an idea close to that of Jung's objective psyche or Self. These terms are reincarnations of the older, religiously derived, soul, a word rejected by scientific orthodoxy. The work of Myers and the early psychical researchers, and the more recent work of Jung speak to the empirical reality of the world-old idea of the soul.

The overarching concern of the early psychical researchers was to found a new science of the soul. As Myers wrote on the first page of his magnum opus, the method of science "has never yet been applied to the all-important problem of the existence, the powers, the destiny of the human soul." Scientific research like this is still somewhat of an outsider, on the fringe of respectability. Still, a steady if sparse stream of researchers has increased the stores of our knowledge.

Transcendent Psi

At first glance, the function of psychic "abilities" is not clear. There are no physical organs associated with them and no real evidence that we can learn to use our psychic abilities in any practical and reliable fashion.

Suppose that the primary function of psi in nature is to mediate an order of reality different from our embodied existence. The consistent elusiveness of these abilities would begin to make more sense. If the function of psi is essentially otherworldly, then we shouldn't be surprised how transient and marginal the effects tend to be in our worldly environment.

We normally rely upon the sensory-motor system for engaging the material environment. Psi's day-to-day survival value in the terrestrial struggle for existence seems to be slight and inessential. The function, in fact, seems to be more about reminding us of our transcendent potential than, say, winning the lottery or making a killing on the stock market. It seems in fact to transcend worldly needs and points toward some dimension the beyond.

What at bottom drives all living things? The goal of life seems to be more life, self-replication with infinite variations. The life process consists of the reproduction, expansion and increasing complication of its genetic legacy. The tendency among mammals, and humans in particular, is toward greater mobility, freedom, and detachment from the environment. Human life is especially mobile and already has begun to move beyond the planetary habitat to explore outer space habitats.

If the goal of life is more life—in a word, survival—the function of our nonphysical psychic potential may be to mediate survival of bodily death. The spiritual world would name the stage where the evolution of life transcends the physical environment. If the goal of life is more life, higher, freer, more complex forms of life, then our psychic potentials represent the power of life transcending its biological template. Psi is the wedge of life driving against the constraints of physical reality, against the boundaries of time and space. Psi is the medium in which new forms of life carry us beyond the boundaries of physical environment.

Human existence is amphibian. As bodies we adapt to the earthly environment; as psi-mediated minds or spirits we shift toward *another* environment, a place free from the limits of time and space. Religion, spirituality, the arts are so many bridges we are trying to cross over into new worlds.

Gardner Murphy, the American psychologist, wondered why, on Darwinian principles, living organisms don't develop increasing psi ability, which would be of great survival value. For instance, an animal in its effort to escape a predator could use a little psi mojo. If psi ability were genetically coded, moreover, we would expect natural selection to work toward a growing incidence of its manifestation, at least among some lucky species.

But there is no evidence of psi becoming a biologically stronger function; further, the consensus among parapsychologists is that psychic ability, unlike most normal psychological abilities, is virtually unlearnable. In fact, almost all the empirical evidence indicates that psychic abilities decline with use; one of the most reliable bits of knowledge about psi functioning is enshrined in the expression, "decline effect." Psi functions in a way that seems to be almost inversely proportional to normal biological utility. Gardner Murphy is right, then, in speaking of psi ability as a "profound biological enigma."[5]

Driven by the paradox of this biologically quirkish psi function, Murphy goes on to speculate that "behind these apparently capricious expressions of a power beyond the ordinary, there is good reason to believe that there exists a deeper level of function, a level at which, perhaps, the paranormal is the normal."

He suggests that there are two modes in which an organism can function: one, the sensory mode, in space and time; another, the psi mode, independent of space and time. In the deeper psi mode, the paranormal is the normal, but this could only be a mode in which the sensory mode were suspended or, as in death, superseded. The psi that appears fitfully and elusively in the terrestrial environment would represent the threshold to the transcendent environment.

The English psychologist, John Beloff, remarked: "There is an evolutionary niche to correspond with almost every conceivable mode of life on Earth and yet, so far as we know, there is no species which depends critically on using extrasensory perception. One is entitled to ask why, if psi is a reality, it has not been exploited in the struggle for existence."[6] Like Murphy, Beloff was puzzled by the biological enigma of psi. How indeed does psychic ability stand with respect to the phenomenon of life?

Natural Selection

The presence of a psychic dimension in nature must fit into the picture of organic life. Some have thought about the implications of psi for the science of life. Others have seriously questioned the validity of the mainline scientific view of life. One outstanding example is Thomas Nagel's *Mind and Cosmos* (2014). If we cannot explain consciousness physically, and consciousness is a feature at least of higher life forms, then the Darwinian account falls short. It fails to account for the greatest mystery of evolution: consciousness.

An attempt to connect psi with the science of life came at the very beginning of modern evolutionary theory. Alfred Russell Wallace, a co-founder of the modern theory of natural selection, was an earnest researcher into supernormal phenomena, even before the founding of the English Society for Psychical Research. In 1874 Wallace observed that natural selection "is not the all-powerful, all-sufficient, and only cause of the development of organic forms." In the Tenth Chapter of his *Contributions to the Theory of Natural Selection*, he cites certain residual phenomena which he thought might be accounted for by psychic factors or, as he said, the operation of "preternatural intelligences."

Wallace describes how by education and temperament, he was exposed to the most hard-boiled materialism. However, he admits that he became acquainted with certain facts that "beat" him. Some of the facts concern the physical mediumship of Mrs. Guppy, a lady whose psi feats gave pause even to the redoubtable skeptic, Frank Podmore. Thus, psi and biological theory were linked from the very start, as may also be seen from Carl du Prel, the early investigator who coined the word "parapsychology." He believed that the next step of human evolution lay in the sphere of psychic development.

English biologist, John Randall, speculates on the parapsychology of life.[7] Randall's strategy was at first to review challenges to Darwinian orthodoxy. He then cites experimental evidence for the influence of psi on living systems. He posits a transcendent psi factor—Randall also calls it Mind at Large. (We children of Aldous Huxley.) This may be the agency that accounts for aspects of life unexplained by reductive orthodoxies. Randall rejects the orthodox view that life on Earth is a by-product of chance. He questions the idea that the immensity of the earth's age renders the chance hypothesis of life's origin automatically plausible. Randall was struck by the gaping discontinuity between life and non-life, and between the not conscious and the conscious.

There are other discontinuities that prompt us to philosophic wonder. Pride of place belongs to the discontinuity between nonbeing and being itself. Why is there something rather than nothing? This may not be a practical question, but asking it arouses a sense of metaphysical amazement.

William James called it "ontological wonder sickness." We are face to face with the ultimate discontinuity. The leap from non-being to being. The traditional way is to invoke a transcendent principle, like God; the scientific response calls it a pseudo-question. There are, of course, other discontinuities, between life and non-life, for example, and conscious from not conscious. It's enough to give you an ontological headache! The mystery of being, of life, and of consciousness.

Does Life Really Need Consciousness?

As with psi, one wonders about the biological utility of consciousness, especially if one says with biologist John Maynard Smith that "The individual is simply a device constructed by the genes to ensure the production of more genes like themselves."[8] Why then have we evolved our intrusive and endlessly problematic consciousness? Surely we don't need consciousness to "ensure the production of more genes".

One wonders about the higher states of consciousness. The heroic self-denial and self-transcendence of saints, yogis and bodhisattvas are hard to see as biologically adaptive. Least adaptive is the conscious refusal to replicate. Yoga, as Mircea Eliade[9] notes, is the willed suspension of all vital functions: thought, breath, sexual impulse. Indeed, the ethics of many (not all) spiritual masters is transbiological. It is oriented toward "overcoming" the world, which can mean discreetly in private ecstasies or radically, by rearranging, challenging, subverting the natural order.

This is hard to understand as the product of a genetic device "constructed" for the sake of replicating itself. It is hard to see such spiritual behavior as adaptive to biological existence in any obviously natural sense. It embraces what is natural but in such a way as to transfigure it.

Life is not a conservative principle. It looks as if some creative principle was using the forms of life not just to maintain the status quo but for the sake of evolving into more complex forms and extended environments. Von Bertalanffy writes that the Darwinian concept of fitness "is the projection of the sociological situation of the nineteenth and early twentieth centuries into two billion years of the earth's history" and adds that "evolution appears to be more than the mere product of chance governed by profit. It seems a cornucopia of *evolution creatrice*, a drama full of suspense, of dynamics and tragic complications."[10]

Natural selection plays a part in evolution, but fails to account for the upward drift of life. Says John Randall: "Whereas Darwinian selection will account for many of the differences between varieties of the same species (microevolution), it is difficult to see how it can account for the emergence of entirely new species." Orthodox Darwinians explain new species as the result of one species splitting up geographically. But splitting may explain how one species becomes two but not how one becomes more highly organized.

The concept of natural selection is suspiciously unfalsifiable, and thus not a scientific hypothesis. If we observe a biological change as adaptive, it can always be said to be naturally selected. Natural selection seems more descriptive than explanatory.

Morphogenesis

If there's anything we could call *miraculous*, it is the unfolding of the micro-fertilized egg into a full-blown organism. Does the chemistry really explain morphogenesis? Or the fact that the form is maintained in spite of lacerations to the embryo, Hans Driesch's maimed sea-urchin embryos being the classic experimental example. Damaged structures are restored. Flat worms divide into parts, which develop into new flat worms; this is another puzzle of morphogenesis.

Even more problematic, though highly controversial, would be instances of paranormal regeneration of living organs. Some well-documented instances of this phenomenon have been recorded at Lourdes and in connection with Padre Pio (now saint), the stigmatist of San Giovanni Rotonda.[11]

Bergson wrote in 1907 that mechanism would be hard to accept if "it could be proved that life may manufacture the same apparatus, by unlike means, on divergent lines of evolution."[12] Yet in *On Growth and Form*, D'Arcy Thompson describes how shapes of animals in the same zoological group express variations of a constant, mathematically defined form. The changes in form seem due less to pressures from the external environment than to the unfolding of an "internal" plan or archetype.

The biologist Sir Alister Hardy confirmed Bergson's philosophic intuition when he said that the "concept of homology in terms of similar genes handed on from a common ancestor has broken down."[13] Thus, the pentadactyl limb pattern is found in the arm of a man, a bat's wing and a whale's flipper. On mechanist principles, such homologous structures must derive from the same gene-complex, but Morgan's experiments with the fruit fly Drosophila demonstrate that homologous organs can be produced from different gene-complexes or different species.

In these remarkable experiments, pure eyeless alleles of the fly are inbred; nevertheless, perfect eyes are formed after a short while, available genes recombining to "deputize" for the missing gene. Randall, Koestler and others take this to imply the existence of an overall plan acting upon the "eyeless" genetic materials.

In 1981 Rupert Sheldrake published *A New Science of Life*, which calls attention to the shortcomings of the mechanist account of morphogenesis. Developing systems are explained by genetic programmes, but Sheldrake argues that genetic programmes imply goal-directedness, that is, teleological causation. Writes Sheldrake:

> The concept of genetic programmes is based upon an analogy with the programmes that direct the activities of computers. It implies that the fertilized egg contains a pre-formed programme which somehow specifies the organism's morphogenetic goals and coordinates and controls its development towards them. But the genetic programme must involve something more than the chemical structures of DNA, because identical copies of DNA are passed on to all cells; if all cells were programmed identically, they could not develop differently.

Sheldrake goes on to postulate falsifiable nonmechanist hypotheses concerning the nature of life, calls attention to the challenge of psi and reckons (like Randall) on the hypothesis of a transcendent causal factor as one way of making sense of the phenomenon of life.

Psi in Evolution

Any attempt to form a revised picture of evolution might ask whether the rogue psi-factor of nature links up in any way. Randall and the American parapsychologist, Robert Morris, provide reviews of the literature, experimental and anecdotal. For our purpose, we note with Randall that evidence suggests a psychic "force" capable of influencing cell division and enzymatic activity, both basic biological processes. We have Sister Justa Smith's experiments with a healer who activated the enzyme trypsin and Bernard Grad's experiments in which a healer increased the healing rate of wounded mice tissue and the growth rate of barley seeds. Grad viewed his results as confirming Henri Bergson's speculations on the existence of a life force, or, as we might say, *psychokinesis*.

The possible role of psi in evolution is indicated when we consider that mutations may arise from single microphysical events. As Von Bertalanffy put it: "As can be shown by mathematical analysis of the experiments, one single hit into the sensitive zone of a gene suffices to cause a mutation. Therefore, the induction of mutations is subject to the statistical law of microphysics." This increases the theoretical plausibility of psi-induced mutations. Conscious or unconscious intentionality might act on the "sensitive zones" in a gene.

The plausibility is further increased by recent discoveries in genetics. In the late 1970's, Pierre Chambon of the Louis Pasteur University in Strasbourg discovered that genes may be split into sections of "nonsense DNA" called "introns." What the purpose of these introns is, and how they are spliced out by RNA, is not yet known; though some geneticists were quick to see that the "nonsense" or indeterminate genetic structures might offer opportunities for rearrangement in the evolutionary process.

Now, it is known that psychokinesis works best on indeterminate systems, i.e., on dice in motion rather than on dice sitting in a stable position. Introns are the indeterminate material of the genetic structure and thus make more suitable targets for psychokinetic action. Introns, the random sequences in genetic materials, may be the target sites of microphysical psi-induced mutations.

Given the gaps in mechanist biology and the experimental evidence that psi influences living systems, Randall states: "There is at least a possibility that parapsychology has discovered the missing factor needed to construct a general theory of life." Randall outlines several possibilities. The most fundamental and radical is that of a psi-factor he calls Mind at Large. Mind at Large intervenes at critical junctures: for instance, the origin of life, the development of new and higher species, instances of "paranormal" healing and in other circumstances where we observe psi at work. For Randall, this hypothesis is a kind of neo-vitalism empirically backed by the data of parapsychology.

Randall is clear that Mind at Large is not the traditional Western idea of God, which implies perfection. Randall's transcendent mind is more like an experimental artist-God who makes mistakes and scratches them out, discovering what it creates as it goes along.

While it would be a mistake to anthropomorphize this floating and unpredictable Mind Factor and suppose that its mode of consciousness, purpose and intelligence were merely an enlarged replica of our own, there is some comfort in the thought that being mental, it may be possible to engage Randall's Mind at Large in some type of meaningful dialogue.

Psi and Life After Death

Back to John Beloff's question: if psi is a reality, why is it not exploited in the struggle for existence? Psi may indeed come into play in the struggle for existence under special circumstances. But its overall function, if I understand Randall, is to direct and oversee the upward thrust of the evolutionary process and to maintain the total balance and ecology of life. Robert Morris suggests a number of ways this might happen, as a "homeostatic regulatory device" among populations; Morris is also led to consider the possibility of a "supra-intelligent regulatory aspect in psi functioning . . ."

The function of psi may be to mediate the origin, evolution and regulation of life, though the sheer maintenance of life, the conservative mechanisms, would be governed by the laws of chemistry and physics. Since the mass of observable life processes is conservative, mechanists can suppose they hold the key to understanding all of life. That is, as long as they ignore the discontinuities: the mysteries of creativity, mystical states, and phenomena described as paranormal or supernormal.

How does this relate to the survival problem? The need of life to transcend the physical environment as such. There are signs of transcendence and transformation. Technology is the most obvious expression of the will to dominate matter, to make matter plastic, malleable, and transparent to the aims and whims of consciousness. Space travel, genetic engineering, satellite television, the giant computers, the great microscopes and telescopes, cyberspace, every technical instrument, every machine speeds up the psychosocial evolution of the body. It's always finding new ways of escaping the constraints of the physical.

18

In this sense, technology is the material analogue of spiritual transcendence, a techno-expression of the Incarnation, of the quest for freedom from death and finitude. Given the quite shocking super-ingenuity of consciousness to master, subdue, deform or reform the home planet, why should its evolutionary conatus toward unlimited life stop short with the death of the body?

If there is an extended mental factor that somehow pervades and perhaps regulates biological evolution, as Randall, Morris, and Sheldrake suggest, the plausibility of post-biological survival increases. Whatever bears the life-originating information might well survive the life-bearing vehicle.

Pre-adaptation

There is a problem for the mechanist theory of evolution— pre-adaptation, the emergence of structures before they are used. Pre-adaptation, says G. R. Taylor, "completely explodes the theory of natural selection."

For example, a tree-climbing apparatus developed in frogs before they began to climb trees. Or, as expert on the biology of amphibians, G. Kingsley Noble, says: "A detailed analysis of the many 'marvelous adaptations' in the Amphibia will reveal. . . that in most cases the modification arose before the function."

If such pre-adaptations are genuine, how do we account for them by natural selection? They look more like expressions of a plan, as if they were made for the sake of future use. We have already mentioned the problem of explaining psi in terms of evolution. Psi, I suggest, may be thought of as a pre-adaptive potential, metaphorically, a "structure" or "organ." But for what future need or later development?

Now the idea that psychic ability may be oriented toward the future of evolution has already been suggested by Robert Morris who speculates that "psi may facilitate temporary expansion into new ecological environments, until the organism or its species develops completely effective adaptive mechanisms."

The question then is what new ecological environments might psi be pre-adaptive to? The first thing to note is how difficult it must be to guess this in advance, especially when we consider advances in earlier stages of evolution. Could the reptiles have foretold that one day they might fly? Could the fishes of the sea have divined that one day they would give rise to creatures that wandered freely on the surface of the earth? Or what hints could blind matter have had that in one distant day it would see the light of the sun?

The lower forms could never have cognized their higher futures or been able to predict them in terms of the "logic" and "paradigms" of their existing worlds. It would have required a genius-seer of a reptile to know that the soarings of seagulls and the flights of eagles were their destiny.

Had any one of them—perhaps some inspired archaeopteryx sensing the power of its mysterious feathers—announced a vision of flight, no doubt the most rational fellow reptiles would have given him the hardest time.

With us who are super-clever, things are different. Given the superior powers of reason and analogical thinking we possess, it may be easier to see correctly the shape of things to come. The first thing that comes to mind, our psychic abilities are pre-adapted for psychic survival in the post-biological environment—also known as the land of the dead.

So we have psychic potential not to win the lottery or play the stock market but as part of our capacity to survive in a post-mortem world. Psi is the extraphysical factor in and around us that connects to the post-death environment. Psi, we may think of it as our passport to the next world.

A Note on the Noosphere

Teilhard de Chardin spoke of an ecological environment he called the Noosphere. The Noosphere includes the collective life of all higher forms of consciousness. It is a place we can and do sporadically visit: through practice or grace, breaking the barriers of time, space, matter; expanding into a new spiritual environment.

We humans, astraddle biosphere and Noosphere, are metaphysical amphibians. In this picture, we exist at the dividing line of two environments, two ecologies, a twilight zone where only occasionally we catch hints of what lies beyond the enchanted boundary. Crepuscular creatures we are, neither fully awake nor fully in our dream.

We are trying to form a picture of psi linking to survival. The suggestion is that the function of psi is realized in the post-biological phase of our existence. Our pre-adaptive psi ability makes possible the transition from the biosphere to the noosphere.

If there were a master plan or cosmic intelligence acting upon the biosphere, it probably wouldn't permit the untrammelled use of psi among living organisms. Untrammelled psi would wreak havoc on the ecological system. For instance, if large numbers of animals could use psi to escape their predators, it would subvert all manner of eco-systems.

Far worse is conceivable on the human scene. Psi power suddenly available to people with realpolitik mentalities, is a distressing thought. If there is a master plan or cosmic intelligence—unless malefic or stupid—it would be averse to humans acquiring extensive psychic power.

Freeing Up the Psychic

The suggestion is that restraints on psi ability are built into the ecological system, which would explain the marginal, hard to harness and unlearnable character of psi.

And yet psi does erupt into everyday experience. The early British Census of Hallucinations showed that people have veridical hallucinations of individuals in life-threatening circumstances. It is as if dying tears open a veil, enabling paranormal communication.[14]

Precognitive dreams tend to precede accidents or sudden death. It's as if the restraints on psi are lifted just when the practical advantage is minimized. There are rare exceptions to this, but my impression is that in the majority of cases, precognition of death and disaster usually serves no purpose.

Much the same can be said for apparitions, hauntings and mediumistic phenomena; drawing near death seems to allow these weird openings of perception to occur. Ernesto Bozzano collected cases in which psychokinetic events (clocks stopping, bells sounding, paintings falling) were coincident with the moment of death.[15]

The Outer Limits of Discipline

Sometimes individuals come close to death, not through illness or accident, but through willed discipline. Yogis, prophets, mystics, and the like know how to surrender their all to the Transcendent.

The saint, the yogi, the shaman—all develop the ascetic impulse. The body, appetites and modes of perception, becomes targets of studied indifference or even fierce abuse. Styles vary, quasi-scientific to moralistic, but the goal is the same: control of biological forces through fasting, sexual abstinence, and complete mind control.

Mastery is exercised through the will by direct inhibition of normal bodily impulses. Fasting may assume extreme, prolonged forms, even to complete inedia. Joseph of Copertino[16] and Francis of Assisi went to extremes to detach themselves from whatever was grudgingly ingested. Herbert Thurston, a student of the physical phenomena of mysticism, describes how saints were so averse to normal eating that the mere smell of food would make them sick and cause convulsions. Or, like Jean Marie, the famous French Convulsionnaire, our seeker may indulge in coprophilia.

What is driving these brutal self-lacerations? Is the war waged against the body mainly pathological? The modern, life-affirming humanist or religious liberal is likely to see nothing but morbid self-abuse here. What to think of men and women who make a fetish of physical suffering? Wearing hair shirts, flagellating their bodies, submitting placidly to the abuse of superiors?

For Nietzsche the ascetic war against oneself was inspired by the will to power. Documented cases attest to yogis who survive for days in airless, underground pits or who, under medically controlled conditions, can stop their hearts at will.[17] This of course is power over oneself, which I think is what Nietzsche had in mind.

Spiritual athletes struggle against the insuperable power of sex. The war on sex is the most unabashedly frontal attack on life. Widespread success here would lead to the end of the species. The ascetic impulse is impossible to reconcile with a mechanist view of life. According to that view, the supreme law of life is reproduction.

The ascetic impulse is problematic for a theory of life; often the most evolved spiritual beings counsel indifference, even antagonism, toward bodily life.

Control of sexual life and transcendence of death are visible in the Tantric ritual of maithuna. The object is to engage in sexual congress while stopping short of seminal emission; the vital force isn't just suppressed but aroused, played with, exploited. An effect of this erotico-spiritual experiment is to experience the mystic light. A similar mystic light is said to appear at the moment of death, according to Indo-Tibetan traditions.[18]

From near-death research we learn that erotic, mystical lights are sometimes experienced at the moment of death. Overall, ascetic practices seem to be about reversing the current of the vital impulse and channelling it for spiritual purposes.

Thus, in the Katha Upanishad we read, "Though sitting still, it (the Self or Atman) travels very far; though lying down, it goes everywhere."

This is a metaphorical way of talking about the space-transcending property of psi. To have this experience, the bonds between body and spirit have to be weakened. What the near-death experiencer stumbles upon spontaneously, the ascetic and the mystic pursue gradually, deliberately.

The most impressive psi phenomena tend to cluster around great saints, yogis and shamans. Fully a quarter of Patanjali's Yoga Sutras consists of recipes for obtaining siddhis or paranormal powers. The ancient Hindu tradition connects psi power with spiritual development. Contemporary researcher Erlendur Haraldsson gives eyewitness accounts of Sai Baba's ability to materialize objects. Biofeedback researcher Elmer Green observed Swami Rama perform feats of extraordinary bodily control and episodes of psychokinetic influence on a magnetometer. In 1977, anthropologist David Barker gave an eyewitness account of a Tibetan shaman who stopped at will a rain storm in an area where a ritual was taking place.

Some of the most startling evidence for spiritual psi derives from the saints of the Catholic Church. The legalistic tradition of the Church led to methods for deposing and sifting evidence. St. Joseph of Copertino, whom we mentioned earlier in regard to ascetic practices, demonstrated remarkable levitation powers for many years in the presence of numerous credible witnesses. The modern case of Padre Pio, the stigmatized priest of San Giovanni Rotondo, abounds with reports, numerously attested, of various psi wonders: bilocation, telepathy, healings, precognition, the odor of sanctity, the power to vanish, and so on.

Healings at spiritual shrines like Lourdes are sometimes extremely dramatic, such as the materialization of bone tissue and the restoration of sight. Marian apparitions, like those witnessed by thousands at Fatima and Zeitoun, make another striking chapter in the story of religious psi. In sum, extraordinary psychic ability seems to be tied to spiritual struggle.

We noted Gardner Murphy's suggestion that psi is a pointer to a larger sphere of being, an alternate sphere of psychic function. Arthur Koestler comes close when he states that "ESP would then appear as the highest manifestation of the integrative potential of living matter—which, on the human level, is typically accompanied by a self-transcending type of emotion." Nor are we left out in the cold during this psychic expansion of reality: philosopher and psi researcher Ramakrishna Rao[19] concluded that the evidence for psi implies a latent omniscience in every human being.

Using a different approach, Charles Honorton construes evidence for psi as evidence for Mind at Large. Mind at Large, he suggests, may be thought of as unrestricted psi potential, a potential never fully realized in any finite being. Honorton doesn't go quite as far as Randall does in suggesting that this larger psychic entity or process has a purpose of its own, or, as I would like to suggest, that if it is conscious, intelligent and purposive, then it may on occasion speak to us as persons. The idea seems natural enough; for if minds "speak" and communicate with one another, then why not minds with the greater, unknown mind, the boundless mind we mean by Mind at Large?

Honorton recalls a fundamental distinction, made by the Cambridge philosopher C. D. Broad, between psi interactions and psi experiences. The former is clearly the wider category. Broad says we may be continuously interacting through psi at a subliminal level, but that only under special conditions can we detect such interactions. According to Honorton and William Braud,[20] internal attention states are optimal for detecting the psi "signal." Methods for reducing bio-mechanical noise consist of controlling a subject's organic systems: nervous, muscular, respiratory, cardiovascular. The aim is to reduce the "engine" to an "idle." Braud speaks of the psi-conducive syndrome, Honorton of psi-optimizing procedures. Specific experimental studies (over 80) of the psi-conducive effects of relaxation, meditation, ganzfeld or perceptual isolation, dreaming and hypnosis are cited.

According to Honorton, evidence that reduced sensory input enhances the ability to detect psi is "the beginning of an empirical basis of support for the filter theory of Henri Bergson." According to this theory, the brain, normally a "filter" of Mind at Large that helps us adapt to real life, sometimes relaxes its grip, allowing a greater influx of consciousness from the great reservoir.

Bergson, I will add, had speculated that death of the brain would be the final breakdown of the "filter," and would open one up to an expanded mental space. This point about the brain as a "filter" or organ that transmits (not creates) consciousness is a key contribution to a new mythology of transcendence.[21]

Osis and Haraldsson tried to explain some of the odd effects associated with deathbed visions; consciousness, they said, may be gradually disengaging itself from the organism. The upper limit of altered state functioning would be complete elimination of attachment to the brain; death, as Plato taught in the *Phaedo*, frees the soul from the body.

An important model of how psi may work is that of Rex Stanford's Psi-Mediated Instrumental Response (PMIR). According to this conception, constraints—rigid and stereotyped behavior—get in the way of using psi to our advantage. Supporting this, in a massive review of the experimental literature on extrasensory perception, John Palmer found that spontaneity is perhaps the best predictor of human psi ability, associated with the borderline of sleep states.[22]

So it seems that the more cognitively uptight I am, the more I insulate myself from my transcendent potential. Too much anxious effort tightens the filter and contracts perception. Stanford describes the internal strategies that reduce constraints on psi function. They converge on the theme of what he calls the release-of-effort syndrome. We understand this from the common experience of trying to remember something and recalling it only after you give up trying to remember it. This may serve as a clue to how we become happy or enlightened, by renouncing the desire to be happy or enlightened.

2

NOTES ON THE
CRAFT OF DYING

She knew how to live rarely well, and she desired to know how to die;
and God taught her by an experiment.

—Jeremy Taylor

The Muse of Death

Seeking inspiration from the muse of death is an old trope. Leonardo and Montaigne, for example, both arrived at the view that learning how to live was really learning how to die. The oldest story in human history, the Epic of Gilgamesh, is about an ancient Sumerian king's journey in quest of the flower of immortality.

But what of us moderns in the scientific age? What sorts of craft of dying do we practice? What sorts are available? Not very much, it would seem.

"Wonders are there many but none more wonderful than man," cries the chorus in Sophocles' play, *Antigone.* Man is *deinoteron*—"the most wonderful," as it's usually translated (it also means "ingenious, clever.") The chorus sings of everything clever that man can do—farm the land, trap wild beasts, sail the high seas, battle the elements. The one step on which human cleverness founders is death.

But even that may not be quite so absolute. True to the spirit of the age, even science—on a small scale to be sure—has begun to throw out a few searching queries to Yama the Lord on death. Research on death and dying raises basic questions about life and what it means to be a human being. True, the amount of research is miniscule compared with the mammoth outlays for the physical sciences, for industry, and especially for the arts of war. We are pushing open the frontiers of physical space but neglectful of the equally challenging frontiers of inner space.

Knowledge is expanding exponentially, though great mysteries remain—above all, the mysteries of the mind and conscious existence. But too often the fundamentalists of modern science see no mystery at all; death is the end of life, they assert with confidence. But the word "end" is ambiguous; it could refer to cessation or to a new beginning.

The end of life in the positive sense covers near-death experiences, deathbed visions, reincarnation memories; ecstatic, mystical, out-of-body states; the release of supernormal powers—a wild and great spectrum of human experience. The spectrum is our experimental link to what may be beyond life.

Death, it would seem, is the opposite of life. For this reason, the inner side of it should elude our grasp. It seems like an impassable frontier but there may be a way to explore the fringes of this frontier. The question is how. By stipulating we conceptualize death as an altered state of consciousness.

Near-death researchers study the frontier between the living and the dead. The border condition called near-death, as research shows, is found to reveal an extraordinary pattern of experience, a range of archetypal elements and motifs. This pattern may be an important clue, a kind of foothold to what lies beyond, a way of bringing the mystery of death into clearer focus for study. The border condition provides an experimental wedge into a place normally deemed unknowable and inaccessible, and we may detect signals from the undiscovered country from which some travellers do seem to return.

Once we forge this experimental link between the state of death and a mode of consciousness, new ways of thinking result. As we'll see, features of near-death experience may be observed in other queer states of consciousness. In short, the inner side of death is, under special conditions, open to human experience *before* bodily death. There are ways of being in the world that may form a bridge between life and death, enabling us to take some baby steps in Hamlet's "undiscovered country."

Grant a connection between dying and altered states of consciousness, the idea of exploring, preparing for death, acquires a new dimension of meaning. With the idea of preparation, we can speak of a craft of dying. Such a craft might supplement what it gleans from science with the wisdom of the spiritual traditions.

A modern craft of dying, like the ancient Platonic one, would devise strategies for altering the state and quality of consciousness. What if death is an altered state of consciousness?

Philosophy as Deathcraft

The classic pagan craft of dying is Plato's *Phaedo*, which tells the story of the death of Socrates, a model for heroic, philosophical death. Other philosophers went to death for the sake of their ideas. Bruno died a martyr to the new Renaissance cosmology. When the Inquisition burnt Vanini at the stake for his heresies, he is said to have exclaimed: "Let us die happily for philosophy."

But in the case of Socrates, the relation between death and philosophy was deeper than Vanini's accidental heroics. Philosophy itself is defined as the practice of death—the highest wisdom being achieved through departure of the soul from the body, which is none other than death.

At first this may seem morbidly fanciful. How do you go about practicing death? And what's the point? Aren't we supposed to practice life? Yes, but what then of the life after death? Everything hinges on the definition of death as the separation of one's soul from one's body. We can practice death by learning how to separate ourselves from our bodies. Such a program may sound a bit schizoid to modern ears, but when we look closely at Plato's language, the meaning becomes clearer. *Chorismos* is his word for separation, but he also uses *lysis*, loosing or freeing, and *appallage*, which means departure.

The freedom of the soul depends on readiness for departure, on looseness, flexibility, ease of movement. The essence of the soul, of life as the Greek philosophers understood it, was self-movement, autonomy of personal energy. The highest life—the life that is godlike—as Aristotle explained in the *Nichomachean Ethics*, is marked by *autarkia*: autonomy, freedom from servitude to the body and its inordinate needs.

Normally, we live deeply identified with the anxieties and demands of our bodies. We not only have bodily experiences, we attach inordinate importance to them. We become imprisoned by our body-egos, engrossed by our needs for comfort, security and pleasure.

Plato says we can break the bonds of this hypnotic state and learn to anticipate the great "departure" that is death. (Be cheerful readers, good things are coming.) This "loosening" of the soul requires a special way of life, a spiritual discipline. Freedom from mindless immersion in bodily existence is the way to freedom from the fear of death, the basis of courage in wisdom and self-knowledge.

A soul consciously detached from the body, Plato tells us in the *Phaedo*, "is not likely to feel that it will be torn asunder at its departure from the body and will vanish into nothingness, blown apart by the winds, and be no longer anywhere."

The Platonic craft helps us to anticipate the divorce of our self from the body in different ways. For instance, pain and pleasure are said to "nail" the soul to the body. Violent emotions increase our bondage and delusions. "The evil is that the soul of every man, when it is greatly pleased or pained by anything, is compelled to believe that the object which caused the emotions is very distinct and very true; but it is not. These objects are mostly the visible ones . . ."

Plato makes the interesting observation here that worldviews, or metaphysical biases, are state-bound. If we identify ourselves with everyday sensory modes of being, we tend to think of them as the only reality— i.e., as "very distinct and very true."

Materialism would thus tend to be the by-product of a materialist, sense-locked habit of being conscious. A person who broke that habit, who experienced states going beyond the ordinary sensory mode, would feel less bound to materialism as a doctrine. The battle between worldviews is a battle between different kinds of experiences.

In line with this state-driven epistemology, Plato recommends abstention from unnecessary indulgence in bodily pleasure. I know that rings of the unpleasantly puritanical, but it might also ring a bell for people who would like to walk more lightly in the world. Even so, Plato's rhetoric sometimes seems to encourage unwholesome repression; on the other hand, it could be said that Plato was touting the classical Greek virtue, *encrateia*, or self-mastery. A virtue to admire, it belongs in any good mythology of transcendence.

A modern craft of dying should remain true to the needs of the body without succumbing to the delusions of state-bound materialism. An ignorant and sometimes malicious neglect of the body is a fault of the earlier deathcrafts. By condemning the body as an inferior vehicle, we become enemies of a big part of ourselves. Anything that validates the repression of the body also serves to validate the general repression of life.

When the soul separates itself from the body in the practice of death, it does so for the sake of its own integrity. The integrated soul orders itself in tune with the cosmos: the "ornament" or pattern of the universe. In the cosmology of Plato's *Timaeus*, the universe itself is said to be a "single animal comprehending in itself all other animals, mortal and immortal."

Science, according to Plato, teaches us to imitate, not dominate, the cosmic pattern. The goal lies in "learning the harmonies and revolutions of the universe." Intellect, our divine part, strives to "assimilate" these harmonies which afford the model for "the best life which the gods have set before mankind." To the extent that one succeeds in this assimilation, one already shares in the realm of the "deathless." The whole enterprise of science is given to harmonizing individual life with cosmic life.

The Platonic deathcraft, based on the separation of soul from body, is guided by the ideal of harmony with the "divine animal" of nature as a whole. The practice is about living in harmony with the natural world while preparing to depart from it.

The Medieval Ars Moriendi

The late Middle Ages of Western Christendom created a different kind of deathcraft, based on the liturgical office *De Visitate Infirmorum*. The generic title *Ars Moriendi* (art of dying) refers to two basic texts. One is a block book version consisting of eleven woodcuts depicting the death-bed drama of *Moriens* (the dying person).

The other, a longer version, had an English exemplar commonly referred to as the *Crafte of Dyinge*. Both versions were extraordinarily popular. The artistic climax of the tradition was Jeremy Taylor's *The Rule and Exercises of Holy Dying* of 1651.

Historical factors paved the way for the *Ars Moriendi*. The fourteenth century witnessed a rise of virtual necromania. The obsession with death and transience was due in part to the ravages of the bubonic plague in Europe, to war, political upheaval and to widespread apocalyptic expectations. Preaching styles, especially in late-medieval England, savagely stressed the perils of hell and purgatory. The earlier, more primitive Crafte made ample use of such tactics to subjugate the wayward conscience of the populace. Churchmen of the day exploited the gruesome side of death to combat the new wave of secularism. As one scholar wrote: Hence the Last Things easily became emotional bludgeons with which to combat ignorance, individualism, immorality. Closing ranks against these common foes, all the religious orders found that skulls, worms, fire, and brimstone were, in one way or another, singularly useful weapons in the battle for God and the Church.

In the wake of the gruesome Middle Ages, it's no surprise that we moderns are eager to bury the idea of death. A modern craft of dying, while refusing to coddle the impulse toward denial, would avoid the macabre obsessiveness of the medieval *Ars Moriendi.*

Jeremy Taylor's devotional masterpiece on holy dying gets past the shortcomings of the earlier tractates. Taylor would have us meditate calmly on the universal doom of death, meanwhile cultivating a cool detachment from the world. He iterates the common (admittedly dismal) wisdom of the ages: "As our life is very short, so it is very miserable, and therefore it is well it is short." His tone is somber, not fanatical.

The omnipresence of death is a favorite theme in Taylor's craft. Death penetrates to the core of life. Here we find no amiable talk of the "joy of living." Taylor would set us straight with the rhythms of his prose:

> Death meets us everywhere, and is procured by every instrument, and in all chances, and enters in at many doors; by violence and secret influence, by the aspect of a star and the stink of a mist, by the emissions of a cloud and the meeting of a vapor, by the fall of a chariot and the stumbling at a stone, by a full meal or an empty stomach, by watching at the wine, or by watching at prayers, by the sun or the moon, by a heat or a cold, by water frozen into the hardness and sharpness of a dagger, or water thawed into the floods of a river, by a hair or a raisin, by violent motion or sitting . . ..

Language is used to effect in Taylor's *Ars Moriendi.* The point of this "word magic" was not to eject the idea of death from awareness but to focus on it. And yet the prose has a way of lulling one into an almost erotic surrender. Our more rational minds, stripped of metaphor and sounding power, may chafe uncomfortably at this performance. Taylor's relentless realism sharply differs from modern evasiveness.

Although Taylor's deathcraft is otherworldly, it offers "hints" on the art of living. For example, he alludes to a technique of recollection that dates back to the ancient Pythagorean brotherhood. "He that will die well and happily," we read, "must dress his soul by a diligent and frequent scrutiny; he must perfectly understand and watch the state of his soul; he must set his house in order before he be fit to die."

The daily practice of self-observation prevents one from falling into the habit of sin. Recollection is a form of behavior modification. According to Taylor, anyone who dies in good conscience— properly self-recollected—dies well.

In some ways, daily recollection anticipates the hour of death. It is now known, for instance, that persons near death often report having a kind of panoramic memory of their lives. The practice of daily recollection, urged by Taylor, would be a rehearsal of near-death recollection. The near-death experiencer gets a new lease on life as a result of the play-back experience, a chance to "set his house in order." Taylor and the Pythagoreans of old make self-recollection piecemeal, a gradual, daily process.

The lesson of Taylor's deathcraft comes to this: if we hope to make dying a more conscious process, we should begin by living more consciously. Daily self-recollection is a simple exercise to that end.

The general drift of Taylor's holy dying is to devalue worldly existence. "Since we stay not here, being people of a day's abode, and our age is like that of a fly, and contemporary with a gourd, we must look somewhere else for an abiding city, a place in another country." It would seem that "holy," as used by the great Anglican preacher, is less than "holistic" in the modern sense. It is a one-sided "holiness" that celebrates the hereafter at the expense of the here and now. This one-sidedness is the counterpart to the modern secular fixation on present-centeredness.

A Tibetan Manual for Dying

The Bardo Thodol[23], recited by Tibetan lamas over a dying or dead man, is both map and guidebook for the intermediate stage between death and rebirth. The word *bardo* means gap, place of transition, literally "the lake between two islands." Unlike Dante's *Divine Comedy*, also a cartography of the post-mortem journey, the Bardo Thodol is an open-ended manual. The Tibetan picture is more fluid than Dante's, where our afterlife adventures are fixed by the deeds we perform in this life. The East is in no hurry and allows us many lives to learn our lessons toward enlightenment. The West would have us go straight to doom or to paradise, or, if you're Catholic, a period in purgatory.

Church doctrine here is not uniform. For instance, the early Church father Origen held that all souls, even the Devil himself, would by the last days be reconciled with God. The official Church doctrine came out against this optimistic heresy. Protestants also wanted to simplify the afterlife schedule by getting rid of that waffling Catholic purgatory.

The Bardo Thodol describes three stages, gaps or bardos in the post-mortem state: Chikhai, Chonyid and Sidpa. The three stages progress from the high point of the first moment of death downward through increasingly terrible experiences that climax in being lured into reincarnation. East differs from West in one striking way. In the Eastern view, our entry into the world is seen as a greater calamity than our exit.

Everything in the teachings of the Bardo Thodol is directed toward avoiding the disaster of rebirth. Embodied existence is itself hell. This twist, curious for most Westerners, may be seen as expressing either the bleakest pessimism about human life or the greatest confidence in the reality of transcendent life.

According to *The Tibetan Book of the Dead*, the best chance of enlightenment comes during the Chikhai Bardo which occurs at the moment of death. This is our chance to escape from rebirth. At that moment, one is said to behold the Reality of the Fundamental Clear Light "wherein all things are like the void and cloudless sky, and the naked spotless intellect is like a transparent vacuum without circumference or center."

We are instructed to abide in the consciousness of the Clear Light, to merge with and know it to be our true nature.

Not entirely easy, it implies being maximally conscious of the dying process itself. The Tibetan craft requires the dying person to remain conscious, and even describes physiological techniques for staying hyper-alert. Anything detracting from that alertness might interfere with your encounter with the Fundamental Clear Light.

This claim about the need for alertness is confirmed by modern findings; for instance, K. Osis and E. Haraldsson[24] and B. Greyson[25] found that narcotics or organic brain dysfunction decreased the incidence of deathbed and near-death visions. The less impaired consciousness is, emotionally or physiologically, the greater the probability of enlightenment experiences at the hour of death.

In Plato's view, the problem of death is a problem of false identification. We falsely identify with our bodies, which restricts our possible consciousness. In the Bardo Thodol, we falsely identify with our psychic projections. The difficult thing is becoming clear about our projections. (We face a similar problem in life.) The Tibetan craft maps the obstacles we meet in the post-mortem state. After the tremendous encounter with the Light arises the Chonyid Bardo, the stage of the dawning of peaceful and frightening apparitions.

At first the deceased is not aware that he is deceased (an idea confirmed by reports from psychical research); he hovers in an astral or dream body, nearby his corpse, confused, vaguely aware of the presence of mourning relatives and religious functionaries. If, after the first glorious encounter with the Clear Light, we fail to recognize our selves in that Light, the text recommends that we meditate on our guru or tutelary deity with intense fondness and humble trust.

The Tibetan system is flexible. Characteristic of Buddhism, it advocates a path of self-reliance: know that the source and ground, the supreme consciousness, is within. But if we fail in the quality of our spiritual awareness, then it's all right to fall back on devotional practices and use external supports.

The model of the intermediate state: first, we encounter the Clear Light; second, the peaceful apparitions appear; third, the wrathful apparitions. The last, Sidpa Bardo, is the most unpleasant, where we skitter toward the onset of rebirth.

Note the parallel with empirical findings. The Tibetan Clear Light is a good match for the Being of Light of near-death research.

The tone is encouraging, but the teaching offers no easy path to enlightenment. The message, in fact, seems to be that the great majority of us are unprepared for death and the sudden change of consciousness it brings. The cost of enlightenment is a lifetime of cultivated self-awareness. The Tibetan way scarcely differs from that of Plato or Jeremy Taylor: How we experience the afterlife will depend on our worldview, our own thoughts and expectations. In the afterdeath bardos we become our own worlds. In the Chonyid Bardo the terrible phantoms are me; I create and project the images of my enemy. The more unyielding, mistrustful and hostile I become toward them, the more relentlessly they will assail me. In this worldview, I am supposed to figure out how to make friends with my inner demons, and most important, how to recognize them as my own creation whenever I project them outwardly. The wrathful and peaceful apparitions are two sides of the same coin, they reflect unconscious parts of myself, layers I need somehow to befriend and take into myself.

Skills for overpowering and manipulating others would be a hindrance in the Chonyid Bardo. Surviving the "ambushes" in the bardo realms calls for a skill with oneself, especially with the self hiding behind the public personae.

Violence is a self-destroying program in the Chonyid Bardo. "Through the power of anger," the text says, "you will beget fear and be startled at the dazzling white light and will wish to flee from it; you will beget a feeling of fondness for the dull smoke-colored light from Hell." In ordinary life, anger and violence may be profitably exploited; here, in the presence of the "dazzling white light," they are self-defeating.

Certain strategies for coping with hazard and crisis won't work in the afterlife. One has to adapt to a different set of rules, use different mental "skills." If and when we ever enter a spiritual universe after death, quite different principles and laws will most likely be operative. Dreams, art and mythology would assume a central role producing our existence. They could be models for imagining a post-mortem spiritual universe.

To move in that direction—as part of a usable craft of dying in the 21st century—traditional wisdom urges letting go of the obsessions of the everyday mind. The Bardo Thodol advises: "Be not attracted to them; be not terrified; but abide in the mood of non-thought formation." The suggestion is obvious and clear: don't react!

But there is more to this instruction. It goes against the instincts of life to non-do, to do nothing, think nothing, feel nothing. But in fact the idea of creative non-action is widespread. The modern Mexican shaman, Don Juan, channelled by Castaneda, liked to speak of nondoing, of "stopping the world." Turn the other cheek, declares the shaman of Nazareth. Among the Chinese sages, the principle of *wu wei* or non-action is also held in high esteem.

This ancient wisdom appears even in the popular consciousness, for instance, in the Hollywood spectacular *Star Wars* of 1977. The young hero, Luke Skywalker, faces the challenge of his life; he has to fly his space vehicle in a pinpoint attack on the evil forces of Darth Vader, a wrathful divinity of the Chonyid Bardo. About to zero in on the target, Luke's disembodied spiritual mentor commands him to let go of the controls, to trust his feelings and the Force.

This scene inspired contempt in Ben Bova, a science fiction writer who disliked the movie. One reason was the "philosophical" point *Star Wars* made. " 'Trust the Force' is the philosophy of the slave," Bova proudly proclaimed. "Here is a movie produced with the latest and best technology that you can buy and the punch line is that when you're in a crisis, switch off the computer and wait for Alec Guinness to whisper in your ear." The spoilsport would have us trust the computer when we're in a crisis – certainly not the "Force."

But technology, even the "latest and best . . . you can buy," has not resolved any of the crises of value, identity, and meaning that are turning the world upside down today.

In the Sidpa Bardo, or last stage before reincarnation, the soul wanders helplessly, blown about by the "karmic winds." The intellect, having no object to rest upon, "like a feather tossed about by the wind," is driven toward re-embodiment, desperately seeking to lose or entrap itself in a new body. Thus are we sucked into a new cycle of suffering. The job of enlightenment is to shatter the bonds of repetition compulsion.

An important theme of the Tibetan deathcraft has parallels in Plato's Allegory of the Cave: Humankind cannot bear too much consciousness. The reincarnated body and Plato's cave are symbols of retreat from the anxiety of the Clear Light. We flee from the Greater Consciousness, as Plato's Allegory shows. The cave-dwellers prefer to kill their liberator, Socrates, unwilling to step out into the pure light of the sun. If Plato and the Bardo Thodol are right, what we fear in death is not extinction but being overwhelmed by consciousness.

The Bardo Thodol is not just a guidebook for a possible afterworld journey. Human relations, personal and political, are prone to the same projections, the same ignorance, aggression, and flight from responsibility. The Tibetan deathcraft is a craft for conscious living. Existence is transitional, bardo-like. Making our way through the "gaps," across the "lake between the islands," is our common lot, both here and possibly hereafter.

Earth in Transformation

A glance at some historical examples of deathcrafts shows one thing clearly: any attempt to talk of practicing for death leads to questions about how to live. We would like to see ourselves as more than helpless victims of a dark implacable power.

If the Platonic strategy was to master the body by deserting it, the Christian strategy was to transform the body, materialize a new spiritual body, and in this sense we can speak of a kind of Christian materialism. This is how Paul of Tarsus reasoned: "If in union with Christ we have imitated his death, we shall also imitate him in his resurrection. We must realize that our former selves have been crucified with him to destroy this sinful body and to free us from the slavery of sin" (Rom. 6:5).

The anastasis or resurrection of nature begins with the gifts of the Holy Spirit. The transfiguration of death-and-matter is highlighted in the deeds of Jesus. Thus the first miracle at the feast of Cana is a sign of this new power at work: the changing of water into wine. Healings and raising the dead are more dramatic signs of the coming resurrection of nature. This new power is not restricted to the agency of Jesus; thus, at the prompting of Jesus, Peter walks on water. The power is awakened in Peter himself—although in a faltering way, due to hesitancy and lack of trust.

In Acts of the Apostles, we read accounts of a new spiritual principle unfolding. Reports abound of miraculous healings and escapes, of prophecy, telepathy and other prodigies. Peter himself is now said to have raised the woman Tabitha from the dead (Acts 9:36-38.) Early Christians believed in the revelations of a New Spirit.

During the first outpouring at Pentecost, the "men living in Jerusalem from every nation under heaven" were amazed and confounded when the Apostles spoke of the "marvels of God" in their own languages: Parthians, Phrygians, Elamites, Cretans, Arabs, Pamphylians, Cappadocians, Egyptians, and even Romans.

Skeptics laughed. "They have been drinking too much new wine," they said (Acts 1:1-13.) Others were possessed by the New Spirit. Thus the community grew on the wings of a miraculous new power, a new kind of intoxication. The world itself, in the title of N. O. Brown's book, is becoming "Love's Body." In the chapter titled "Resurrection," Brown writes:

> To rise from history to mystery is to experience the resurrection of the body here now, as an eternal reality; to experience the parousia, the presence in the present, which is the spirit; to experience the reincarnation of the incarnation, the second coming; which is his coming in us.

These words sum up the forgotten Christian craft of dying. For Brown, true Christianity means the death of the fundamentalist adherence to the letter and the rebirth of the polysemous spirit, Spirit incarnate, spirit alive in a loving body.

The Christian deathcraft is the practice of being radically alive in a loving body. The ultimate goal is to spiritualize the body, to create what Paul called the *soma pneumatikon.*

Modern liberal Christianity is embarrassed by miracles; it shies away from signs and wonders. But to the first Christians, sensible signs were essential. It was the experimental "proof" of the reality of the new spiritual power. The early Christians were radical empiricists. They needed concrete evidence of the Higher Power they worshipped and trusted. Lofty ethical ideals and philosophical reasons were by-products of an encounter with a living Force, experiences that "sounded like powerful wind from heaven," noises that "filled the entire house," the appearance of "tongues of fire" (Acts 2:1-4.) The roots of the Christian story of life and death were powerful transformative events.

The need for concrete evidence of the supernatural continued throughout the Middle Ages and is part of the Roman Church to this day. Miraculous power is surely not the whole story of heroic sanctity, but it is consistent with the belief in the resurrection of Jesus, in the power of a new transcendent force in nature.

The rules of canonization call for evidence of miraculous power in all candidates for sainthood. Levitations, bilocations, stigmata, healings, discernment of spirits, prophecy, bodily incorruption and other saintly phenomena may be construed as evidence of the resurrection effects of nature that follows from the *ars moriendi.* A powerful indicator is the phenomenon of bodily incorruption, it deserves to be investigated; reportedly, many Catholic saints after they die have either escaped or delayed the natural course of bodily corruption. Cases have been meticulously attested by medical reports and eye-witnesses. Normal accounting for these preservations is neither easy nor obvious.

The incorruptibles—a distinguished company, including Theresa of Avila, John of the Cross, Francis Xavier—are dramatic retroactive expressions of the body's spiritual potential. They express a unique power that raises objections to the dominion of death. Here is one of many possible examples: St. Andrew of Bobola. The description is from Joan Carroll Cruz's[26] study:

> Prior to his martyrdom he [St. Andrew] was partially flayed alive, his hands were hacked off and his tongue was torn from his head. Splinters of wood were driven under his fingernails, and his face sustained such

mutilations that he was scarcely recognizable. After hours of further tortures and mutilations, he was dispatched by a sword's blow at the neck. His body was hastily buried by Catholics in a vault beneath the Jesuit church at Pinsk, where it was found forty years later perfectly preserved, in spite of the open wounds, which would normally foster corruption.

Although the grave had been damp, causing his vestments to rot, his body was perfectly flexible, his flesh and muscles soft to the touch, and the blood that covered the numerous wounds was found to be like that which is freshly congealed. The preservation was officially recognized by the Congregation of Rites in 1845. Even though the relic was roughly handled during its numerous translations, the body remains after more than three hundred years in a state of preservation.

These accounts of dead bodies that refuse to behave like dead bodies symbolically suggest the presence of a power protesting the finality of bodily demise. A power above "normal" nature likes to show itself off in a wide assortment of "miracles."[27]

Evidence of high weirdness periodically erupts into our world: the levitations of Teresa of Avila or Joseph of Copertino, so well documented; the stigmata, anomalous wounds born of a passionate imagination; countless reported healings and bilocations of Padre Pio; the dried blood relics of Januarius that periodically, inexplicably, liquefy in the Naples Cathedral in response to the chants of local aunts and grannies.

Dramatic phenomena are claimed by modern charismatics today.[28] Examples are plentiful for those willing to investigate the facts. Beginning with the resurrection story, the engine of the movement for centuries, we have accounts of extraordinary events based on significant, even compelling, testimony. Liberal theologians may have demythologized Christianity in modern times. Nevertheless, it was belief in the living story of the resurrection and the reality of the miraculous that propelled and inspired the early Christian communities.

The Lure of the New Age

The Christian deathcraft is tied to the idea a new age, a powerful force in the modern consciousness movement. The new age, the new testament, were grounded in the idea of a new mind, metanoia rather than paranoia; *metanoia*, the "afterthought" that triggers psychic transformation.

Ideas like this of group awakening turn up in all historical epochs and the lure of the future draws us eternally on. "And I saw a new heaven and a new earth; for the first heaven and the first earth were passed away," wrote John of Patmos, and further, "Behold, I make all things new," (Rev. :21). Out of this came the idea that the world would witness a final conflict; God would triumph over the wicked, the elect would be saved, and nature would be pacified and spiritualized. "And God shall wipe away all tears from their eyes; and there shall be no more death." (Rev. 21:4)

Radical New Age promises inspired historical movements, animated by the belief that a new world was coming. The writings of the eleventh century Calabrian mystical prophet, Joachim of Fiore,[29] devised a system still echoing in the historical unconscious.

According to Joachim, history unfolds in three stages, each stage dispensed by one of the three persons in the Holy Trinity: the Father, the Son and the Holy Spirit. The Father signifies the reign of law and servitude; the Son presides over the age of faith and filial concern; under the aegis of the Holy Spirit the last stage of history shall unfold, and be marked by freedom, friendship and contemplative joy. The Church will wither away because in the age of spiritual consciousness, the boundaries separating us from the divine source will have melted away. Reliance on authoritative interpreters of scripture and the Church as mediator of God will no longer be necessary.

Joachim was a loyal son of the Church, but the Joachite philosophy of history appeared in secular theories of social evolution, reaching as far as the 19th century German idealist philosophers. Lessing, Schelling, Fichte, Hegel, Comte and Marx were all influenced by the Joachite view of the ages and stages of history. Some scholars even trace the spirit of National Socialism to the trinitarian archetype. Thus, according to Norman Cohn, the idea of the Third Reich, "adopted as a name for that 'new order' which was supposed to last a thousand years, would have had but little emotional significance if the phantasy of a third and most glorious dispensation had not, over the centuries, entered into the common stock of European social mythology."[30]

The fact is that Joachim's thought—quite apart from the author's intentions—lent itself to anti-ecclesiastical sentiment. The Church was identified with the fearful and submissive stage of history. The vision of spiritual apocalypse spawned millenarian cults, mystical anarchists and eschatological revolutionaries: movements like the Flagellants, the Franciscan Spirituals, the Brethren of Free Spirits, the Amaurians and many others. What these movements had in common was a belief in the power of a new form of consciousness to renovate human life and society.

Belief in a new spiritual body took the form of release from conventional sexual restraints, and the quest to abolish bodily death became a search for the erotic innocence of Adam and Eve before the fall into self-consciousness. If overcoming death were not immediately feasible, one could at least try to recapture the paradisal potential of the human body.

The theme of new age erotics recurs in Herbert Marcuse's *Eros and Civilization*[31] and in the writings of Norman O. Brown. The problem of transcending death becomes the problem of bodily resurrection: the recovery of the erotic body, freed from repression and death-anxiety. The new dispensation, the new heaven, was pictured as a liberated sensuous existence on earth.

Feuerbach's Vision of a New Age

German philosopher Ludwig Feuerbach's critical vision of a new age was closely tied to his philosophy of death. In his *Thoughts on Death and Immortality* (1830), he worried about the divided consciousness—which Marx in 1844 called alienation—being cut off from our authentic selves and vital interests. How does this come about?

The false pietism of Christianity, he believed, causes us to project our spiritual energies into a vague future state. Sentimental fantasies of an afterlife drain life from present embodied existence. We become alienated from our true powers, enthralled by the abstractions we forge. The worst abstraction is the selfish ego, which hinders us from participation in communal life.

For Feuerbach, the concrete human community is the locus of love and liberty, and the abstraction of God gets in the way and must be overcome. God is the projection of our highest powers onto an alien, phantasmal framework: God is thus the supreme symbol of the divided consciousness. So we must set about to recapture the displaced energies of our bewitched consciousness. We need to become aware that we are the source of divine reality. Feuerbach was on to something.

But the divine is not only a projection of the psyche; it also has a life of its own in a world beyond time and space. This is hard for the enlightened Western mind to entertain nowadays. Jung once commented: "But though the European can easily explain away these deities as projections, he would be quite incapable of positing them as real." Still, Feuerbach was no doubt justified in railing against the false piety of his day.

Here is one of his epigrams: "For these gentlemen, religion is a life-insurance company. Even sacrifice relates only to one's good; and God for them is the grease on the squeaky wagon of life that makes the wheels turn more easily." Religious ideas are exploited for selfish reasons. Religion becomes an instrument for disguising and inflicting one's neurosis on the world. Fear, even hatred of life, hides behind religious fervor; human energies are vainly spent on the ego-spawned effusions of low-order religious experience.

The German Hegelians liked to make trouble. Governments are also projections, they understood, and we can free ourselves from their enchantment. Since we made them, we can unmake them. Ultimately, the authority of government is not rationally justifiable, the anarchist argues. The first step is to recognize that gods and states are human constructs, solemnly defended fictions. When they become nightmares, we are entitled to "wake up" from the spells cast on us. We sink into the lower bardo of global politics, confused and terrified by our own awesome fake news. Through our own labor, as Marx said, we create the world that oppresses us. Our hope is to devise ways to uncreate the nightmare we have bought into.

But Feuerbach got snared in one of his own projections, namely, "religion." He exhibits a fundamentalist cast of mind when he states, "As they posit a future life, they negate the actual life." Really? Why must it be either/or? "For if there is life after death," he goes on, "there cannot be life before death; one excludes the other; the present life cancels the future life, the future life cancels the present life."

But there is no incompatibility at all. We can be faithful to the earth and we can be scanners and ponderers of next and alternate worlds. Feuerbach needs to stop obsessing either/or and dig a little both/and. He did, to be fair, distinguish between false piety and a more authentic religious consciousness he associated with primitive Catholicism. He once remarked that a "senseless visionary" is more equipped to understand the Bible than a scholarly theologian.

Feuerbach's revulsion against false piety resulted in a disabled openness to the Transcendent. Nevertheless, Feuerbach, like Nietzsche and other rebels against traditional religion still craved to see the "heroic shapes of reality." His writings quiver with talk of infinity, immortality, universality. But he struggled to squeeze all the old categories of transcendence into the shrunken frame of material existence.

Deathcraft in the Nuclear Age

The crisis of nearly dying is also a stage of intense growth. The terminal situation is a challenge, shakes up the basic structure of personality, and throws open the door to new possibilities of perception and relationship. Now if indeed civilization is starting to look terminal, then we are facing a collective challenge to personal growth. By terminal civilization, I mean a civilization realistically, credibly threatened by the prospect of nuclear war and/or climate catastrophe. There is, however, a good side to all this; it forces us to face the necessity of inner change.

And there are many signs of this from different sources: secular and religious peace movements, the scientific search for a new paradigm, the consciousness revolution. It is reported that millennials are racing away from the established religions in droves, but not because they are flaming atheists or diehard materialists. The reason for the migration seems to be more about wanting to create new spiritual communities.

It is taking all forms, like small groups deciding to provide sanctuary for victims of unjust deportation or enclaves of friends that meet to discuss their spiritual interests and concerns, or groups who eager to practice drumming, or chanting, or meditating. These eddies of free-floating spiritual energy, these currents of consciousness may be converging, however discreetly and haphazardly, toward a collective, more unified response to the steadily mounting global dangers.

One of the great dangers is the way science is used to serve special interests. With science we are heating up the atmosphere and filling the planet with weapons of almost limitless destructive potential. Technology, in so many ways a boon to humankind, is rapidly evolving into a supreme danger to the entire biosphere.

We need a new term for the unprecedented situation we have created. The term is *technocalypse*,[32] which I have defined as the convergence of technology and the apocalyptic imagination. What this term is meant to emphasize is the historical convergence of two explosive forces, one mental, the other physical. The wild fantasies of a final battle between good and evil, God and the Devil, now have wild technologies to act out their grandiose visions of the climax of history (that's the second).

What is the second? Science has contributed to the creation of technology that specializes in murdering people with pinpoint precision or murdering them en masse. Science needs to recover its *conscience,* and its *consciousness.* A glance at the etymology of these words is illuminating: science, conscience, consciousness. They all stem from a common root: scire: to know. To be "whole" all three words belong together and need each other. Science, we might think, *should* serve conscience and consciousness. But science is sometimes tempted to bracket its conscience, often for a price, cash and status, especially. At a time when everywhere the danger of mass destruction is increasing, we need a new philosophy of life and death, an enriched mythology of transcendence. In it, the conscience of science and of consciousness would be firmly intact.

3

REPRESSING IMMORTALITY

I know you want to keep on living. You do not want to die. And you want to pass from this life into another in such a way that you will not rise again as a dead man, but fully alive and transformed. This is what you desire. This is the deepest human feeling; mysteriously, the soul itself wishes and instinctively desires it.
—AUGUSTINE:
SERMON 344.4

Je me revolte contre la mort.

—ARTHUR RIMBAUD

The ancient myths of transcendence, which sheltered us from disquieting thoughts of our mortality, have among the educated masses been crumbling since the 17th century. They helped us manage the anxiety caused by our conscious existence; they were aids to living and kept the terror of death at bay. But they lie in ruins after the storm-blast of the scientific revolution.

Mythic humanity, living in harmony with the collective wisdom of life, was as vulnerable to the fear of death as rationalist folk presently are. But the sharp awareness of individual existence, the sense of being rent from the bosom of nature, was not nearly as acute or unsettling.

47

Of course, our brave materialist friend will correctly say, even the most comforting illusions are still illusions.

But let's not beg the question—which is, are all the beliefs about life after death illusions? Is the core belief that there is such a life false and illusory? So it is believed by many, usually with a cocksureness commensurate to their academic degrees. This of course tends to throw water on beliefs and experiences intensely meaningful to countless human beings.

My view is that logic and certain matters of fact should discourage that kind of hasty dismissal. The official view of these matters amounts to little more than ignorant dogmatizing.

Far from being neurotic and escapist, the belief in life after death seems very much like a reflex of life itself. It voices the fate of living substance: the self-replication of DNA, the branching out and evolution of living forms. Life, as we find it, appears designed to replicate, multiply, reproduce. If that is true for our physical life, why should it not be true for our mental life?

In a prepersonal way, the idea of immortal soul merely echoes the fact of immortal DNA. Indeed, there is an uncontroversial sense in which we are immortal. We are all part of immortal DNA. But it's not an appealing form of immortality. It only describes the physical and narrowly genetic continuity of living forms.

The immortality that interests us is the immortality of consciousness. The truth is that modern science has wrecked the shelter, the buffer against feeling helpless before mortality. Its sole offering is belief in a vacuous physical immortality; but has no regard for our mental or spiritual immortality.

The Hunger for Immortality

If a pebble on the beach became conscious of itself, would it resist the prospect of being eroded by the waves? It seems that way with most people, who instinctively resist the idea of becoming eroded by time into extinction. We try, of course, to reconcile ourselves to our pebble fate.

Nevertheless, I think we are haunted, driven—often unconsciously—by what the Spanish philosopher Miguel de Unamuno called the "hunger for immortality."[33] Any attempt to think on the riddle of human behavior needs to face the problem of this hunger. In a pregnant phrase, Unamuno speaks of the "immortal origin of this yearning for immortality."

A yearning so powerful becomes problematic from the standpoint of scientific skepticism. What are we to make of this "hunger"? Is the cause of it the fear of death? Or is it based on some intuition of our soul life, our instinctive resonance with something transcendent?

Freud focused on sexual repression. But following Unamuno's suggestion, but what about repressing our "hunger for immortality." That repression may reveal itself in unsettling ways. Unamuno wrote in 1921 of the "tremendous struggle to singularize ourselves, to survive in some way in the memory of others ..." The urge to be singular, to stand out, to be noticed at all costs, becomes, after the decline of medieval faith in immortality, a struggle that is "a thousand times more terrible than the struggle for life." The periodic mass killings in America and the murderous and suicidal terrorism of religious fanatics come immediately to mind. What surely drove them all was a terrible need to "singularize" themselves—stand out, make a mark, be noticed.

Hegel may have had this in mind when he said that consciousness craves recognition more than it craves love. Recognition makes one feel "real," providing a kind of extended life for us through others. It affords hope of survival in the great (albeit fickle) memory of human experience. If I want to "survive" in this sense, I must make myself known, famous or infamous. I have to be able to count on the spotlight staying on me.

Resistance and Illusion

Free and enlightened spirits like Thomas Jefferson recoiled from the idea of discourse with spirits of the unseen world. The point is to master oneself; stand up and apart from "comforting traditions." Jefferson saw Jesus as a great moral philosopher. But he had no respect or interest in what actually drew people to Jesus and his story, the belief, for example, in the resurrection of the dead.

So confident was Jefferson that all the miracle stories were fraudulent that he produced an edition of the New Testament with all the miracles excised and bowdlerized—a startling early symptom of totalitarian scientism.[34]

Nietzsche, who seemed to understood the need for healing fictions, believed the fictions of Christianity were corroders of human potential, and strove to conjure new fictions such as Superman and Eternal Recurrence, substitutes for God and Immortality. Jung brings us even closer to understanding these life-sustaining "illusions" of human culture, as we'll see in our discussion of the archetype of death and enlightenment.

In *Denial of Death and the Double*[35] Otto Rank marshals examples from film, literature and anthropology, illustrating the phenomenon of the human double. Rank explains the idea of the "soul" by the same mechanism responsible for producing the psychic double.

According to Rank, a severe threat to the self can cause one to create an alternate or shadow self. Death is the most catastrophic threat to the self, "The idea of death, therefore, is denied by a duplication of the self incorporated in the shadow or in the reflected image."

The belief in immortality, he says, is a reflex effect of denying death. Religion, superstition, modern cults (including spiritualism) are all creatures born of "the increasing reality-experience of man, who does not want to admit that death is everlasting annihilation." Rank comments on what he deems the narcissistic pathology of writers like Wilde, Maupassant, Hoffman, Musset, Dostoyevsky and others, explaining their preoccupation with doubles.

As usual none of the empirical studies of survival research are cited. If we accept Rank's thesis, the greatest believers in the immortality of the soul must be the greatest narcissists. This would include famous saints and yogis, despite their often obvious fame for transcending the "narcissistic" ego. Anyone who knows about their lives would find it incredible to pronounce Teresa of Avila or Joseph of Copertino "narcissists".

The denial of death remains a problem for a theory of culture. The argument, developed by Freud, Rank and others like N. O. Brown, Alan Harrington, Herbert Marcuse and Ernest Becker, is that the entire dynamism of human culture—works of art, religion, philosophy, politics—represents a revolt against death, a disguised quest for immortality. The great achievements of civilization are all at bottom byproducts of trying to compensate for mortality.

Eros and Life

According to Norman O. Brown in *Love's Body*, the insatiable need to produce and hoard treasure is demonically driven by death anxiety, by the inability to let go, to spend oneself on life and fully experience the erotic body.

The way to halt the demonic dialectic, and be released from the compulsion to shore up power, is to liberate the body's erotic potential. More than a matter of genital gratification, Eros possesses the whole body and mind; it opens one to a radically responsive *mode of being*. Eros affords a model for embracing concrete existence in all its messy multiplicity.

Issues With Annihilation

A brilliant study of this problem is Alan Harrington's *The Immortalist*.[36] The emotional honesty of this book is rare. Harrington, echoing Unamuno, exposes the bad faith in repressing our hunger for immortality. Harrington takes the new consciousness of death very seriously and writes of the "problem of meaningless annihilation having become so urgent in our time, threatening world-wide violence and madness ... All around us we have the spectacle of overflowing millions no longer praying but grasping for salvation, behind all faces of sophistication and toughness, each in his own style, every man for himself ... an imperious demand to be rescued from nothingness."

There have always been people bothered by the latent absurdity of the human condition. Skepticism, atheism, nihilism have in the past been badges of iconoclasts. What makes it a matter of evolutionary significance today is that the specter of annihilation is piercing the "general consciousness." Harrington traces every upheaval, every menace to this growing sense of nihilism: the obsession with achievement, being on "top," gratuitous violence, paranoia on the rampage, sensuality disturbed, art and philosophy grimly irrelevant. "An unfortunate awareness has overtaken our species: masses of men and women everywhere no longer believe that they have even the slightest chance of living beyond the grave." Harrington adds, "The species must solve the problem of death very soon, blow itself up, or blow its mind."

Harrington neither denies the immortalist project nor the consequences of its frustration. He then proposes his solution. Well, given that death is causing such a problem, let us just abolish it! After all, science has unlimited potential—why not summon the gods of medical technology, unite the human race in a great war on death?

I would say that even if we succeeded in prolonging life far beyond its present span, death by accident or murder would remain a possibility, and the anxiety would remain. Neither would merely prolonging life solve the peculiar modern problem of the meaning of life. Endless meaningless life is not an endearing concept. I say nothing at all of the ethical niceties of who would enjoy the benefits of "immortalist" medical technology.

But in fact science, or rather many scientifically trained individuals, some of them quite famous in their fields, have studied various kinds of evidence of postmortem survival. Anyone interested in the problem could begin by tackling the extensive literature on life after death.[37] Harrington provides such a keen diagnosis of the sickness: why ignore potentially good medicine?

Assuming the magnitude of the problem—its tremendous implications for the future of humankind—why did Harrington and others ignore over hundred years of research on mind, body and death? Is the dogma of physicalism so powerful?

We could ask the same of Ernest Becker, another brilliant theoretician of death. Becker's *Denial of Death*[38] is a landmark study of the psychological problems of 20th century humanity. His analysis of Freud's character illustrates. According to Becker, Freud toyed with the idea of yielding to higher powers. His character, however, stood in the way of the act of surrender. His basic stance toward reality, like that of many men, was antagonistic to the idea of yielding.

But "Freud not only played with yielding but actually longed to be able to shift his center elsewhere." Becker quotes a conversation between Ernest Jones and Freud on psychic phenomena in which Jones said: "If one could believe in mental processes floating in the air, one could go on to a belief in angels." Freud then said, "Quite so, even *der liebe Gott.*"

Jones was disturbed by the quizzical, almost receptive tone of Freud's remark. But Freud remained ambivalent toward the idea of yielding to any principle beyond his rational grasp. The root of Freud's ambivalence was explained in these terms: "To yield is to disperse one's shored-up center, let down one's guard, one's character armor, admit one's lack of self-sufficiency." To yield is to risk losing one's defences against anxiety. It is easy to see, in this light, why so many educated people (and not only) ignore or resist the evidence of paranormal realities. If such things are afloat "in the air," it opens the door to angels, God, and all manner of possible creepy unknowns.

Such powers threaten the self-sufficiency of one's character, one's carefully wrought system of defences. They also bring the challenge of new, perhaps unwelcome responsibilities. The powers invite us to yield, to let go of the hold, however precarious, that we have won over ourselves.

An illustration is novelist Graham Greene's encounter with Padre Pio. Greene was deeply impressed by the Padre's mass, by his stigmata and by a "small miracle" he experienced. The novelist had prayed to the Padre for a distressing personal relationship to clear up and he obtained a seemingly miraculous result. Greene had the chance to meet with Padre Pio but backed down.

His reasons throw light on the question of resistance to psi and transcendent power in general: "I was so convinced of his powers of goodness that I refused to approach him and speak with him. I explained to the friends who had brought me along that I was too afraid that it might upset my entire life." Upsetting one's "entire life" is equivalent to dispersing one's character armor, one's customary way of coping with existence.

Ironically, the fear of death is the very thing what keeps us in a bind and stands in the way of transcendence. The bind lies in the great difficulty we have in admitting the "hopeless lack of genuine centering on our own energies to assure the victory of our life," as Becker wrote. Death makes such a victory impossible. Admission of this is hard for modern people, as seen in Harrington's desperate biomedical immortality project.

It's hard to admit, writes Becker, that "there is no strength within oneself" to bear the overwhelming fact of life and death. "To yield is to admit that support has to come from outside oneself and that justification for one's life has to come totally from some self-transcending web in which one consents to be suspended ..."

Becker's book ends with a plea for a fusion of science and religion. Again, as with Harrington, Brown, Marcuse and others, there is no reference to the possible role of parapsychology in bringing about the essential changes of mind. But parapsychology is the most obvious candidate for laying the foundations of a science of the Transcendent.

The fear is that if we renounce the armor, the illusion of scientific omnipotence, we might end up cheated, deceived, without armor or protection against death-anxiety. To renounce physicalist science for the sake of transcendent psi would be psychologically risky. Psychic science is probabilistic. To stabilize anxiety, we need something unequivocal, repeatable on demand—if at all possible.

But a repeatable experiment on demand eludes parapsychology. Psi is elusive and blows around like the unpredictable wind. Most grown men—grown into the radical insecurity of existence—crave more secure relationships. Like Lysias, in Plato's *Phaedrus*, modern rationalists prefer manageable and profitable relations with their lovers to those riskier, more truly romantic affairs that move us beyond ourselves.

Becker and Brown made the case that the *causa-sui* project won't work: that is, the hope of achieving total independence from transcendent powers. Scientific technology transcends the old mythologies. Yet neither peace nor plenty have come to pass from all the Promethean efforts. I'm afraid there is even more bad news. Science has helped invent and produce the machinery that makes it possible for the human race to commit suicide with the click of a button.

If science is our technological armor against the fear of death, it's not doing a very good job. In fact, it's doing the opposite, not only ripping to shreds the old life-guiding mythologies but creating the technical machinery for the physical control, reorganization, and destruction of our lives. The supernatural has been trashed, the natural exploited, the unnatural and the inhuman installed as what is becoming the basis of mundane survival.

The Dead-End of Thanatology

Thanatology has made death an academically respectable subject. The trouble is that talking about the sociology of the funeral, the psychology of mourning, the ethico-legal status of the death certificate, skirts around the edge of the basic question of what death actually is. Volume after volume is produced by the academicians of death. Mountains of data are amassed, but to what end?

In one example from the academy of death, the authors lavish attention on the details of the burial process. We are provided with the following fascinating observations which are typical of this volume:

> Most persons choose earth burial, where the body is placed in a casket and buried beneath the ground; a stone monument or marker is customarily placed above the grave to mark its location . . .

The writers continue to discuss the materials used in the construction of coffins, the options for design, etc. It seems a good way to deaden the consciousness of death. In the middle of the book we find a one page section dealing with the question of life after death. A mere page devoted to the ultimate question!

Thanatology, supposedly the new science of death, is a stillborn discipline. The professors of thanatology mostly work within a framework which assumes, without hesitation, that death is annihilation of consciousness; but surely a science of death should be open to all the data, including the relevant transpersonal and paranormal data. Unfortunately, most of the new wave of death experts show little acquaintance with this broader material.

One study examines the relationship between death and the creative life.[39] The author, Dr. Lisl Goodman, a psychotherapist, ran interviews with highly self-actualized people, famous and successful artists or scientists, as well as with numbers of "failures," people who are "drop-outs" or who lead "aimless lives." Are the successful, the self-actualized, those who fulfil their potentialities, better able to deal with death?

The writer concludes from her interviews that it is possible to win the race with death by achieving a kind of "immortality" through "self-fulfilment." This is an important idea, though everything depends on what you mean by self-fulfilment. Goodman's model is, in a curious way Hegelian insofar as it relies on the notion of recognition. All her self-actualizers are public, productive personages. Those who perform, achieve, and excel according to established standards are rewarded with the badge of self-actualization: their photographs appear in popular magazines, they have epiphanies on network talk shows, live comfortably, even opulently by world standards. We know all the telltale signs of the great self-actualizers.

But there is no room for the "drop-outs," the unfortunate mass of botched and bungled humanity. Since money is a handy tool for self-actualization, the rich seem to stand a better chance of grappling with the nuisance of mortality.

The author has a vague, worshipful attitude toward human potential. Says she, "... to one who has succeeded in reaching self-fulfilment by giving form to all the latent possibilities within, death no longer presents a threat: one has won the race with death." I doubt if any highly conscious creative person would believe that he or she had ever realized "all the latent possibilities within" them.

In any case, "all" the latent possibilities within must include much that is wicked, brutal and repulsive. One thinks of the ancient Greek self-actualizer, Herostratus, who put the torch to the temple of Artemis wishing to immortalize his name. For the vast majority of human beings throughout history, the race with death is lost.

Was Leonardo da Vinci a self-actualized man? Perhaps in the eyes of those who worship the aura of fame and "immortality." But not in the eyes of Leonardo apparently! Thus, at the end of his life, he reproached himself bitterly and said, "I have wasted my days."

And what of Goethe, another giant self-actualizer? Goodman herself reminds us of Goethe's obsession with death, how he refused to see his wife on her deathbed or go to her funeral. And this was after living with her for three decades. This hardly seems like a man who has won the race with death. It seems more like denial, shabby defensiveness, behavior we might expect from neurotic failures.

The truth is that we can neither assign any limits to human potentiality nor can we say that any amount of self-actualizing enables us to "win the race" with death. Human beings are self-transcenders, not just self-actualizers. Neither the dream of indefinite life-extension nor the secular ideal of self-actualization are bread to satisfy the hunger for immortality.

A Stimulus to Self-perfection

Western philosophers, long before modern humanists, were passionate about human perfectibility. The old masters of the tradition saw the connection between human perfectibility and life after death. Death was seen as a major step in the evolution, not the extinction, of human potential.

In the *Phaedo*, Socrates puts his finger on a good motive for disbelieving in life after death. About to drink the fatal hemlock, he says:

> We ought to bear in mind that, if the soul is immortal, we must care for it, not only in respect to this time, which we call life, but in respect to all time; and if we neglect it, the danger now appears to be terrible. For if death were an escape from everything, it would be a boon to the wicked, for when they died they would be free from the body and from their wickedness with their souls. But now, since the soul is seen to be immortal, it cannot escape from evil or be saved in any other way than by becoming as good and wise as possible.

Immortality here becomes the basis for a mythology of self-perfection and self-transcendence. In other words, the belief in a life after death is compatible with the great assumption of human potential.

On the other hand, the belief in a life after death can be used as an instrument to bully, threaten, dominate and even justify holy murder. So there is a dark side to transcendent ideas.

Item: In general, the idea of judgment of the dead, of postmortem rewards and punishments, is not in favor with the modern mind.

It is a more credible story of hell to say, as Sartre did, that it's Other People. Attitudes vary a good deal. Some fanatics object to current near-death research because it fosters a picture that death is judgment-free, and worry because dying is presented as just too pleasant.

And what of all that judgment talk? We could call it an archetypal projection of humanity crying out for justice. One concession is possible: once in a while, punitive imagery of hell could be a booster for the morally challenged.

Modern secular morality has freed itself from the threats and sanctions of a future life. Is this a moral boon or does it open the door to nihilism? If God is dead, isn't anything possible?

Marxism broke with French and American revolutionary traditions and proclaimed that religion was the opiate of the people. But the fear of hell, the acute sense of personal responsibility, and the ideal of spiritual perfection hardly seem like opiates. As far as opiates, in the sense that we deceive ourselves about what the world is like and what we are, Hannah Arendt wrote:

> Modern ideologies, whether political or psychological or social, are far better fitted to immunize man's soul against the shocking impact of reality than any traditional religion we know. Compared with the various superstitions of the twentieth century, the pious resignation to God's will seems like a child's pocketknife in competition with atomic weapons.[40]

In the past, mythologies of a future state actively served as more or less useful moral guides for the populace. And I'm sure that for some they still do. But such mythologies are out of fashion today among the educated and the derivative popular culture.

Loss of belief in a future state has various effects. It may be thought of as a spur to authenticity, in the spirit of Heidegger; on the other hand, nodding to Unamuno, it may intensify the drivenness, the ferocious need to singularize oneself, to make a memorable mark on the world, no matter how. The hunger returns to inspire fantasies of computerized immortality. There are people who think they can load their souls into a computer chip and make themselves immortal. As for crazy fundamentalism, it's no answer to a missing mythology of transcendence.

Death and a Lonely Child

I'll end this chapter with an example of how extensions in the concept of mind may be useful in forming a new myth of death. The following was written by a thirty-year-old student in a class where I had discussed types of evidence for an afterlife:

> The greatest problem that death presents, in my opinion, is its finality. When I began this course I had feelings of anger, desperation, fear and confusion. My daughter, age six, is dying of leukemia. Her fears were hard enough to deal with, but compounded by my own fears, the task was next to impossible.

> The night we discussed children's reincarnation memories was the turning point for me. I began to see there were many possibilities I had never considered before. People must examine their innermost thoughts and feelings to come to terms with death. Now I feel that when the end comes, I will still feel pain but I also feel that my child may go on to another dimension.

> She will not be alone; there will be others to watch over and guide her to the next life. I have been successful in conveying some of these more positive feelings to my daughter. Now she also seems more relaxed and the anxiety she had is greatly diminished. We're both more comfortable with what's coming.
>
> My thanks, Mary

I had no idea, until the end of the semester that Mary's child was dying. I had presented some data in support of the survival hypothesis. My conclusions were tentative, even skeptical. I did, however, stress that there were grounds for believing in life after death, even though a complete proof was unavailable, at least not yet.

Mary described her child's terror of going away, of dying lonely. With regard to her daughter, the world looked bleak. The empirical findings—the stories shared in class—helped her form a new story she could share with her child. A story that allowed them to hope. Maybe in the end it will be all right after all.

Part Two: Potential to Respond

4

ON GOING IN AND OUT OF THE BODY

Our religions make promises to be fulfilled beyond the grave because they have no knowledge now to be put to the test, but the ancients spoke of a divine vision to be attained while we are yet in the body.

—AE

THE CANDLE OF VISION

As far as revising the prevailing mythology of death, the out-of-body experience (OBE) ranks as a real step forward. The phenomenon plays a role in traditional thought, has spiritual and therapeutic significance, and helps us picture human nature in novel ways. It even provides fodder for speculating on our evolutionary potential.

Defining out-of-body experience can be tricky. You are clearly aware of yourself located somewhere outside, or at a distance from, where you know your body is located. Your center of awareness has shifted. In an out-of-body state, awareness is extended in space, it is de-localized. In the two or three out-of-body episodes I had, I can describe how it felt: light, mobile, electric, ecstatic—at the same time, possibly angst-inducing, in my case, the instant I found myself outside. I feared getting lost in mental space. Mental space, I knew, could be *anything* and *anywhere*. The possibilities were infinite; I recoiled and snapped back into my body.

No doubt an odd experience, it comes in many flavors. I would wonder about this talent for escaping the constraints of time and space. What does it mean? Does it bear on the hypothetical future existence?

We can say that veridical, information-bearing OBEs are very important. They prove that the experience is objectively real. This is not easy to explain and points to a certain independence of the eye of the mind from the eye of the body. This is enough to upset some guardians of Establish Science.

But there is something else about the OBE. There is the ecstatic dimension of the out-of-body experience. Interest in this was piqued by my study of the Joseph of Copertino (1603-1663). Ecstasy is altered state linked to extraordinary phenomena like levitation. This prompts me to ask: If the soul in ecstasy can carry the body high in the air, it seems like the sort of something that could exist without the body.

I have spoken with many who claim to have "left" their bodies, as in the following.

A Curious Night Visit From a Lady

In 1976 I made the acquaintance of a student of anthropology, Mrs. E.S. of Belleville, N. J. More than once she experienced being out of her body, for instance, during her second childbirth. Mrs. S. didn't claim much control in starting her out-of-body flights, but once they had begun, she had control over where she went.

I casually suggested that she try "visiting" me in her out-of-body state. Nothing more was said of the matter.

Within a few weeks, the following occurred. But first I need to say that at that time I had begun playing the flute; in the morning I practiced for about an hour. A music stand stood by a large bookcase in the living room. I deliberately kept the stand in the same spot, so I was puzzled one morning when I awoke, went for my flute but found the stand in the middle of the living room. I had no idea how it got there; no one else was in the house nor had I received any visitors the night before. I was puzzled for a moment but assumed I unconsciously moved the stand myself.

Within an hour, I received a telephone call from Mrs. S. Without my mentioning the music stand, she recounted the following. The night before—it was well past midnight—she found herself out of her body and decided to try to "visit" me. She did this merely by concentrating her attention; suddenly she found herself observing me reading in the kitchen. (I was, in fact, reading in the kitchen at that time.) My out-of-body guest hovered nearby but was unable to make any impression on me.

She wondered how she could leave her mark. After straying through the house, feeling a bit frustrated, she came upon the music stand and took hold of it with her out-of-body "hands," appearing to herself to succeed in moving it to the center of the living room. She then returned to her vacated body in Belleville.

Here we have at least a remarkable chain of coincidences. On that morning, I unwittingly moved my music stand. Mrs. S. hallucinated paying me a visit, coincidentally noting just what I was doing at the time, and coincidentally imagining she moved the music stand I unwittingly moved.

The alternative to coincidence is to say that somehow she actually did "leave" her body and was able to displace a physical object in my room. The story is one of many reported out-of-body flights; I cite it because I was an eyewitness to a displaced metal music stand weighing (with music sheets) over two pounds. What to make of it? Did Mrs. S.— and can people—really "leave" the body? And while out roam around in space and move physical objects?

The Importance of Being Out-Of-Body

For an excellent account of the phenomenon, the history and the experimental literature, see Carlos Alvarado's historical overview.[41] In a global cross-cultural survey, Dean Shiels[42] found that ninety-five percent of the world's cultures believe in OBEs. According to Shiels, the belief in OBEs is strikingly uniform; a recurrent phenomenon of human experience. Other surveys vary, but it is clear that large numbers of people, millions perhaps, are having out-of-body experiences.

For many years I've asked students of various ages and ethnic backgrounds about OBEs. About ten percent say they've had the experience. OBEs have seeped into popular consciousness through reports of near-death experiences.

The idea of being able to split up, form a double of oneself, and wander freely in time and space, describes the essence of magic—if by magic we mean certain uncanny kinds of mental power. This sort of experience, when I first heard about it, was very surprising. It didn't tally with the idea that my conscious self was identical or hopelessly entangled with my brain.

If people have experiences from outside their brains, I thought, it was very interesting. It inspired a sense of freedom, of expansive optimism. That was the giddy side, but there was also a philosophical side. *Leaving the body* is a very odd locution. What to make of it?

The Mind-body Problem

Besides all the problems of life, there is a thing called the "mind-body" problem. What we find when we look around and look within are two different kinds of stuff. When we look, touch, listen, taste, smell, we sense all sorts of things through our sense organs—computers, coffee cups, patches of blue, flashes of gold, windows, a plane in the sky, a ground hog.

When I shift my attention and look within, I find sensations, reasons, dreams, memories, images, a fuzzy thing I call *my* self, along with moods, memories, beliefs, and desires–stuff like that. What we find inside we call mental; everything else we meet outside is physical.

So what's the problem?

The problem is how the two kinds of stuff relate to each other and which if any is more basic or derivative. Oceans of words have been spent trying to give answers. Some philosophers focus on the least conceptually disturbing aspects of mental life, like itches, pains, or afterimages. These are mental happenings that *seem* close to bodily happenings. It is just under the left shoulder blade that I want so badly to scratch.

The throbbing ache in my tooth is right here and now in my mouth and not afloat in the heaven of Platonic Ideas. The truth is that even these near-body mental events are not easily digested by or identical to anything physical. Even our most localized sensations depend on attention. If I dwell on, anxiously expect my bad knee to hurt, the more pain I tend to feel. If my attention is yanked elsewhere, my pain is up and away. We ourselves or a good hypnotist can decrease our experience of pain by manipulating attention. When Joseph the ecstatic went into trance, the brothers would poke, jab, shout, or torch him without any indication of him noticing. Some sort of a plug was pulled—Joseph was elsewhere.

Problems increase for materialism when we turn to higher activates such as reasoning or imagining or making moral judgments. Difficulties further multiply when we look at paranormal and transpersonal mental occurrences. None of the foregoing can be identified with any known brain process, and even if there were fixed correlations between brain events and mental events, it would not explain much.

Suppose a person whose body is located at X has a correct mental impression of something at location Y., Y being in a separate room or town. This would suggest that my mind is not localized in my brain or body. There are knots to untie here, but if such things happen, they challenge our view of mind as brain-dependent.

The out-of-body phenomenon sheds light on the shamanic roots of religion. Shamanism is the archaic response to the Transcendent, which Mircea Eliade describes as the quest for ecstasy. The shaman is the master out-of-body explorer of higher and lower worlds who rescues lost souls, curries favor with gods, spirits, and other emissaries from the beyond. The shaman is the transcendent experimentalist, poet and namer of gods and demons, mapper of psychic geographies.

The present stage of evolution of life on earth and its looming dangers suggest a mandate for a new consciousness. Out-of-body research points to new environments of exploration. There are no *a priori* limits we can place upon future directions in the evolution of life, and for all we know, the out-of-body state may be matrix for one possible direction of evolutionary development.

Consciousness delocalized suggests the possibility of a prolonged or even permanent out-of-body experience—also known as the *afterlife.* The idea is simple: if a person can be conscious and out of the body while living, the condition may persist after bodily death. The idea takes on reality when a person has a close brush with death in a car accident, say, and observes his body pronounced dead by a bystander yet continues to be conscious and to feel alive, indeed, to feel intensely alive. The temptation to embrace the idea of an afterworld can be quite strong after having such an experience.

Things look different from the outsider's viewpoint; perhaps the experience was just an interesting hallucination. The "outsider" is not compelled to accept the claims of people who have these unusual experiences. But it would be unwise to dismiss them out of hand, and experiences of my own have forced me to be a little more open-minded.

I was vacationing on the small Greek island of Aegina. My plan was to "astral project" by loosening my imagination and learning to linger on the border between waking and dreaming.

I pictured myself flying above my house, floating over the outdoor cafés, tracing in my mind's eye the crooked moonlit streets leading to the shore's edge. I did this internal work several nights in a row, which left me in a twilight state of phantasmal alertness, never quite yielding to sleep.

In the back of my mind I kept musing about Gilgamesh of the great Sumerian epic who after a long journey finally found the plant of immortality but fell asleep, allowing a serpent to steal it from him. With my efforts I succeeded in producing a startling effect at least once. Half-dreaming, sensing vague presences, faces, murmurs, all at once I shot with a swish through the top of my head straight up through the roof into the sky. I looked around as I whirled through space; down below was the sea and the streets of the town. It looked familiar but it was dark. I was awake and clear about what I was experiencing. Then in a flash I was back in my body. Was it a dream? An illusion? Or a short leap of the spirit out of the prison of my body?

Conceptual Disarray

Psychological theories hold that the OBE is like a dream, a memory or episode of the imagination. Parapsychologists suggest that some OBEs can be verified as objectively true. Some think a conscious entity separates from the body, moves around in space, and observes events from viewpoints distant from the body.

Remember Cary Grant's double cavorting about in the classic ghost-story, *Topper*. Or we might recall the astral, spiritual and radiant bodies of the Platonic and New Testament traditions or the fluidic bodies of 19th century mesmerists. G. S. Mead outlined a history of the doctrine of the subtle body. According to the separation theory, the subtle body is sometimes detectable and appears localized.[43]

OBEs often occur during sleep and dreams, and so may be a special type of dream. Moreover, dreams are psi-conducive, which explains why some OBEs have psi ingredients. OBEs show perceptual mistakes, as do memories; hence OBEs may be a type of memory. There are psychoanalytic approaches in which fear of death creates the illusion of doubles. Still others say that in the twilights of waking life called hypnogogic, we create a body-image that may cause us to imagine we are out of our body.

Is the person out-of-body located *somewhere*? A localized out-of-body perception would differ from ESP. To test this, Karlis Osis, of the American Society for Psychical Research, used a special optical device by which subjects could correctly identify targets, but only from a specific position within a few feet. The evidence from these tests supports the idea of a localized out-of-body presence.

Harvey Irwin, an Australian researcher, tested versions of the psychological theory and found nothing to show that fear of death correlates with having OBEs. Irwin has also produced evidence at odds with Susan Blackmore's reductionist theory; OBErs are not better at imaging tasks than non-OBErs, which they should be, if the experience is a product of the imagination, as Blackmore believed.

What does it mean to leave or be out of one's body? All experience is mental. My experience of the room my body is sitting in now is mental; the objects in my room, the desk, the computer, my brain are all in physical space, but my awareness of them is not. All experience implies being out of the body. So what about the OBE we are discussing?

We might turn the question upside down and ask why we experience ourselves as *in* the body at all. If all experience is essentially "out" of the body, why do we normally feel located "in" our bodies?

Most of our normal waking life is spent using, expressing, and caring for the needs of our bodies. As I switch lanes driving on the highway, survival depends on attending to the immediate sensory environment. While I play tennis, eat lunch, control my keyboard—in short, use my body—I am compelled to attend to and identify with it, enjoy its pleasures and suffer its pains.

As Plato said in the *Phaedo*, our use of the body causes us to identify with it, and think it most "real." When we attend to normal bodily functions, to events on the plane of life, we experience ourselves as in, about, and bound to our bodies.

But things happen that disrupt the normal sense of being connected to our bodies. Routines are shattered, there are breaks in the flow of sensory input and motor output: dreaming, deep relaxation, extreme stress, any violently unexpected situation. Forced to disidentify with our bodies in critical situations, consciousness may slip out-of-body.

Some OBErs report experiencing themselves in duplicate bodies, some in cloudy diaphanous envelopes, still others as balls or points of light. Yet others lay claim to a pure bodiless state. Some report the sensation of moving from X to Y; others say passage is instantaneous. Some claim they can "see" their physical bodies; others do not. For some, getting in and out is attended by sensations of electrical vibrations; for others, transition is smooth and unconscious. Some OBErs claim passage in parallel or higher worlds, in fantasy worlds, in normal space, or in outer space.

Finally, some out-body sojourners tell of environments that mix the normal, the fantastic and the transcendent. OBEs are voluntarily induced; more often they occur involuntarily. Some are subjective, like dreams; others involve veridical perception of the physical world. This is a pretty slippery phenomenon, and it almost seems we're sliding in and out of our body all the time.

Many describe the experience as hyper-real, brilliantly vivid and intense. But so are some dreams and visions real in this sense, and dreams like OBEs may produce striking aftereffects. There is no scientific consensus on the nature and function of dreams. Francis Crick and Graeme Mitchison seem to dismiss the idea of dreams having any cultural value. But had Descartes, Kekule, Poincare, and other scientists done so, science would be the poorer today. To dismiss the role of dreams in history, religion, anthropology; in the arts, psychotherapy, and mythology would stunt our mental horizons.

Dreams vary in degrees of vividness, coherence, and meaningfulness: lucid dreams, high dreams, archetypal dreams, group dreams; telepathic, precognitive, and near-death dreams—dreams that elide into full-fledged out-of-body experiences.

Remarks of Colin Brookes-Smith are worth quoting in the present context:

> The reality and nature of mind may always remain an unresolved enigma, but the fact of its psychical ability to organize chemical atoms into temporary amorphous or structured forms to perform particular tasks or even to replicate by ideoplastic materialization human faces and clothed bodies as in apparitions will no longer be doubted ... The evidence suggests that if a volitional impulse demands action or seeks information beyond the range of limbs or senses, then an appropriate tenuous-matter structure is temporarily exteriorized which not only performs mechanical tasks but also acts as a sensory organ.[44]

This describes in a plausible, economical way how psi may account for paranormal out-of-body effects. Yet it is easy to see the appeal of the idea of a double, of a fixed entity or "tangible something." Persons, it might be thought, need some sort of double as a vehicle for inhabiting the postmortem world. Without that self-identifying vehicle, we might evaporate into nonentity. We need to think of ourselves in solid terms. We gravitate toward the thinglike, toward substance and mechanism.

But psi is all we need to account for tangible signs that a person has "projected" out of the body. In one study, Karlis Osis and Donna McMormick found that when star OB projector Dr. Alex Tanous exteriorized himself to a specific location, sensitive strain gauges nearby registered an unknown physical force. Tanous wasn't informed of the presence of the strain gauges; this suggests that the effects he produced were not the result of expectation but that something of Tanous was localized at the target site, something with energetic effects.

It looks as if Tanous deployed his PK to produce a transient physical extension of himself that influenced the strain gauge. The idea of psychokinesis duplicating a transient "double" or symbol of the body is enough to account for ghostly manifestations. Even the worlds we enter in our dreams might be subtle creations of our PK. We don't really know what dreams are or how private they are.

In the 1960s, Stanley Krippner and Montague Ullman at the Maimonides Dream Laboratory performed experiments proving that outside agents could influence the dream life of experimental subjects.[45] So it appears we can get out of ourselves and we can also get inside others through their dreams. This fact may disturb people who believe in the kind of security afforded by the idea of walls.

Art, Ecstasy and Out-of-Body Experience

Ecstasy is another word for the out-of-body experience—meaning, literally, standing outside oneself. Ecstasy is of all states of consciousness the one most intimately related to transcendence. Ecstasy figures in religion, art, and history where we find a trend toward a higher, freer, more elastic body. William Butler Yeats was hinting at something like this when he wrote these lines in *Sailing to Byzantium*.

> Consume my heart away; sick with desire
> And fastened to a dying animal
> It knows not what it is; and gather me
> Into the artifice of eternity.

Going out of the body is about finding a new body, an artifice of eternity, a transformed mode of existence. Making art and music is one way this can happen. Art and music represent worlds distilled, re-ordered, and transformed by the creative imagination.

There is a psychology of the aesthetic perspective, summed up in the phrase—the pathos of distance.

The British psychologist, Edward Bullough, in a classic paper on "psychical distance," argued that the aesthetic attitude consists of maintaining the right degree of psychical distance from the object we contemplate. Psychical distance disconnects the object from the real world and turns it into material for aesthetic construction and enjoyment. "Distance," Bullough wrote, "is obtained by separating the object and its appeal from one's own self, by putting it out of gear with practical needs and ends."[46] As with the out-of-body state, attention is sharply deflected from the plane of life.

Two problems with the aesthetic attitude are *under-*and *over-*distancing. Suppose I'm watching a play; the villain reminds me of someone I know and dislike; I overreact and cuss under my breath. The aesthetic quality of the experience is ruined. It became *too* real. Under-distancing is marked by excessive involvement: envying or adoring the heroine, viscerally loathing the villain. As for its general utility, psychical distance favors the cultivation of wider sympathies, a definite plus to our nascent mythology. Broadly speaking, a detached, inclusive perspective on things will almost always be useful in the rough art of living.

Speaking of art, when it's great, we neither hate the villain nor adore the hero, but see them both as part of an interesting and bigger human story. If we over-distance, we may feel nothing at all, an unfortunate model for the art of living.

Like Bullough, Kant the philosopher saw in aesthetic awareness a suspension of the category of existence. "The beautiful is that which pleases in disinterested contemplation," he wrote and went on. "Disinterestedness is pure contemplation independent of concern for the real existence of the object."[47] Interest is based on desire, which fuels our passion for pleasure and good or bad. In disinterested contemplation, we rise above the opposites of pain and pleasure, evil and good.

Through art and the spell of beauty, we learn to detach ourselves from existence. Immersed in the struggle for survival we spend our energies; in art we gather our internal forces for the sake of active, free play. Artistic and aesthetic activity are for the sake of self-enjoyment. Released from the compulsion to succeed and singularize oneself.

The free play of our psychic powers – laying aside the rational and the practical — was Kant's idea of the aesthetic potential of consciousness.

Aesthetic activity was said to be "purposive without purpose", and not restrained by rules. "The cognitive powers are here in free play, because no definite concept limits them to a definite rule of cognition." This is a rare space to savor and enjoy.

Arousal without cognitive and emotional restraints, lack of ego-involvement, spontaneity and playfulness, all these are congenial to success in psi tasks, and in fact it seems that many talented psychics are gifted artists; just as artists are tuned to the psychic.

Einbildungskraft—"power of imagination," according to Kant, consists of power to negate nature, the given reality, *and* to create another, a better, in its place. From the material supplied by nature, genius creates something that transcends nature. Genius implies "freedom from the law of association," and art is a vehicle for exploring the outer limits of the possible. For W.B. Yeats it was about creating artifices of the imagination for glimpsing William Blake's "eternity."

The philosopher Arthur Schopenhauer, influenced by Kant, believed in the healing power of art: a power employed to free us from the blind will to exist, a procedure for questioning our raw instincts and automatic assumptions—for stopping us in the tracks of our existence.

Art becomes a way of disengaging from the constraints of everyday life, of beginning to create, concretely and symbolically, another nature, a transcendent environment. A work of art is a sensuous embodiment, an autonomous world, constructed in accord with the "rules" of the imagination. A landscape of Nicholas Poussin or a still-life of Giorgio Morandi are both symbols and sensuous embodiments of a higher order, a more perfect world in which form, line, color and psychic energy blend into one harmonious whole.

Kant's philosophy of art took off in other directions with F. Schiller's *The Aesthetic Education of Man* and with the 20th century theories of Herbert Marcuse. According to Schiller, the aim of art is to educate the whole person. Without the sense of beauty, the rational and moral side of human nature develops out of proportion. The effects can be hazardous. Beauty humanizes reason and tames morality. Reason without beauty becomes mechanical; morality without soul heartless.

This theme was taken up by Marcuse, who stressed the erotic side of the beautiful. The aesthetic sensibility foreshadows a new type of humanity, a new reality-principle based on the spirit of song and play, the charm against aggressive competition. With Marcuse the critical function of art was uppermost. Art creates images of a possible world, images that indict and negate established social realities.

Art is the free spirit of the imagination reconnoitering the realm of the possible. It points to us and says with critical passion: this is what life could be like! Why not make life like a Mozart clarinet concerto or a painted garden of Matisse? A world subdued by aesthetic form, the energies of greed and aggression sublimated.

Negation under the banner of art proceeds by different routes. Each authentic artwork is an outcry of the imprisoned spirit, a cry for wholeness. The more completely the artwork expresses internal coherence, the more it reminds us of how sordid and disjointed daily life is. Like the out-of-body traveller—light, luminous, rejuvenated—the artwork exhibits an alternate world, enlightened by the harmonious free play of the spirit.

Marcuse ends by objecting to Kant's view of art as disinterested. He objects to art as merely contemplative. The visionary world of art foreshadows a new society on earth. *Eros and Civilization* (1955) was an inspirational text to the revolutionary 1960s. One of the questions it poses: What will our bodies look like and feel like in a world freed from oppression and exploitation? The new body will be defined by its erotic, not its "productive" potential. A similar argument appears in N. O. Brown's *Love's Body* (1966). Here too we encounter the body transformed by love into an instrument of aesthetic delight.

In an essay *Art as a Form of Reality*, Marcuse wrote: "It seems that the aesthetic sublimation is approaching its historical limits, that the commitment of Art to the ideal, to the beautiful and the sublime, and to the 'holiday' function of art, now offends the human condition."[48] Art should not sublimate but transform existence, serve as a tool to re-fashion a new sensibility. Marcuse wanted to see the human body become a vehicle of human satisfaction, not a tool of corporate profiteering.

The Metaphysics of Modern Art

Yeats's concern for an "out-of-nature" body gets us to the metaphysics of modern art. Modern art, freed from the idea of itself as imitation, embraced a metaphysics of sovereign creativity.

Ad Reinhardt, for instance, a master of minimal art, was steeped in Zen thought. His final, "black" paintings, where the visible hovers on the threshold of the invisible, were evocations of the dark night of the soul, meditations on the tunnel that leads to the Being of Light. Reinhard's art was to minimize the visible, make an image of no image.

It was an art dedicated to the transcendence of art. Few artists were less willing to rely on the visible world for his art than Ad Reinhardt, painter of the mystical *via negativa.*

Metaphysics in modern art is evident in all the major movements: cubism, in its quest for the geometry of the fourth dimension; expressionism, in its revolt against reliance upon external reality; dada, in its assault on conventional logic; surrealism, in its desire to incarnate dream life; conceptual and environmental art, breaking all boundaries, bringing art into the foreground of life itself.

The great Surrealist, Georgio de Chirico, nursed his art on the thought of Nietzsche and Schopenhauer. In his 1912 *Meditations of a Painter,* Chirico quotes the following from Schopenhauer: "To have original, extraordinary, and perhaps even immortal ideas, one has but to isolate oneself from the world for a few moments so completely that the most commonplace happenings appear to be new and unfamiliar, and in this way reveal their true essence."

We are back to the idea of deflecting attention from the plane of life, defixating attention from the struggle for survival.

Modernist art revolted against everyday perception, everyday reality. Art was a transcendent act, a raid on the fourth dimension, a destruction of the solid and the familiar.

In a famous letter, the poet Arthur Rimbaud described his method of becoming a clairvoyant, a seer. "Je est un autre," he wrote: "I is another." Rimbaud's method was to subject his senses to a *dereglement,* literally, a deruling. His method was diametrically opposed to Descartes', which was to filter our perception of reality through a small, incorrigible set of rational rules.

Marcel Duchamp epitomized the revolt against the rule-bound mind. His gesture was, first, to refuse to repeat himself. It was his way of purging the habitual and the mechanical from his art. The final gesture was to renounce painting itself. Duchamp chose to do nothing, to act only from a motive of "amusement." Art became a game played with the will, a game of chess, a diverting manipulation of reality tokens. One work consists of a photograph of himself playing chess with a naked woman: a portrait of the artist practicing psychical distance.

Duchamp cultivated a form of painting he said was in the "service of the mind." Dada, he wrote, was "an extreme protest against the physical side of painting. It was a metaphysical attitude. It was a sort of nihilism to which I am still very sympathetic. It was a way to get out of a state of mind—to avoid being influenced by one's immediate environment, or by the past: to get away from clichés—to get free."

Aesthetic consciousness is a way of dislocating oneself from the habitual stances and postures of the body. It aims to create psychical distance, to disengage from practical reason, to learn to see things in their isolated thinghood, to destabilize the rules of ordinary perception, and so on. All these phrasings point to one task—in a word invented by Dante, *trashumanar* – "to transcend humanity." Art then is one way that consciousness carries on the search for ecstasy—for "getting out of a state of mind," as Duchamp put it. Art is one way of "getting out." It's not the only way.

The Spectator of All Time and Existence

According to Plato, the philosopher is a "spectator" of all time and existence. Strange view of philosophy! And how different it is from today where philosophy labors in such highly specialized ways.

The ancient philosophers placed a high value on the contemplative life. The modern world is very much about the active life and nothing is more definitive of humanity than being a "productive" member of society. We rarely hear folks being praised for their contemplative virtues. Without dedication to the active life, it would be impossible to maintain the rate of economic growth necessary to the system's survival. One may not say with Walt Whitman: "I loaf and invite my soul."

Given that the mainline ethos isn't very contemplative, it's no wonder that claims of transcendent experience are suspect. In fact, people who nearly die sometimes report becoming spectators of their whole life, and, they insist, in minute detail. The experience is deeply transformative.

The philosopher-parapsychologist, Ramakrishna Rao, states, in light of his research:

> Every subject is a microcosm, potentially capable of reflecting the whole cosmos. This potential is not realized because we are habitually and constitutionally given to respond to and interact with our environment rather than to probe within to discover hidden knowledge. Psi events do seem to indicate, however, that this is not an irreversible process and that on occasion knowledge can be had by tapping our inner resources. Thus we are led to postulate an omniscience inherent in our very being.[49]

The language of unlimited capacities, and perhaps the language of divine powers, seem based on the assumption of unlimited psi potential, and point for all we know to future human evolution. The psychological difficulty of accepting the reality of survival must in part be the result of seeing the dominant culture of action, productivity and achievement as defining what life was about.

The kind of life we lead and the kind of experiences we have shape our view of the nature of reality. In this chapter, we're looking at one type of experience that jolts minds into embracing a greater spiritual reality.

Greek Shamanism

The image of the spectator is primordial. It came through strong with Plato and Pythagoras. We should glance backward at the shamanic wise men of early Greece. Shrouded in obscurity and older than Thales or Heraclitus are the figures of Abaris of Hyperborea, Aristeas of Prokonnesos, Hermotimos of Klazomenai, and the Cretan, Epimenides. Ecstatic seers and cathartic priests, they were great fasters capable of prolonged out-of-body journeys.

Aristeas, for instance, was a man of high rank in his native city. According to Suidas, "whenever he wanted, his soul left his body and returned again." Or from Maximum of Tyre we hear that while his body lay as if dead, his "soul going out of the body sailed into the aither." In this state, he was "seized by Phoibos" and given mantic knowledge of past and future.

The case of Hermotimos is intriguing. It was said that he could go out of his body for prolonged periods of time. According to Pliny and Plutarch, the enemies of Hermotimos, enlisting the help of his wife, set fire to the seer's deserted body, thus making it impossible for his soul to return from its voyages.

Hermotimos, however, also figures in the history of philosophy of mind; for according to Aristotle in the *Metaphysics* (948b), Hermotimos was among the first to clearly distinguish between pure Mind and matter. From the town of Klazomenai came another philosopher-shaman, Anaxagoras, condemned to death because he theorized that the sun was a red-hot meta. But he too had an insight into the fundamental nature of Mind. In the twelfth fragment of Simplicius, he wrote: "All other things have a portion of everything, but Mind is infinite and self-ruled, and is mixed with nothing and is all alone by itself." Anaxagoras grasped the notion of mind at large, nonlocal mind, transpersonal mind.

But what was the source of these ancient insights into the infinite and autonomous power of Mind? The words of Irwin Rhode, the great classical scholar, might shed some light:

> ... when it is related of Hermotimos that he, like his countryman Anaxagoras, attempted a distinction between pure Mind and matter, we can see very clearly how this theory might arise out of his special experiences. The ecstasies of the soul of which Hermotimos and this whole generation had such ample experience seemed to point to the separability of the soul from the body—and indeed to the superiority of the soul's essence in its separate state over that of the body.[50]

Behind the Platonic concept of *theoria*, the condition of being a spectator of all time and being, lies this tradition of primal Greek shamanism: special "experiences" of ecstatic flight beyond the body.

Husserl, Jung and Reduction

The image of the spectator reappears in the phenomenology of Edmund Husserl (1859-1938). The basic technique of phenomenology is the reduction (not to be confused with materialist reductionism). Husserl's reduction is a kind of meditation; it requires practice and resembles Plato's practice of death, a psychic "drilling" that suspends what Husserl calls the "natural standpoint."

Phenomenology is a discipline whose goal, says Husserl, is to "go back" (*re-duce*) to the field of pure consciousness. In the reduction, we make an effort to detach ourselves from all assumptions of what is real, true, objective, natural; and learn to describe, to observe, to see, to record a presence: *not* to explain or evaluate.

"Go within," said Augustine, "the truth lies there,"—words quoted by Husserl in the *Cartesian Meditations*.

The goal of the phenomenological reduction, as Husserl wrote in *Ideas*, is "the winning of a new region of being." Husserl, like Descartes in the seventeenth century, sought a fresh point of departure for grappling with the problems of philosophy. Like Descartes, he began with the attempt to doubt everything. To doubt everything is to express "our perfect freedom."

Husserl borrowed a word from the ancient Greek skeptics— *epoche*, which means abstention. The aim of this abstention from beliefs, opinions and knowledge claims is, among other things, therapeutic. Zen masters say much the same thing: only cease cherishing opinions, and truth will enlighten your mind. The same could be said for those mind-exhausting meditative devices called koans.

Let us rehearse this inner work, and lay aside all aspects of conditioned mind that bind our consciousness, the entire standpoint of the natural world. In the words of Husserl:

> Consciousness in itself has a being of its own which in its absolute uniqueness of nature remains unaffected by the phenomenological disconnexion. It therefore remains over a 'phenomenological residuum,' as a region of being which is in principle unique, and can become in fact the field of a new science—the science of phenomenology.

The field of this science is absolute consciousness, what remains after the objective world is disconnected. The task Husserl set for himself was to purify the foundations of knowledge, to create a new science of the spirit. The reduction is the first step; it brackets the natural standpoint, a technique for dislocating consciousness from its everyday assumptions; it asserts the freedom of spirit over the claims of the natural world. In a related vein, C.G. Jung wrote:

> Not only do I leave the door open for the Christian message, but I consider it of central importance for Western man. It needs, however, to be seen in a new light, in accordance with the changes wrought by the contemporary spirit. Otherwise it stands apart from the times, and has no effect on man's wholeness.[51]

Husserl and Jung, each in their own way, tried to stand outside the "body" of tradition. We may speak of an "out-of-tradition" experience. Just as we normally identify with our bodies, we normally identify with our traditions; we have routine relationships, perhaps stereotypical attitudes toward our bodies, as we do toward our traditions. People inhabit the body of Christian tradition; Jung sought to step outside that body in order to see it more clearly.

Like Husserl, he had to deal with the category of existence. Does God really exist? Do angels and demons, heaven and hell, really exist? Since they don't exist the way atoms and genes exist, or any measurable bodies, their place in the scheme of things is uncertain.

Husserl and Jung tried to renew our sense of reality by introducing methods of suspending cognitive rigidity, the sense of existence itself. Husserl used logic to discredit the primacy of material existence. The only certainty and principle of all philosophy, is transcendental subjectivity, the most logically primitive form of "existence." Jung took a therapeutic tack; what is real, effective and fateful is the psyche; the way we think, sense, feel and imagine the world.

Here is an example of how the "reduction" might help us retrieve meaning from a controversial experience. Suppose somebody says she "saw" an apparition of some mysterious form, a ghost, let's say. But, if I assume that such things don't exist, I automatically destroy my relationship to the phenomenon. I invalidate it before it even begins to speak to me.

The reduction allows the phenomenon as a phenomenon to reveal itself. A discipline of listening, it helps us cultivate the art of understanding that comes before attempts at explaining. What did seeing the apparition mean to Jones as it appeared to her? What was its appearance? How did Jones experience it? The experience surely exists; it is a datum. Jones' apparition, however elusive, lives! Let us adopt a nonviolent attitude toward it; a metaphysics that begins in the nonviolence of understanding.

Something unpleasant is going on: being subjected to the subtle violence of scientific explanation. Whole worlds of meaning are trampled by muddy boots. It is possible to learn to listen, however, to try to understand first, to pause and place ourselves inside the other. Husserl's "reduction,"—the opposite of materialist reductionism—is a prescription for dialogue. It asks us to listen and understand before we judge and explain—listen and observe before we categorize, objectify, and reach for the holster.

The Mystic as Artist

We have been looking at ways that consciousness may be dislocated from its ordinary relationship to the body. We noted how a shift may occur in the context of art and philosophy. Now a word about the mystic quest. The mystic assumes a special attitude toward the body, a progressive detachment from the plane of life where bodily survival is a consuming priority.

A. R. Orage[52] speculated on the idea of the "superman"—the mystic as artist whose artwork is himself. According to this scheme, the difference between human and animal consciousness is a difference in degree of inner detachment. Lower forms of life identify with the external environment; humans, by contrast, dis-identify and transcend. In the interests of ultimate unity, the mystic artist learns to disidentify from the body *and* from one's internal worlds.

The evolutionary charge, if Orage is right, lies in learning to disengage from our interior environments as we at earlier stages of evolution learned to know ourselves and disengage from the external environment. The "superman," according to Orage, stands outside his own mental life the way an ordinary man stands outside the world of external objects.

The arts become spiritual disciplines, imaginative rehearsals for spiritual adventures in possible worlds, whether here or even hereafter. Biologists like Sir Alister Hardy, Ludwig Bertanaffy and John Randall have likened the "intelligence" behind the evolutionary process to that of an artist's. Speaking of the mechanisms behind the transformations of life, Hardy, for instance, wrote: "It seems to me that they have all the appearance of a definite mental conception like that of an artist or designer—a pattern outside the physical world which in some way has served as a template or gauge for selective action."[53] If Mind at Large is an artist, and the forms of life are works of art, then the artist in us reflect the meaning of the story of life.

The Mystic as Witness

The idea of the mystic as witness appears in the writings of Vedanta. Our basic perception of the world is riddled with illusion, according to Vedanta; if we could rid ourselves of the illusion, we would experience ourselves as one with Brahman, the source of true being. Shankara likens this awakening from the illusion of normal mental life to the sudden realization that a frightening snake was really a harmless piece of rope. Our deepest fears spring from persistent cognitive error.

Here is Shankara from Swami Prabhavananda's and Christopher Isherwood's translation of the *Crest-Jewel of Discrimination:*

> There is a Self-Existent reality, which is the basis of our consciousness and ego. That Reality is the witness of the three states of our consciousness, and is distinct from the five bodily coverings (the senses).

Atman is the name of this Self-Existent reality; one of its chief functions is to "witness." As with Orage's superconsciousness, the Hindu self or Atman is said to be the "inner controller."

Besides being "witness" and "controller," the Atman is blissful by nature. Pure consciousness, according to Patanjali's Yoga Sutras, isolated in its "own" form, and unmixed with impressions of the external world, is inherently positive and blissful.

This is a remarkable claim. If true, we don't have to *do* anything in particular to "achieve" enlightenment; rather, it is the "karmic" chain of our needs, desires, memories that obscures our authentic being. The Hindu formula is *satchitananda*, the ultimate one entity— being-consciousness-bliss. We needn't go outside ourselves or acquire new knowledge to attain the saving state. In fact, our strained efforts to do so get in the way.

Shankara and Patanjali return in various ways to the theme of the witness, the seer, the observer, the spectator. The ordinary OBE, I believe, provides a kind of spontaneous episode of consciousness as pure witness. It seems there is no direct way to seize this greater reality of the Self. Letting go, renouncing, forgetting, non-doing suggest the right attitude.

One knows a man who is free in this life, Shankara says, by the sign that "he has no feeling of ownership."

We'll pass by the implications of this remark for economic philosophy. It would be more in line with our discussion to notice how it dovetails with parapsychological findings that "ownership resistance" is psychologically unfavorable to success in performing the magic tricks we know and describe as psychokinesis or telekinesis. Not having the feeling of ownership frees consciousness to experience itself in its naturally blissful condition, according to Shankara.

It also appears to be a condition conducive to psychokinesis. The consciousness that is "real being," the ground of true human felicity, is "real" subjectively–but, it is also real *objectively*. In short, it's causally effective. It can make things happen in extraordinary ways, but we are not to be fooled by these powers into believing they guarantee enlightenment.

"Life flows by," says Shankara, but the man who is free "watches it like a disinterested spectator. He does not identify himself with the body, sense organs, etc. He has risen above the idea of duty. That is how you may know someone who is free even in this life."

Once more, this is a striking bit of counter-intuitive news: Nothing we can do, no external action by itself, can be the equivalent of the actual experience of the Atman, the radical emancipation of one's consciousness.

The great discipline is simply to remain alert. The great art is to take a stand outside the world. "One who remains continually absorbed in the consciousness of Brahman is freed from the tyranny of the objective world." The whole objective world, along with the imperative for action it normally demands, is turned off, discounted, disconnected. Even duty and ritual action are ultimately valueless.

Attitudes like this are potentially very subversive. Just concentrate on the One Being who is eternal bliss; look on all things as matters of indifference. Like the surrealist, the Vedantin sage is describing a technique for de-realizing the world, increasing distance, de-automatizing responses.

Max Scheler describes this aspect of spiritual discipline as Buddha's "technique of de-actualizing the world and the self."[54] The mystic quest in this way is practical metaphysics. Not just the critical examination of fundamental concepts, it aims to change our experience of the world. Marx got it: the philosophers have sought to understand the world; the point is to change it.

What surrealizes or de-realizes our ordinary sense of reality? Reducing resistance, says Scheler. "For all reality," he writes, "because it is reality, and regardless of what it is, is a kind of inhibiting, constraining pressure for every living thing. Its correlate is pure anxiety, an anxiety without object. If reality means resistance, the cancelling of reality can only be the kind of ascetic act by which we suspend the operation of the vital impulse." The sense of reality and the amount of resistance provide an index to our anxiety. For Scheler, the Buddha had a technique for overcoming suffering, a means of "cancelling reality through suspension of desire," a way of making the "sensory world and the physical and mental processes disappear and fall away piece by piece, along with the sensory qualities, shapes, relations and forms of space and time." Buddhists call this state of mind *nirvana*.

It is a way of getting out of the normal body, creating a new relation to space, as in this Buddhist text:

> Herein, a certain person, by passing completely beyond consciousness of form, by paying no attention to consciousness of manifoldness, thinks, 'Space is infinite,' and reaches up to and stays in the sphere of infinite space.

79

This is not the whole story, but a new experience of space, a dislocation of consciousness from the body, is a feature of Buddhist spiritual discipline. The same can be said for Vedanta where the *atman*, understood as witness, radically deflects attention from the plane of life—back into its unplumbed depths.

Conclusion: Mind as Wayward

Creating psychical distance, becoming a spectator, becoming a witness—all these metaphors for spiritual discipline speak of methods of deflecting attention from obsessing over *what is happening to me*.

Mind, however, is on the way, refusing to be arrested, constrained, defined, predicted, or annihilated. However we interpret the out-of-body process—as a denial of death and a re-duplication of the self, as a way of sustaining the image of self and reconstituting the world during times of crisis and confusion, or as authentic flight of the spirit into worlds beyond time and space—it attests to the reality of Mind as rebel against the established worldview.

The waywardness of Mind is shown in a paradox: the finest flower of life, mind can be careless about life and make light of its needs. Mind, when not weighed down with the cares of matter, prefers adventure to security and loves the unknown more than it craves the familiar. Wayward mind scorns the surrogate, the mechanical, the stereotyped.

It likes to shape novelties from chaos, itching to make visible the invisible. Mind likes to play with fate and chance, whether in games of power or by trying to elevate the conditions of life. The waywardness of Mind is revealed by its resistance to bodily death. In that case, let's have a closer look in the next chapter.

5

NEAR-DEATH EPIPHANIES

In the name of truth, Are ye fantastical,
or that indeed which outwardly ye show?

—MACBETH

Introduction

One day some years ago, I was driving into Manhattan with a friend. Upon merging with traffic, we struck an embankment. The automobile careened, and spun like a top across several lanes, describing a complete turn of 360 degrees. We landed unscathed on the other side of the road, escaping collision with several trucks that came after.

While the car was spinning out of control, several psychologically interesting things occurred. I could see clearly the danger; it was the kind of situation impossible to imagine without flinching. And yet I didn't flinch at all. It was as if I was a spectator at an interesting show; the instant I realized there was *nothing* I could do, I experienced no fear, only tranquil curiosity. Indeed, the sensation was pleasant, almost erotic. My sense of time dilated and the instant, by all odds pretty frightening, swelled with a leisurely euphoria.

It was strange to note my unexpected shift of awareness. I was some-how being prepared for the emergency; something was already there to assist me in the midst of a life-threatening crisis.

I wondered how deep this adaptive mechanism was and what its ultimate significance was. I noted the discrepancy between my con-scious image of what nearing certain death might be like and what my spontaneous response actually was. Only at a later date did I realize that I had been through a very shallow but none the less instructive near-death experience (NDE).

In this chapter, then, I want to look at the near-death experience, and ask how it contributes to the attempt to create a credible mythology of transcendence. After the incident on the highway, where I caught a glimpse of something I never expected, I was drawn to study near-death phenomena, examined old case history collections, followed the new research and collected reports of my own.

Consider, for example, the near-death experience of a sixty-year-old Roman Catholic nun. The report is based on information I obtained from three nurses from Christ Hospital in Jersey City, N. J.

Sister B. M. entered the hospital in February, 1981, complaining of weakness and pain in her right side. She had the pain for a long while but hoped that with prayer it would end. According to the nurses, the patient suffered quietly. Her religious medal, scapula and small white head-covering she wanted on at all times; she became anxious if they were removed for any reason.

A diagnosis of cancer was followed by surgery. The next day, Sister B. M.'s heart rate became rapid and unsynchronized, threatening her life. A Code Blue was called and she was resuscitated. The patient appeared to recover, spoke of her religious life, was pleasant and co-operative except in regard to her religious articles. She was anxious about losing them.

Several days later, the patient was sitting in bed when the nurse no-ticed a sudden jerking of arms and legs, the head dropping to the right. Another Code Blue was called. When the coronary care unit responded, no spontaneous respirations or pulses were noted, skin color was dusky, cool to the touch; the cardiac monitor showed a morbid arrhythmia.

During the resuscitation procedure, the nurses observed tears in Sister B. M.'s eyes.

Again the patient recovered, but this time she described the experi-ence she had during her resuscitation. First, she remembered floating out of her body toward the ceiling. "I could see my body and everyone around me; they were upset," she said. She described how she felt herself leaving the room, surrounded by the most complete blackness, and how she passed through a tunnel into a dazzling bright light. There she "saw" a beautiful garden, filled with colorful trees and flowers, and was filled with peace and serenity.

And then she found herself back in her body. The Sister explained the meaning of her tears. She was trying desperately to say not to save her, that she was happy where she was and didn't wish to return to her body. One of the nurses commented: "So they were tears of a different pain than we imagined."

The most interesting point in this account is that when the nurses attempted to put Sister B. M.'s medal, scapula and head-covering on, she waved them away, stating they were no longer important to her, that they were only objects and that her faith was deeper now. Forty-five minutes later, the nun's eyes rolled back, her body stiffened; she went into a coma and expired three days later.

The report confirms a strong finding of ND researchers: the close encounters with death deepen the inner spiritual sense, not conventional religiosity. This seems proven from the nun's story. She caught a glimpse of the deeper spiritual reality of which her medal, scapula and habit were symbols. Her experience helped her see the foundation of her faith, which loosened her attachment to its symbols and conventions.

NDErs experience a reduced sense of sin, a fact that disturbs some religious-minded people. The Being of Light is not into righteous condemnation, but presents itself as a gentle instructor—a little bit like your Sunday school teacher. It encourages taking on the tasks of life, learning to live and work through problems; it promotes confidence that in the end, all will be well.

Some of the deeper experiences involve acquiring a sense of love with a cosmic twist. In this way, the new value system echoes that of Plato's *Symposium*, Dante's *Divine Comedy* and Whitman's *Leaves of Grass*. At the same time—and perhaps to the satisfaction of the theologians of wrath—there is a small percentage of near-death meetings with demonic, hellish and decidedly unpleasant apparitions.

One young man reported to me that he overdosed with a drug and had a hellish near-death experience. The image he described in great detail was of a mass of ghoulish entities that kept grabbing and pulling him down into a black seething pit. There were none of the positive elements of the NDE, and yet the result of the experience was transformative, cured him of his various addictions, and set him on a responsible path of education that he demonstrated in my class. I still recall having an impression of somebody who managed to combine sobriety with radiance.

The NDE is sometimes a catalyst of spiritual consciousness. It is clear from Pim van Lommel's comprehensive study, *Consciousness Beyond Life* (2010), that Sister B.M. is not alone in having such an experience. NDE literature contains similar reports of persons shedding traditional beliefs as a result of transformative insights.[55]

Given the fractious world around us, this is an interesting finding: an experience that brings people to the heart and soul of their religious beliefs, and detaches them from all the extraneous and unspiritual stuff that separates them from others.

The experience in question is a template for the transformation of sectarian minds into beacons of catholicity. What could be more useful? What could be more necessary? What could be more impossible?

We need to look at the various strange and sometimes wonderful effects and aftereffects of this phenomenon, which could turn out to be the most important in the history of psychology. The NDE is a metaphysical paradigm-buster, a recurrent phenomenon that points increasingly toward undermining a presumption of science since the 17th century revolution of mechanistic science: the recessive role of mind in the great scheme of things. NDEs challenge that presumption, and recall mind to the metaphysical stage, now to play a central role in a new story.

NDEs: World at the Edge of Existence

The near-death experience (NDE) is a striking anomaly—meaning, it's very difficult for the experts to explain how it is possible and what it means. The experience is recurrent and available for research. Although psychical researchers have long been aware of reports of unusual experiences on the threshold of death, since the 1970s medical and other professionals have focused on near-death phenomena.

It seems correct to say there is a near-death movement. IANDS, the International Association of Near Death Studies, has chapters in cities all over the world, and represents a network of sources of information revolving around the idea of transcendence.

Van Lommel in 2001 suggested that about 25 million people since 1975 have had near-death experiences. Clearly, millions of people have had near-death experiences, and millions have something to add to a modern mythology of transcendence. Today's techniques of resuscitation enable greater numbers of people to return from the threshold of death, and report what they experienced and how it transformed their lives.

There are two types, the first consists of deathbed visions. The subject, usually ill, often bedridden, at the hour of death suddenly has a vision. He or she often "sees" apparitions of deceased relatives or friends. The experience may be accompanied by an elevation of mood. Usually, the dying person is in a state of clear, wakeful consciousness.[56] Apparently, organic dysfunction does not correlate with these experiences. The clearer, the less impaired the consciousness, the greater the likelihood of an experience. Early collections of deathbed visions were compiled and studied by E. Bozzano,[57] J. H. Hyslop[58] and W. Barrett.[59]

The second type of NDE results from cardiac arrest, near-drowning, mountain-climbing falls, suicide attempts, auto accidents or other life-threatening incidents. Raymond Moody brought the subject to public attention with his book, *Life After Life,* in 1975. Moody formed a model of the experiences he studied. The common elements he found were ineffability, feelings of peace and quiet, entering a dark tunnel, being out of the body, meeting with others, having a panoramic memory of one's life, encountering a being of light, reaching a border or limit and, importantly, undergoing lasting changes of value and outlook. Less common but still important elements cited by Moody are hearing transcendental music and having a "vision of knowledge."

The subsequent work of Kenneth Ring,[60] while supporting Moody's findings, describes five stages of the "prototypical" core experience: euphoric affect, an out-of-body state, entering darkness, seeing an unearthly world of light and entering into that world of light. These stages seem like parts of an ordered and developing sequence; the final stages, experienced less frequently. At any one of these stages, there might occur what Ring calls a "decisional process;" for example, the person "decides" to return to life. And this is truly a difficult decision, since subjects often express emphatic displeasure over being dragged back into their bodies.

In addition to the five stages and the decisional process, Ring's cases include the other features of classic near-death experiences such as meeting with others, the panoramic memory and so forth. We should note here that there is never a perfect manifestation of the pattern, but different conditions allow for partial manifestations of the various elements.

There is an initial paradox. One wonders about what possible biological function could we ascribe to having *any* experiences near death. As long as one is functioning, it would not be surprising if the brain continued to produce adaptive responses. Albert Heim, a geologist, described mountain-climbing falls accompanied by accelerated mental processes; the increased alertness might have some survival value.

But once clinical death begins, e.g. no respiration, flat EEG, etc., the occurrence of *any* experience is surprising, because under these conditions, consciousness could not occur in an oxygen-deprived brain. But they do occur.

Three things about the prototypical NDE are puzzling: the apparent pattern they generally exhibit, a pattern that seems independent of individual variables; their psi components; and their profound psychospiritual aftereffects. For the student of the natural history of the mind, the NDE appears as a distinctive finding, a coherent, spontaneous psychism. Firsthand accounts derive from all kinds of people. In case after case, pretty much the same set of themes, though coded differently, emerge in the experiences.

What appears is a common pattern of phenomena filtered and personalized by the experiencer's constructs. Osis and Haraldsson, as well as Ring, found that religious beliefs influence the interpretation, not the content, of the experience. The experiencer says she saw a light, and subsequently places a label on the light: maybe God or an angel or whatever.

An important point about the NDE: it can occur in situations without actual life-threatening events. The pattern of near-death experience appears in a much wider variety of contexts than literal organic disruptions—for instance, depression or the belief that death is imminent. However, it seems that circumstances of clinical death, especially cardiac arrest that disables the brain from functioning cause the most dramatic and powerful experiences.

About the NDE, can it be explained physiologically, as a defence mechanism, a benign evolutionary illusion, a possible pointer to a transcendent life beyond the grave, or what?

Paranormal Aspects of NDEs

Some dismiss NDEs as fantasies produced against the terror of death. The limitations of that view are apparent when we consider the paranormal side of the phenomenon.

For example, in so-called "Peak in Darien" cases, the dying person sees the apparition of a person not known to be deceased. Nobody present was aware that the person whose apparition was seen was in fact dead, thus ruling out telepathy from people at the dying person's bedside. Most Peak in Darien cases come from the older literature, but more recently Craig Lundahl[61] and Kenneth Ring offer examples of this type of phenomenon.

The most commonly reported psi comes in the form of veridical out-of-body experiences. For example, cardiologist Michael Sabom systematically examined the out-of-body part of near-death experiences. Thirty-two of his patients gave accurate descriptions of cardiopulmonary procedures performed on them while they were clinically dead.

Sabom tested the idea that cardiac patients could provide pseudo-veridical accounts of CPR procedures based on "educated guesswork." So he interviewed twenty-five "control" patients with medical backgrounds similar to those who had OBEs. He found that twenty-three of them made at least one major error in their descriptions of the CPR procedures. In contrast, none of the out-of-body patients made any serious errors in their descriptions. Six of the thirty-two provided specific, verifiable details in their reports. Sabom obtained further verification from relatives who witnessed the event. Here are some specifics:

(1) A security guard from Florida was able to give the correct sequence of steps in a CPR procedure: chest thump, cardiac massage, airway insertion, medications and defibrillation. This patient rejected Sabom's use of the term "paddle" but gave an accurate description of the object itself.

(2) A sixty-year-old housewife described how an "express team" entered her room with a resuscitation cart, how her chest was thumped and an oxygen mask was placed on her face; she observed her carotid pulse checked, eyelids lifted to check pupillary response, arterial blood gases drawn from her hand, and a nurse collecting and labelling her personal effects for a move to the intensive care unit.

(3) A forty-six-year-old laborer observed a nurse touching two defibrillator paddles together, a technique for lubricating the paddles and insuring good skin contact with the chest. The patient also described how everyone moved back to avoid being shocked, and how his body jumped a foot high.

(4) A retired Air Force pilot gave an accurate description of a fixed and moving needle on a defibrillator as it was being charged

with electricity. The meter described is no longer in use but was common in 1973, at the time of the patient's cardiac arrest. During his interview, the patient used medical terms like "lidocaine pushes" and "watt-seconds," terms he had heard for the first time during his CPR ordeal.

(5) As a last example, a sixty-year-old man, during resuscitation, was able to observe from his out-of-body vantage point his wife and two children. The interesting fact is that his family was located some distance down the hall. According to the man's wife, whom Sabom interviewed, she and the two children came to the hospital unexpectedly and were stopped "at least ten rooms down" from where her husband was. Moreover, his face was pointed away from them at that moment. The distance factor destroys the possibility that the patient, semi-conscious, glimpsed his wife and children through normal means.

All these detailed and specific observations were made by individuals who were externally unconscious or clinically dead. Events such as these are impossible, according to the mainstream picture of the world.

There is discussion of hypercarbia: increased levels of carbon dioxide in the brain. Experiments with elevated levels of CO_2 are cited in which experiences closely akin to NDEs were produced: photic and OB effects, panoramic memories, ineffability, religious presences and so forth. As Sabom notes, however, we don't know if the CO_2 surplus is the cause of the near-death experience or just one of its physiological correlates. It might be part of the cause, but only in the sense of serving to release a latent potential.

To complicate matters, in the one case where the patient's carbon dioxide and blood oxygen levels were measured at the very moment of his near-death experience, the oxygen level was above normal (thus ruling out hypoxia), and the carbon dioxide level was below normal (thus ruling out hypercarbia).

Hypercarbia intoxication, one may see, offers a useful line of research into near-death experience, for it is a method, free of serious risk, of mimicking, fairly closely it would seem, important features of the near-death experience. The controlled use of hypercarbia intoxication might find itself useful in a modern deathcraft.

A recent PBS documentary describes efforts to use psychoactive MDMA and psilocybin to treat post traumatic disorder and deep depression, and the same agents have been used to induce the kind of mystical and ecstatic state often reported by NDErs.

In other words, it may be possible to experimentally induce some or even all of the elements of NDEs, for which there is massive evidence of transformative potential. I'm amazed that cadres of philanthropists aren't lined up to support what could be the most important research project on earth—a kind of neo-Manhattan Project for the expansion (not the annihilation) of human consciousness.

Now let's turn to OBEs in deathbed vision cases. Here separation may be more gradual. Osis and Haraldsson write, "While still functioning normally, the patient's consciousness might be gradually disengaging itself from the ailing body." In Barrett's early study, witnesses are cited who "saw" dying persons' "doubles" split off and disappear at the moment of death.

There are gradations of depth in the NDE, as Ring's model suggests, ranging from euphoric detachment to profound absorption in transcendent worlds. Psychically, as well as physically, dying seems like a gradual transition. There are clues indicating that consciousness begins to disengage in advance of bodily death—often through dreams just prior to dying. People begin to talk of deceased friends and relatives, have slips of the tongue suggesting preoccupation with them, spontaneously put their affairs in order, settle accounts, and the like. Preparation.

There is an example I observed when I was visiting an elderly man, who was, in fact, not in a critical condition, after an operation. The man's wife was present; suddenly, he spoke of his mother (long dead) bringing him dinner. He meant the nurse, of course. The man died the next morning. In this case, it would seem as if something "broke through" not by means of a vision but by a slip of the tongue. Perhaps his mother was standing by. Or perhaps it was a dream.

In the aftereffects, however, what researchers find is increased spiritual sensitivity. In the case of a man whose experience I recorded, the following aftereffects were noted. This person, a skeptical academic with a hard edge mind, had an NDE in 1979. The changes were clear and dramatic: being in touch with his feelings; being less egocentric; being more aware of others, especially of their needs; greater psychic sensitivity (he claims to obtain impressions from touching articles belonging to people); increased perceptiveness; increased zest for life; increased energy level; and a great single-mindedness of purpose that he never had. It was a striking syndrome of changes.

This example is bolstered by more organized studies. For instance, Richard Kohr[62] found that near-death experiencers tend significantly to report psi and psi-related states more frequently than non-NDErs. Kohr's studies indicate a global increase of sensitivity, greater access to states of mind normally unconscious; among "psi-related" experiences are listed deeper, more subtle access to dream life, meditation and apparent memories of past lives. Mystical and more deeply meaningful experiences were also reported more frequently among NDErs.

These studies were confirmed by the work of psychiatrist Bruce Greyson, who concluded: "The NDE appears to be not only psi-conducive for the duration of the experience, but psi-enhancing for the individual's subsequent life."[63] Finally, Kenneth Ring studied the psychospiritual aftereffects of deep NDEs.[64]

Elements of Near-Death Transformation

In Van Lommel's account of the twelve elements of the NDE, there is no fixed order in which they unfold. There does appear, however, a discernible directedness about the NDE; it seems geared toward the transcendent horizon of consciousness.

The first three elements seem like immediate reactions to being violently disrupted, resulting in awareness of being dead, profound feelings of peace and quiet, and freedom from pain. The state is so rare and strange right from the start that one lacks ordinary words to describe it, hence the often cited ineffability of the experience. The next element marks the beginning of transcendence with the experience of leaving the body, as we saw, sometimes with veridical out-of-body perceptions.

The fifth element involves entering a dark space that seems like a prelude to yet more dramatic elements: the sense of passing through a tunnel, seeing a dot of light in the distance, or running into a rare frightening or hellish experience.

The interlude in darkness more often leads to the most expansive elements of the experience. One may now encounter deceased persons, usually but not always family, occasionally relatives or old friends not known to have died. Clearly, this for many is the most significant emotional element of the NDE.

Next, we find reports of what sounds like the transcendent visionary element in which the near-death traveller has perceptions of an unearthly environment of extraordinary beauty, sometimes accompanied by strains of otherworldly music and color.

The next three items are grouped together because they seem to be about the most transformative elements of the NDE. First in importance is the encounter with an all-embracing, all-loving light presence—Moody spoke of "beings" of light.

Equally transformative for individuals seems to be the often reported experience of a panoramic life-review of oneself. One seems to see one's whole life flash before the mental eye, all one's deeds *and* their effects on others. It's all there, your life in review. Transformation could be likened to the effect on Scrooge (in Dickens' classic tale) of being taken by the spirit of Christmas past back to view his early life.

Less frequent are reports of flash-forward experiences where one glimpses one's future, and sometimes the future of the world at large. The last two elements cited by Van Lommel include the perception of a border and the conscious choice to return to the body.

My question is whether this process of transformation, awakened during individual near-death crises, is a latent potential of all human beings in a wide range of crises? NDEs occur universally to people independently of age, culture, and type of cause of the experience. This suggests the phenomenon indicates a general human capacity.

If so, might there be circumstances that could awaken these potentials for large numbers of people? Is something like a collective near-death experience with collective after-effects conceivable, likely, or even perhaps inevitable?

The search for a transcendent story is a reflex of consciousness facing uncanny crisis. Global trends are converging toward the creation of new dimensions of disaster, so it appears to increasing numbers of people that large-scale change of consciousness may be the only hope for humankind. Real forces are in play driving societies everywhere toward growing chaos and instability.

Money and technology aren't going to save us; if anything they are what threaten to destroy us. So I find myself imagining something like a collective near-death experience triggering a revolution of consciousness. My view is that the closer we edge toward plunging into apocalyptic mayhem, the more the archetypal energies of spiritual rejuvenation are likely to awaken and begin to transform us en masse. How this will take place is anybody's guess. We can be sure though that the imagination of the species will come up with all sorts of surprises to astonish us.

Elements of NDE are sure to play roles in the formation of a new mythology of transcendence. I am trying to make explicit—trying to imagine—what it would mean if the elements of this phenomenon were to unfold into a widespread trend of consciousness, if the imagery and metaphors were given space to proliferate and incarnate in whatever ways support the creative advance.

To return to the story of the nun's near-death experience; it involved a shift from external religious particulars to a freer spiritual outlook. The point was not about sweeping rejection but subtle detachment, a move that would alleviate fanaticism and celebrate diversity.

Van Lommel defines the living core of the NDE as "an overwhelming confrontation with the boundless dimensions of our consciousness." That is the essential transformation that the times call for, a great awakening of human consciousness.

A crucially related aftereffect noted by all researchers is a loss, or significant reduction, of the fear of death. Fear of death deforms character as well as institutions. Imagine a society without people driven by the will to power or the need to puff up their self-image at the expense of others.

A consistent aftereffect researchers report is detachment from superfluous wealth, material goods, status-manufactured culture, fame the drug, or power based on authority. The unfolding in society of a more refined capacity for enjoying life would diminish the spell of consumerism and the glitz of capitalism. In the "boundless dimensions of our consciousness," we will learn to "see eternity" in everyday life and experience.

Van Lommel describes the difficulties NDErs have living the way they want, indeed, need to, having been deeply changed, no longer caring about many things that friends, family, and co-workers attach so much value to.

The full transformative potential of the NDE is likely to be lost if it is not understood or appreciated or integrated by society at large. Despite the fact that well over 25 million people worldwide have had the experience, the meaning and the message it contains is attacked or ignored by mainstream materialist culture.

I found in my study of Joseph of Copertino that his rapport with his belief system—the symbols, dogmas, various art forms—was in part the essential basis of his wonders and achievements. A highly evolved mystic with unusual psychophysical talents, he was surrounded by a culture that reinforced his belief-system, even as it tested and often tyrannized him.

A person who by chance or trauma becomes suddenly enlightened or vividly awakened to transcendent reality needs some kind of social support to reap the full benefits of the experience. Even the desert contemplatives of the early Christian movement who practiced in solitude on pillars in the blazing sun or in dark secluded caves knew they were participating in a movement with a tradition that had roots.

Nowadays many explorers of the transcendent are improvisers, loners, eclectics that hang out at the edges of recognizable zones of authority. The near-death experience is my template for the possible evolution of human consciousness. It has no theological pedigree, but it has been reported, discussed, analyzed and well published. Igniting a revolution of consciousness may be utopian, but Oscar Wilde said, "A map of the world that does not include Utopia is not worth even glancing at."

Osis and Haraldsson have reports of sudden elation that follow deathbed visions. In the earlier case histories, compiled by Barrett and Hyslop, the change in mood was often so striking that it spread to friends and families witnessing the deathbed scene. Moody's "glimpses of eternity" were reportedly shared spontaneously by bystanders. Interesting examples of psychic contagion or the group high.

My question concerns the possibility of awakening the transformative elements of the NDE *en masse*. I also have the recurrent phantasy, or if you like, speculation, whether an evolutionary quantum leap is a credible scenario, in light of the NDE template.

A Non-Lethal Science of Spirituality

In imagining a new mythology of transcendence, we anticipate the rise of a new kind of science. The enterprise of modern science is not above critical misgivings. One distinguished critic, Wolfgang Pauli (1900-1968), abstained from joining Bohr, Fermi, and Oppenheimer in the creation of the atomic bomb. He objected to the Baconian formula that knowledge is power, and was known for the "purity" of his quest for knowledge. It was this rebellious purity, his qualms about science and the bomb, and his extraordinary dream life that led to an intellectual friendship with C.G. Jung.[65]

During the arms race atomic weapons proliferated among the superpowers. Pauli wrote of the dark side of science: "I believe that this proud will to dominate nature does in fact underlie modern science, and that even the adherent of pure knowledge cannot entirely deny this motivation. We moderns are once again becoming 'afraid of our likeness to God' . . . [and] the anxious question presents itself to us whether [even] this power, our Western power over nature, is evil."[66]

Pauli believed that the "magical-symbolic" and quantitative-mathematical descriptions of nature were compatible. He wanted, he needed to retain the spiritual dimension of science, rejecting the use of science as serving the will to power.

Paul Feyerabend carries on the critique of modern science in his first book, *Against Method*, and later with *Science in a Free Society* (1978). The author argues that Western science has evolved into something dictatorial, megalomanic, and oppressive. He argued that in major advances of science, from Galileo's experimental physics to quantum mechanics, scientists did not adhere to rules of reason or established principles but bore down on a problem or a hunch with intuition, guesswork, imagination (as Einstein stressed)—whatever it took. Creativity likes to improvise and doesn't bow to authorities.

From the tyranny of what Feyerabend called "Methodism" follows the tyranny of what we can know and how we can know it. He thought voodoo, acupuncture, and psychic healing in their traditions were valid forms of knowledge, and had much to teach scientific experts, if they weren't mentally locked down by their presumptions.

Feyerabend mocked what he called "small gangs of intellectuals" dictating to the press and halls of power what is worthy of scientific sanctification. He thought the flight to the moon a worthless boondoggle. At immense cost to the public, what did any citizen benefit? The public was told it was a "giant leap for humanity." Really? How so?

The idea of science dictating to the public what is important and what it should support with taxes, he attacked as undemocratic. He was not in favor of relying on experts in matters of moment to society at large. "Ignorant and conceited people are permitted to condemn views of which they have only the foggiest notion and with arguments they would not tolerate for a second in their own field."

Feyerabend opposed the conceit of scientific materialism. The overpowering influence by means of technology on consciousness in service to the state and corporate power is something we should resist. Instead of Satan roaming about seeking the ruin of our souls, Feyerabend feared totalitarian scientific memes "killing" our minds. He saw what ontology dictators could pull off: "We concede that our epistemic activities may have a decisive influence even upon the most solid piece of cosmological furniture—they may make gods disappear and replace them by heaps of atoms in empty space."

Combining the two critiques, if we are willing to face them, a bleak picture emerges. Something has emerged, a monster with a life and will of its own. It controls the official worldview and mainstream consciousness.

Meanwhile technology propagates the ideas, images, attitudes, and fantasies of what is possible and what is real. Science, in short, ends up by leaving us to be redefined and exploited by the ever-grinding engines of reductionism. The outermost reach of profit-driven metaphysics is reduction to the inhuman.

In *Understanding the Present: An Alternative History of Science* (2004), Bryan Appleyard critiques the extravagant claims of science, and its positioning itself as the salvation of humanity. He also dwells on science's "ultimate inability to solve the most important problems we face" (p.xi).

The book is neither anti-science nor does it question the extraordinary contributions of science. What it disputes as disastrous is the hubristic triumphalism. Like Feyerabend, Appleyard wants to position science as one of many human institutions. It is not the one and only master template of human virtue and culture. The author goes at length into the human consequences of the severance of value from knowledge.

Appleyard captures the human predicament in his comments on Joseph Conrad's story, *Heart of Darkness*: "For we have not only inherited that century's (the 19th) legacy of the cold shock of a meaningless universe, we have also to cope with the discovery of a range of potential evils unknown to the world before the advent of science and technology."

Appleyard argues that the scientific way of doing things seems always to be the inevitable outcome. His main and very major point is that "modern liberal-democratic soiety has been created by the scientific method, insight, and belief," but his second major point is that this method is inadequate as a guide for human life. Established science, the way it currently operates, "is incapable of co-existence" with other traditions or conceptions of ultimate reality and how to live.

In all questions of moment, the assumption is that we must always look to science for answers. But science has created more and new problems, and has proven less than useful in helping the human mass live satisfying lives in harmony with the natural world and with each other. Liberal reason and science combined have totally failed to heal the wounded human condition. In fact, their frigid marriage have made hell on earth proliferate so that Earth now seems bent on returning the favor, in the form of extreme weather events.

The conclusion is hard to avoid, as far as I can see. The stage we're imagining as some kind of mass renaissance of consciousness will honor science but a science in service to democratic humanity, not to the state or special financial interests. This can only succeed as a communal task. Science, art, and spiritual practice need to come together in new forms of partnership.

Concluding Reflection

In my opinion, the NDE is to psychology what quantum mechanics is to physics: both powerfully challenge their respective fields of study.

According to cardiologist Van Lommel, cardiac arrest stems the flow of oxygen to the brain and ought equally to stem the possibility of any conscious experience. In fact, the reverse occurs and subjects report an immense expansion of consciousness that seems on the face of it to another dimension of reality.

Likewise, quantum mechanics raises questions about the ultimate nature of physical reality, revealing a nonlocal realm of potential being whose discrete manifestations seems to depend on the awareness of observers. So neither brains nor any manifest form of physical reality seem to be the ultimate players in the ontology game; rather, in ways that remain a mystery the mental and the conscious seem to occupy the ground floor of actual existence.

One last comment on shoring up the coffers of our transcendent worldview. There is now a subset of near-death testimonials I want to mention that seems to me of special interest. I am referring to near-death experiences of medical or scientific professionals, especially people trained in the neurosciences. The names I want to mention are of individuals whose worldview was transformed, indeed upended, by their near-death experiences.[67]

6

THE COSMIC DETECTIVE STORY

I confess that at times I have been tempted to believe that the Creator has eternally intended this department of nature to remain baffling, to prompt our curiosities and hopes and suspicions all in equal measure, so that, although ghosts . . . and messages from spirits, are always seeming to exist and can never be fully explained away, they also can never be susceptible of full corroboration.

—William James

The cosmic detective story, what's that? It is about tracking clues to exploring the mystery of mind, trying to determine the scope of its outreach in nature, and as far as ourselves, the soul's fate after the body perishes.

In this chapter, we'll talk about claims regarding the belief in a life after death. This is a key part of the new story of transcendence, and the two previous chapters were steps that move us in that direction. Absolute proof may forever elude us, at least until the final experiment; but meanwhile the subject is full of interesting surprises.

Remarks on a Peculiar Paradox

It seems a paradox, but the main obstacle to belief in life after death is not lack of evidence. In fact, there was never a time in history when (in relative terms) there was more organized data suggestive of post-mortem survival. But still, among the educated masses, belief in an afterlife is probably at an all-time low.

And even among those who have studied the evidence closely, the claims are often hedged and qualified. So, for example, after years of study, Gardner Murphy concluded: "To me, the evidence cannot be by-passed, nor on the other hand can conviction be achieved."

In speaking of survival data, apart from OBEs and NDEs, I refer to mediumship, apparitions and hauntings, and studies of the reincarnation type. And among these broad types are further sub-divisions. Compiled and analyzed by various societies for psychical research, the scientific study of these phenomena are ignored, played down by most scholars and scientists.

There is much to learn, if you are willing to do some homework. For example, there is the work dealing with so-called *cross-correspondence* case material (a sub-division of mediumship), much of which remains unanalyzed and unpublished to date. It comprises a small library.

Several things in the background of modern life account for the near absence of interest in these matters. I would say the main thing is the iron curtain of materialism that has been draped over the average human consciousness.

The Global Reign of Materialism

The prevailing climate of thought militates against rational belief in survival. The official party line of the academy is that all things are at bottom material, more broadly, physical. The prevailing creed varies in expression; some of the older and cruder forms (behaviorism) are no longer in vogue. Identity theory, however, which identifies mind with brain mechanisms is held by some votaries of neuroscience.

The life sciences, medical and biological, remain attached to the dogmas of physicalism. So powerful are these that ministers and theologians play down the "supernatural" side of religious experience. The idea of a mental entity enjoying autonomy and, wilder yet, surviving the death of the body, is treated as inherently implausible or just irrelevant. Dualism, in some form essential to the idea of survival, is viewed as the worst scientific heresy.

Materialism as a metaphysical doctrine implies nothing as to the way one might actually live. Metaphysical materialists might be unworldly in morals, devoted to lofty causes, real benefactors of humanity. Conversely, those who profess lofty spirituality may be, and often have been, the worst enemies of the human race.

That said, the supreme values of many are not just declared to be material as a matter of dry metaphysics, but are pursued with passion in daily life. The hard driving materialist values of financial and political powers are regularly the cause of conflict, international politicking and military adventurism. Think of the horrific situation of the Middle East today and think one word: oil—a word that epitomizes rank materialism in action.

As far as the quality of everyday life, practical materialism in everyday life leaves little space to encounter the Transcendent. Techno-modern cultures are increasingly mediated by numbers, passwords, wires, screens, logos, etc., etc., Non-machine-mediated experience is gradually disappearing. In classical and archaic societies, the rite of passage offered a chance, opened a space, to those leaps we call transcendent. Ego-death, incorporated into ritual, was part of the fabric of social existence. The rite of passage made consciousness permeable to alternate realities. Also, pre-modern attitudes toward the dead strengthened the sense of continuity with another dimension of reality.

Ancestor worship in Shintoism, for instance, or the practice of saying Mass for the dead are ways of cultivating our links to the unseen. Materialism as a climate of moral perception neglects the unseen dimension, exalting the immediate and the visible. Egoism is a by-product of myopic materialism, and serves to keep us distracted and unaware of the Transcendent.

Absence of a Coherent World View

The presocratic philosopher, Xenophanes attacked the theology of Homer at the dawn of Western philosophy. Instability of worldview has been widespread in Western consciousness ever since. The rise of critical reason represents one of the most fateful events in human history. It threw open new pathways to change and progress, but also brought along new evils and new dangers.

This in part is clearly due to the relentless impact of scientific progress and technology, as Bryan Appleyard describes it so vividly in the book cited above. The inability to see life as a coherent whole is increasingly difficult. The inner perspective is confused and overcrowded. This contrasts sharply with the technical ability to manipulate the forces of material nature. Technical success in all fields of experience has distracted us from questions of meaning we might otherwise feel moved to reflect on.

The Parapsychological Obstacle to Belief in Survival

Having stated some general reasons for the lack of hospitality to survival evidence, we should look at the substantive objections. It is a paradox that the great obstacle to belief in survival comes from within the field of parapsychology.

Students of the best survival evidence—from the founders of psychical research to now—have been driven to various conclusions. After eliminating everything due to fraud, poor reportage, paramnesia, cryptomnesia, and so forth, one retains two options: either that some form of survival is a fact of nature or that the appearance of survival is engineered by deceptive psi from living agents.

After immersing oneself in the details of the mediumship of Mrs. Piper, Mrs. Leonard and other gifted mediums, we are forced to decide between one of two options; no obvious third course seems tenable. Either option is momentous: the reality of an afterlife or the reality of a massive unconscious conspiracy to produce illusions of an afterlife.

Psi permits us to believe that what looks like a message from another dimension is in fact a seductive deception. After all, we know of psi among the living, the creative powers of the unconscious, the fear of death, and all the rest. We don't know about discarnate existence; it's a disposable hypothesis.

The argument cannot be ignored. The problem is that there is no way it can be falsified. One's "reasons" will prevail over every contingency of fact. But then to assume unlimited psi ability in human beings already provides a hospitable climate for an afterlife. For if mind is up to performing with unlimited ESP and PK (which is what super-psi implies), the idea of survival gains a new air of credibility. If the mental apparatus of a human being can shapeshift reality so effectively, it might well be able to operate without a body.

The claim that deceptive psi accounts for apparent survival evidence runs into another problem. There is no experimental evidence for the existence of such godlike psi abilities. Yet we are asked to believe that mediums (like Mrs. Piper) or children with detailed reincarnation memories, skills and behaviors, and who do poorly at ESP tests, suddenly acquire extensive, copious and complex psi abilities, exclusively in contexts that suggest survival.

The powers of unconscious self-deception must be vast and relentless. That should give us pause about all our cherished beliefs and theories. We are all liable to be duped by that "incomprehensible enchantment" and "all powerful force" of which Pascal wrote concerning self-deception. If we are that subject to the deceptive powers of our own subliminal selves, we should be radical skeptics and suspend *all* our beliefs and judgments.

It is best in this area of study to take each case as it comes and examine it for fraud, cryptomnesia, psi influence of the living, and so on. This is the general method of Ian Stevenson and is the basis of Alan Gauld's book, *Mediumship and Survival*. Gauld's book is a sustained critique of the superpsi attempt to explain survival evidence, making explicit the assumptions in specific cases where deceptive psi competes with the survival view.

Take a relatively simple case, frequently cited, perhaps because it is written in the legal history of North Carolina. My summary is based on the report made by W. H. Salter, who prepared the case for publication for the English Society For Psychical Research,[68] and who exchanged letters with the American lawyer engaged in the probation of the will.

In 1921, a farmer, James Chaffin of North Carolina, died accidentally from a fall, leaving all his property to his third son, Marshall, who himself died about a year later. In June, 1925, James, the second son, began having vivid dreams or waking visions of his father at his bedside. On one occasion his father, wearing a familiar black overcoat, said, pointing: "You will find my will in my overcoat pocket."

The coat was found in the older brother's house, and inside a sewn-up pocket was a roll of paper which read: "Read the 27th. Chapter of Genesis in my daddie's old Bible." The Bible was found in the presence of witnesses, and a new will dated January 16,1919, was discovered, dividing the property equally among his sons.

At first, Marshall's widow contested the will but yielded when she saw the documents. The second will, though unattested by witnesses, was admitted to probate and validated by the State. Although the Testator's action with his second will seemed odd, the lawyer assured Salter there was nothing suspect in the case.

Although it's not clear why Chaffin senior paltered with the second will, it is easy to imagine what may have happened. Chaffin seems to have favored the third son, Marshall (shown by his first will), but was moved by duty and Bible to produce the second will. The devious manner of disposing the second will reflects the farmer's lack of resolution.

The alternate interpretation is that young Chaffin, who stood to gain by discovering the second will, used his clairvoyance to retrieve it. (Recall that no living person knew of the existence of the second will.) But why do all this through the halting procedure of a series of dreams or waking visions of his father? Why not a hunch or a dream or a well-timed "accident" targeted on the Bible itself? If Chaffin had been using his own clairvoyance, he would have had to have "cognized" the location of the will hidden in the Bible, because the rolled paper in the overcoat said nothing about a will. All it said was something about reading a passage in the Bible. The assumption that Chaffin used his psi ability here strains credibility because it is too complicated and because it presupposes (in a man not known for any psi ability) an extraordinary and sudden capacity for psi.

The term I've been using is "deceptive psi." In all cases of apparent survival, the superpsi explanation assumes an unconscious tendency to engineer deception. Once we make this clear, we can make another assumption more explicit: where there is deception, there must be a need for deception. Deceptive psi in survival cases must be need-relevant. Consider the Chaffin will case. No one could deny the need to use psi here; young Chaffin obviously stood to gain by using his psi. However, it turns out that Chaffin continued to have apparitions of his father even after the latest will was recovered.

The need for deception could be at work in many cases of apparent survival, but not in all. For instance, a teenager reported the following. She was about to step into a room at a funeral parlor where her father lay dead; she was distressed and disconsolate. As she approached the casket (along with her mother and brother), an apparition of her father, radiant, smiling, appeared before her. The girl's mood lifted dramatically. Clearly, need is apparent in this case. It might have been the hallucination of a needy soul.

But not all apparitions of the dead are obviously need-relevant. Consider the following (abbreviated) account of a story I investigated.

A young couple moved into an apartment in Irvington, N.J., in 1979 and had been living there for six months. During that time, Grace would often wake Alan at night and say she heard the closet door opening and slamming shut. Alan usually heard nothing and, in fact, was annoyed.

One day, after Alan had gone to work, Claire was hanging draperies in the bedroom. There was no one else in the house, but Claire heard the living room door open and close. She poked her head outside the bedroom into the living room and saw a strange man sitting on the couch looking at her. She panicked, ran into the bedroom and grabbed a hammer; meanwhile, the closet door in the living room was heard to open and slam shut. It became silent, and Claire peeked into the living room. Nobody was there. She ran off to her mother who lived nearby.

The incident made problems for Claire and Alan, although the latter's skepticism was soon undermined. Claire was able to identify from a photograph the apparition of the man she saw sitting on her couch; he was the younger brother of Mrs. Lewis, had previously lived in Claire's and Alan's apartment and was stabbed to death in a bar in Newark nine months previously.

The disturbances did eventually cease, and in accord with advice from a local priest, the house was sprinkled with holy water. A Bible was also opened and placed on the living room table. The couple, shaken from the experience, moved away soon after.

After speaking with the people involved, there was little doubt in my mind over the facts of the story. Surely we cannot dispose of this by uttering the magic word, Superpsi! If superpsi is deceptive psi, where is the deception here? One could see deception at work with the teenager who saw a consoling apparition of her father. But Alan and Claire? It seems absurd to say that the young couple needed to have this experience. It served no purpose for them at all, but was, in fact, a very large nuisance.

Deceptive psi seems out of court here. Was it after all an indication that some soul had actually survived bodily demise?

But now comes another twist in the cosmic detective story. Perhaps, it is often said, such haunting apparitions are merely traces without consciousness, echoes of charged moments trapped in the corridors of time and space; inwardly vacant images, with nobody home. But the facts don't fit the theory; the murdered man's apparition didn't behave like a lifeless, psychic photograph; it appeared conscious. It looked directly at Claire. It had an expression of puzzlement mingled with anger.

Three points suggest survival. First, against "superpsi," the apparition seems irrelevant to the percipient's needs. Second, the apparition was veridical; Claire knew nothing of the former occupant of her apartment and yet was able to identify him through a photograph. Third, the apparition displayed a responsive intelligence. It could not reasonably be described as appearing like a detached and mindless psychic photograph.

Reincarnation

Reincarnation is a widely-held form of belief in life after death. The human personality is not bound to the lifespan of a single body. Since the painstaking labors of psychiatrist Ian Stevenson,[69] we have impressive empirical evidence for cases suggestive of reincarnation. Based on extensive travels and on-site investigations, Stevenson collected about 25 hundred cases, a body of data enriching the mythology of transcendence. Reincarnation suggests that we are connected in intimate ways with our past and even our future lives.

But it also raises some difficulties. Suppose aspects of my personality appear to be continuous with a previous personality. Memories, behaviors, skills, even bodily marks may be shared. Does it really make sense to say that the previous personality—or just some isolated trait?—survived in me?

The transformation from one embodied person to another (often with change of sex) is too catastrophic to justify claiming identity with the previous embodied personality. Suppose my burly, gravel-voiced uncle died and reincarnated, with memories and (even say) some behaviors intact, but in the form of a little girl from a nearby town. I would find it difficult, if not impossible, to think of the little girl as my uncle, no matter what memories or behaviors they shared.

Continuity of traits of personality would therefore not entail continuity of person; the former may be thought of as an abstraction, but not as a substitution, for the latter. According to Stevenson, most reincarnation memories fade in early childhood. But if memory is the measure of continuity, then continuity would fail as memory failed. Survival would then be restricted to those short-term memories that are retained in the recipient person. Continuity may exist with a previous personality but just as a faint or occasionally active residue in the new personality.

There is a story that when the Buddha was enlightened under the Bo tree all his past lives came before him. This resembles reports of near-death experiences in which people witness the details of their whole lives flash before them. The Buddha witnessed all his past lives, not just all the events of one life.

Suppose we've been reincarnated many times. Then all the layers of our previous lives must form part of the deep structure of our unconscious mental life. This suggests an intriguing possibility. In a new dispensation of human potential, we might acquire the skills to draw upon the great well of wisdom and experience each of us may secretly be. In the future consciousness we're trying to imagine, we learn to live in rapport with our ancestral selves. We become custodians of our soul history that stretch backward in time and forward toward unknown futures.

Much depends on knowing what we don't know. We may not consciously remember our past lives, but they may still be influencing us. Stevenson believed that phobias, philias (stuff we like), special talents, skills and other personality traits may be traceable to previous lives. His suggestions are based on documented case histories. The carryovers may be quite powerful, even though we consciously forget their origins.

The situation is comparable to memories repressed in this life that influence us. Stevenson cites examples in which memories of a previous life crop up in dreams, which raises the possibility that dreams or other altered states put us in touch with memories of former lives, even though probably not verifiable as such. It's hard to say how pervasive these nonverifiable interactions with past lives may in fact be. The amnesia of ordinary life may be covering up a wide but entirely latent outreach.

Studies by Stevenson along with C. G. Jung's work on transpersonal imagery substantiate Van Lommel's claims about NDEs and their "endless" outreach of consciousness. They add to our attempt to articulate a democratic, science-based, art-inspired, and soul-infused mythology of the Transcendent.

Reincarnation cases cannot reasonably be described as need-relevant, we should add. Consider what Stevenson himself has to say about children caught up in the reincarnation scenario:

> I wish to say that I find it puzzling that anyone should want to remember a previous life ... Persons who remember a previous life are by no means always happier for having done so. The majority seem to

me less happy than other persons until they forget their memories. As children they are often involved in painful conflicts with their parents when they remember a second set of parents, and perhaps a wife and children as well! And many of the memories recalled by subjects of these cases are of unpleasant events such as domestic quarrels, crimes, and violent death.

It makes very little sense to describe this behavior as gratifying any self-serving wishes. Like the apparition of the murdered man that caused a disruption in the lives of Alan and Claire, reincarnation memories seem more like external intrusions.

Winding Up On This

To review survival research as a whole is beyond the scope of a short chapter. I do maintain that we are entitled to remain open to the mystery of death; the records are full of well-documented cases not at all easy to dismiss; there is evidence suggestive of another dimension of being, invisible but sporadically interactive with our mental life.

Evidence exists in various forms and with degrees of persuasiveness. There is one really big issue at stake: Can minds exist without brains? Can they flourish after complete divorce from their brains? Will they, in short, continue to hang around after the last farewell to the body?

Two obstacles to belief in a life after death stand out. One lies in the background of modern intellectual life: the pervasive dogma of materialism, which constrains our perception of the possible. The second comes from parapsychology itself: can evidence for survival be explained by the psychic talents of the living?

The super-psi hypothesis is too vague and barely qualifies as a scientific hypothesis. When it is defined precisely by its deceptive and need-serving function, it seems to apply less readily to much of the evidence, such as certain apparitions and reincarnation memories.

Neither does it easily apply to at least one type of mediumistic phenomenon, the so-called "drop-in" communicator. A stranger to the sitter and the medium intrudes, communicating through the medium, and identifies itself. And sometimes it provides verifiable details of its premortem life. No one present could explain the appearance of these visitors.

It is also hard to see "no-consent" cases reported in Hindu death-bed visions and "hellish" near-death experiences as the products of wish-fulfilment.

Some of these phenomena strongly suggest external agency. I have had several experiences of the sort, and one night was physically attacked by a ghost in a house that was said to be haunted. There was absolutely no doubt about there being something "out there" that came toward and engulfed me, briefly paralyzing my body. It's a stretch to call this wish-fulfilling.

There is another difficulty. No experimental studies lead us to believe that anyone can synthesize from a diversity of sources information unknown to any living person, and reproduce attitudes, points of view, appearances of meaningful intention, and specific skills and behaviors known to belong to deceased persons. On the other hand, we can't say with confidence that this is impossible either.

"Proof" of survival we may not have; but still the cosmic detective story deepens, and we keep finding good reasons for revising our picture of what is possible in nature. And psi, or if you like, superpsi, is itself the single most powerful basis for raising questions about the scope and boundaries of the human personality. Modern science is catching up with the intuitions of the ancient thinkers for whom the limits of the soul were thought to be undiscoverable.

7

THE ARCHETYPE OF DEATH
AND ENLIGHTENMENT

A man should be able to say he has done his best to form a conception
of life after death, or to create some image of it—even if he must confess
his failure. Not to have done so is a vital loss.

—C. G. JUNG

The near-death experience clearly points to another dimension
of being. The experience, I believe, may be better understood
in context of C. G. Jung's theory of archetypes, which is about
a *trans*personal psychic realm. NDEs are evidence for a general psychic function, associated with the idea of dying. This function I call
the archetype of death and enlightenment (ADE). The ADE shows up
in psychedelic experiences, UFO "revelations," ancient mystery rituals,
dreams and hallucinations.

What comes through these various vehicles is the idea of a
death-transcending psychism, a latent potential of the subliminal self.
A lowered threshold of resistance permits an influx of imagery from
dormant regions of our inner life.

Such an archetype might be of interest to "modern man"—solitary,
anxious, driven, traditionless, spiritually uprooted—out of touch with

the symbols and energies of the healing psyche.[70] The NDE seems a clue to finding the healing force within. The answer to the riddle of death is in our own psyches.

Archetypal Near-Death

Archetype, primordial image, psychic dominant—Jung used these terms to refer to organizing psychic structures and associated energies that form the collective ground plan of the psyche. Some similarities to Platonic ideas and Kantian categories are notable, the difference being that the Jungian archetype manifests in primordial imagery. Jung thought of the archetype as a kind of psychic equivalent to biological instinct.

Jung rejects the Lockean notion of the mind as a *tabula rasa*, a blank slate upon which historical or cultural contingencies dictate our existence. Jung thought that human beings have archetypal tendencies, an inner-directed destiny. A principle of self-development presides over our lives, as we shape ourselves into performing individuals. The archetypes oversee the fortunes of our ever-evolving selves.

Jung distinguishes between the "archetype as such" and its particular psychic manifestation. The image that appears in the dream or myth is not therefore the archetype as such, which is never given in consciousness. Archetypes are meaning-endowing psychisms that orient the individual in the endless process of individuation.

Archetypical Situations

"There are as many archetypes as there are typical situations in life . . . [They represent] merely the possibility of a certain type of perception and action," wrote Jung.[71] Dying is one of the typical situations of life; it would therefore be surprising if there were no archetype related to dying. The archetypes express the great forms and psychic residues of the human condition, the permanent impulses, conditions, tendencies that belong to humanity at large: womanhood, childhood, heroism, wisdom, the shadow, the soul, birth, death, rebirth, and so on and so forth.

Now, just as even the lowest organisms are provided with mechanisms to assist in birth, growth and adaptation, so creative evolution has armed the human organism with a "mechanism" for adapting to the end stage of life called death.

The archetype is a psychic dynamism untraceable to the personal history of the subject; the NDE cannot be traced to the personal history of the subject either. The typical features occur independently of personal variables such as age, sex, education, religion and culture. Apparently, the fact or even the belief or feeling of being near death may precipitate the archetypal pattern of experience. The near-death pattern seems, so to speak, "built-in" the deep psyche, which is why it often shows up in the experiences of children.

In one account, a seven-year-old girl, deathly ill, heard a chorus of heavenly voices, experienced peace, went out of her body, met beings who sparkled like stars, sailed through a dark tunnel, at the end of which saw a robed Christlike figure. Children, even much younger than this seven-year-old, report having similar experiences. I'm sure we under-rate the riches of childhood spirituality.[72] It's unlikely these images were based on personal history, on the personal unconscious or anything previously learned by the subjects. They seem rather like crystallizations of some "preformed faculty" of the mind.

The archetypes, according to Jung, "appear under infinite variety of aspects." This makes discussion of them a tricky business. "A kind of fluid interpretation belongs to the very nature of the archetype," he said, and further, "no archetype can be reduced to a formula . . . but they change their shape continually." Despite this fluidity, it is possible to pick one archetype from another, so we can talk of the Shadow, the Wise Old Man, the Anima, and so on.

Still, fixed labels are pale reminders of the richness of archetypal experience. The often reported ineffability of the NDE comes as no surprise. Archetypes mark a point between the personal and the collective experience of humankind. Charged with a surplus of meanings and associations, they reverberate with memories, nostalgias, aspirations. The excess and overflow of meaning leave subjects unable to evoke or describe their experience.

Jung spoke of a category of archetype that, in addition to personified imagery (the Trickster, the Child, the Hero), consists of "typical situations, places, ways and means ..." These he called archetypes of transformation. The NDE clearly reflects an archetype of transformation; death, any way we look at it, is certainly a case of transformation.

We find not one discrete thing with sharp boundaries but a family of overlapping psychic processes. In the near-death experience it is personifications, guides, light-beings, deceased relatives, religious and mythical figures, voices and presences.

We also observe situations, ways and places such as coming to a border, beholding heavenly (and sometimes infernal) landscapes and cities; hearing the music of the spheres; passing through tunnels, cones, whorls, caves; resting in darkness before entering the light, having prophetic visions of global catastrophe forcing a renaissance of human consciousness.

The common thread of the various elements of the near-death archetype is the theme of transformation. The type of prophetic NDE described in the work of Ken Ring consists of powerful images of transformation on a global scale. If archetypes express the timeless, universal configurations of human consciousness, a prophetic, futuristic character of the NDE ought not to surprise us. It is this prophetic/futuristic strand I'm trying to tease out of hiding.

Archetypal Reality

These highly colored formations of the deep mind express themselves spontaneously through dreams, trance, psychotic delusions, reveries of childhood, active imagination, and the like. A weakening of ordinary waking consciousness is a condition for their appearance; near-death drastically weakens ordinary consciousness and for that reason is likely to activate archetypal motifs. In theory, being near death should be optimal for activating the ultra-personal (and quite frankly mysterious) powers of the deep unconscious.

The argument for archetypes has the following general form: somebody, a child, say, or an uneducated person, has a dream. The dream contains imagery, symbols, not traceable to the dreamer's experience but parallel to imagery and motifs found in mythology, alchemy, mystery rites of antiquity, and other obscure, world-old sources.

There are other ways of explaining such cases. Sometimes it's reasonable to invoke coincidence. There is also cryptomnesia, or unconscious memory. Another possibility is reincarnation memories. Ideas and images might also be picked up via telepathy.

These may occasionally apply, but the millions of near-death experiences, the spontaneous uniformity and universality of the imagery, the profound similarity in the aftereffects suggest the presence of deep psychic structures.

Archetypes behave autonomously; they have a life of their own and "come upon us like fate." This tallies with the near-death experience in which the figures, the messengers from beyond, have a life of their own. They come like fate, apart, as the facts show, from religious beliefs and expectations. However, although the visions intrude from the outside, their interpretation is conditioned by prior beliefs.

The autonomous nature of ND archetypes is shown in many ways, often contradicting the beliefs and expectations of the experiencer. Osis and Haraldsson cite a case of an avowed atheist who had a deathbed vision of Christ. According to the theory of archetypes, the forces of the collective unconscious are called to compensate for the one-sided conscious mind.

One thinks of St. Paul on the road to Damascus, having a psychic encounter with the figure whose followers he planned to oppose. Paul's world-historical auditory hallucination had many motifs associated with NDEs, such as a powerful out-of-body experience, and the conviction of having seen heaven.[73]

According to Jung, atheism would be an extreme state of psychic one-sidedness, a state of alienation from the powers of the unconscious. So a vision of Christ might well occur to an atheist, to compensate an impoverished psyche caught up in a crisis.

But most NDErs who have a vision of Christ are Christians. Yet even here, there is support for the autonomy of the near-death imagery. The literature is full of anecdotes about dying persons whose visions conflict with their conventional expectations. Christians may expect to see angels with wings but instead encounter light beings in human form. Archetypes, like NDEs, just happen, in spite of, and even because of, the limitations of the personal ego.

The autonomy of near-death archetypes is evident from the following remark of Osis and Haraldsson: "It seems that apparitions show a purpose of their own, contradicting the intentions of the patient." The apparitions are not projections of the personal psyche. They exhibit a purpose of their own: to "take away" the dying person to another world. Emotions of peace and serenity correlated significantly with otherworldly messengers having a take-away purpose.

The Numinous Trumps the Will to Live

Nothing better testifies to the power of the archetypes than the negative feelings felt by those returning to life from their out-of-body voyages. People catch glimpses of something more attractive than life itself. Like spellbound sailors caught by the song of the Sirens, those near death hear a strange melody that weakens their grip on life and calls them to the beyond. What could reverse the instinct for self-preservation? So much anxiety is spent in the course of life struggling to fend off death, yet on the verge of death, all the struggle and anxiety vanish, and life in the body turns into a reason for regret. That to which we clung so grimly all our lives, we're now ready to let go. Research shows that "encounters with ostensible messengers from the other world seemed to be so gratifying that the value of this life was easily outweighed."[74]

Jung himself had a remarkable near-death experience. He had a heart attack after he broke his foot. "I felt violent resistance to my doctor because he had brought me back to life," he wrote in his autobiography. He said it took him more than three weeks to make up his mind to live again. He regretted having to return to this "gray world with its boxes." The other world he glimpsed was fuller, not broken up into bits of time and pieces of space. "Although my belief in the world returned to me, I have never since entirely freed myself of the impression that this life is a segment of existence which is enacted in a three-dimensional boxlike universe especially set up for it."

During his near-death encounter, Jung had a vision of Zeus and Hera consummating a mystical marriage ceremony. The contemplation of such awe-inspiring images, and the cosmic feelings associated with them, might be numinous enough to weaken the ordinary will to live.

The Feeling of Immortality

Closely related to the reduction of the will to live is the experienced feeling of immortality. We've discussed the positive aftereffects of NDEs. Chief among them is a dramatic reduction of the fear of death. That may be ascribed to what people call feelings of immortality. I have on several occasions had such feelings while listening to the music of Claude Debussy and Johannes Ockeghem. I recall thinking, as I was listening at the moment, that it would be perfectly fine to die. "The feeling of immortality," Jung wrote, "has its origin in a peculiar feeling of extension in space and time."

Ancient deification rites were group techniques for projecting archetypal imagery: Dionysos, Persephone, Isis, etc. Using hypnotic suggestion, right-hemisphere languages, sensory overload, psychoactive drugs, trance-dancing and the like, celebrants entered altered states, and had exalted visionary experiences. Temporary psychic union with the archetypes seems to produce the sense of immortality, often with profound and long-lasting effects.

A twenty-eight-year-old woman who nearly died during an emergency caesarean section wrote a report of her experience. The experience profoundly changed her sense of self-identity; she claimed to have discovered she was a spiritual being, an idea entirely foreign to her previously:

"I was in excruciating pain, physically exhausted, and in labor for fifteen hours. Dr. R. said, 'I'm sorry, M., I'm going to have to put you to sleep.' The next thing I remember was being above the room. I looked down and could see everything and everyone, including my body with Dr. R. and two nurses standing over it. I felt terrified and panic-stricken at first, but then the feeling passed. I realized I was very big, I was taking up the whole room.

"I also felt very, very good. Better than I've ever felt before or since. The feeling was extreme, extreme exhilaration. I felt brilliantly, totally alive—like all my senses were tuned to maximum awareness. I was very interested in what was going on. Dr. R. yelled: 'Her pressure is still dropping!' The anaesthesiologist started squeezing a black rubber ball that was connected to an apparatus over my face. Dr. R. said some numbers I can't remember, and then, 'OK, she's stable.'

"His forehead had been creased above the mask and it seemed to smooth out; I could hear him letting out his breath. My husband was sitting in the corner. He looked scared and had a very sad look on his face and tears in his eyes. A nurse was wheeling in a bassinet on wheels that squeaked a little. She said to another nurse in the back: 'Is everything all right?' The other nurse said, 'Yup.' It was like watching a movie. I started thinking the baby will be a girl, which is what I wanted.

"The next thing I can remember happening was being awakened by the nurses washing me. I felt awful, shaking all over—headache, nausea. They said, 'You had a girl.' I asked my husband if the people said the above things and I told him what I saw. I also thought the room was very, very bright. That was the only thing he said wasn't so. It was light but not brilliantly light, as it seemed to me."

Metanoid Near-Death

Reduction of the fear of death is only part of a larger pattern of transformation. The experience has all the earmarks of a kind of religious conversion. We could describe the full-fledged NDE as a natural conversion. The convert undergoes a pervasive change of value and outlook. The word for such is *metanoia*.

This metanoid component of the NDE is sometimes expressed in terms of unconditional love. In the words of one experiencer: "I would describe this love I encountered in dying as *unconditional*. It was so powerful, so complete, so forgiving, so all-knowing, so encompassing, it transcended all forms of earthly love ..."[75] The awakening of this all-encompassing, unearthly love makes the NDE uniquely interesting from a theoretical viewpoint.

Clearly, this kind of inspired, universal love is a rare phenomenon. As far as the evolution of human consciousness, it may be reckoned as part of our human potential.

P. Atwater tells how normal emotional relations were disturbed by her NDE. Customary attachments became an obstacle to further growth. The experience released a force that disrupted her routine relationship. A rather different, transpersonal dynamic of love was set in motion. The restless dynamic of this new love-driven self is reminiscent of the daimon Eros that Plato describes in his great dialogues, *Phaedrus* and *Symposium*.

Deep experiencers become obsessed, as though something was gestating within them, a painful pressing outward toward new life. They complain of loneliness and find it hard to adjust to a world that falls short of the perfection glimpsed. Experiencers return to ordinary life haunted by a sense of incompleteness, a nostalgia for the paradise that pained them. The positive and dangerous effects of archetypes are inseparable. To minimize the risk, experiencers need a helping community open to and understanding the process.

The Self and the Near-Death Archetype

On the threshold of death, the ego may for the first time come face to face with its unknown self. The larger psychic reality submerged below the threshold of everyday life Jung calls the Self or Objective Psyche.

This Self comes upon us, as if from the outside, a force transcendent. Ring also thinks that the being of light, the voice, the presence experienced during near-death states, is the larger pattern of oneself. "It is not merely a projection of one's personality, however, but one's total self, or what in some traditions is called the higher self. In this view, the individual personality is but a split-off fragment of the total self with which it is reunited at the point of death."[76]

In his study of alchemy, Jung remarked, "... the archetypes have about them a certain effulgence or quasi-consciousness. . . . and numinosity entails luminosity." Near-death experiencers therefore sometimes conclude that the "being of light" is God. "We know that an archetype can break with shattering force into individual life . . . It is therefore not surprising that it is called 'God'."

In the Western tradition, to claim identity of Self with God rings of blasphemy. But in light of NDEs, we can see how some might be led to proclaim this identity. Jesus was accused of blasphemy because he claimed a special intimacy with the Father (John: 10:33). The Hindu doctrine of the oneness of Atman and Brahman is not shy about asserting the lofty equation. Tibetan Buddhist teachings say we must recognize that the Divine Light before which we stand in awe is a projection of the Self.

Gnostically inclined Christians, Sufis and cabalists of the Islamic and Judaic traditions, all drew their inspirations, often at great risk, from the mystical well of this supreme identity. Such experiences could, in hardy spirits who trusted their own instincts above tradition, form the kernel of a new authority, a new interpretation of reality or a new myth of identity. However, archetypal encounters have a malevolent potential. Mix the inner urgencies with more disreputable instincts, and the energies of spiritual transformation work their way into the dark side of history.

Being near death sometimes activates an archetype of the collective unconscious, a constellation of motifs about an enlightenment process, a passage toward greater consciousness of the Self.[77] We're calling this constellation the archetype of death and enlightenment (ADE). Near-death is not the only context in which ADEs constellate. Any crisis of transformation, spontaneous or artificial, individual or collective, might awaken the process.

Near-death imagery describes becoming a Self: moving from darkness to light, from unconsciousness to consciousness. Light from darkness is a universal symbol. Rembrandt and Caravaggio are the master painters of this numinous configuration. John (1.5) speaks to the paradox. "And the light shines in darkness; and the darkness comprehended it not." (John: 1.5)

Or the Bradaranyaka Upanishad: "From non-being lead me to being, from darkness lead me to the light, from death lead me to immortality." In near-death states, the sequence is also from darkness to light.

We find it in creation myths: in the Rig Veda, Hesiod's Theogony, the Old Testament, and the Scandinavian Eddas. For Jews, Arabs, Germanic peoples, Celts and others, day begins with night; darkness precedes the dawning of the light. Light is a primordial image of consciousness; and it always rises from the depths of darkness, the not yet conscious.

Another near-death motif is passage through caves, canals, holes, tunnels, and the like, all moving into a clearing: birth and rebirth, a passage to a higher plane of being. The Allegory of the Cave in Plato's *Republic* (Bk. 7) is a landmark in Western philosophy. Enlightenment is portrayed as escape from a cave into the light of the sun. A change of consciousness is required. The cave motif appears in the Myth of the True Earth in the *Phaedo*, the great dialogue on immortality. There is a struggle to emerge from the mist and shadow of the false earth, with the task of learning to endure the light of the true earth. Plato's myths contained deep insights that reflect the idea of ADE.

These experiences throw down a gauntlet before common sense and scientific materialism. Dying, as it appears to the rational materialist eye, means the end, total loss, personal extinction. In the eyes of the archetypal imagination, it represents a gateway to greater knowledge and self-realization.

The ego is normally in the dark with respect to the light of the Self. Perhaps the "image" that cuts across all near-death imagery is that of Light, symbol, I suppose, of consciousness. The light is not just symbolic but literal fact, an intense experience. It may appear as formless illumination or as jewelled cities of light, human figures or "angels" brightly clothed, or landscapes bathed in celestial radiance.

Mircea Eliade wrote about the mystic light: "Experience of the Light signifies primarily a meeting with ultimate reality: that is why one discovers the interior Light when one becomes conscious of the Self (Atman) or when one penetrates into the very essence of life and the cosmic elements, or, last of all, at one's death."[78]

Intentional, directed, dynamic, the ADE compensates for the ego's one-sided view of death. Affectively, this means overcoming the fear of death. Existentially, it means that the end is perceived as a beginning, that what is coming is a change in the state of one's being. Cognitively, it signifies an expansion of conscious capacity; a psychic constellation that heralds a new mode of being. Here are Jung's words:

> Hence it would seem to be more in accord with the collective psyche of humanity to regard death as the fulfilment of life's meaning and as its

goal in the true sense, instead of a mere meaningless cessation. Anyone who cherishes a rationalistic opinion on this score has isolated himself psychologically and stands opposed to his own basic human nature.

This is a bold claim. But let's not fool ourselves. The idea that death is somehow the transcendent goal of life runs totally counter to the modern outlook. It also runs counter to common sense.

Nevertheless, it's the message that comes out of the near-death archetype, echoing the mythic claims of the collective psyche of humanity.

The case can be made for the unhealthy consequences of being, as Jung says, in conflict with our own nature.[79]

What we call death is archetypally portrayed as the road to a greater reality than what we know in life—in its way, a Copernican revolution. It places the sun of the Objective Psyche at the center of spiritual reality, challenging the illusion of the conscious ego: that bodily death swallows up all.

Literal near-death is only one possible ADE trigger. Any situation threatening ego-death, major life changes and transitions, might mobilize this imagery and their energies. The kind of crisis and the context would determine which factors of the constellation came to the fore. For instance, deceased relatives are more likely to appear in a crisis of literal near-death; in nonliteral "ego-death", the epiphany may be more subtle and indirect.

Let's glance at some examples. Imagery—that is what archetypes are about—other than literal near-death: in dreams, mysticism, mythology, initiation and mystery rituals, psychedelic experiences, and UFO "revelations." These by no means exhaust the spectrum of possible sources.

Mystical—The resemblance between NDEs and mystical phenomena has been noted many times. Russell Noyes wrote that the mystical consciousness "seemed not so much a distinct element of the altered state under examination (that is, the NDE) but rather its more extreme progression."[80] The elements of this mystical extension cited by Noyes include feelings of unity, transcendence of space and time, release from ego-driven fear, heightened sense of the value of truth, and extreme emotions.

Some mystical experiences result from practice or discipline and show a connection with near-death states. Plato's view of philosophy as the practice of death comes to mind as does the picture of yogis who put themselves into deathlike trances. Eliade gives us medical testimony showing that "the reduction of respiration and cardiac contraction to a degree that is usually observed only immediately before death" is something yogis are able to accomplish at will.

About the supernatural Christian ecstasy, one scholar wrote:

> ... the physical life approaches a deathlike state, the breathing is reduced, the heart and the pulse become slower, the vital warmth disappears, the limbs stiffen, the outer and inner senses are wholly bound. It is as if the soul, as in death, were separated from the body.

I have noted and like to repeat: The awakening process may be precipitated by purely psychical causes. The story of the modern Hindu mystic, Ramana Maharshi, shows the relationship between *ego-death* and the enlightenment experience. Ramana, quite young, was in perfect health. One day he became panic-stricken that he was about to die. He wrote:

> The shock of the fear of death drove my mind inwards and I said to myself mentally, without actually framing the words: 'Now death has come; what does it mean: What is it that is dying? This body dies.' And I at once dramatized the occurrence of death. I lay with my limbs stretched out stiff as though rigor mortis had set in and imitated a corpse so as to give greater reality to the enquiry. I held my breath and kept my lips tightly closed so that no sound could escape, so that neither the word 'I' nor any other word could be uttered. 'Well then,' I said to myself, 'this body is dead. It will be carried stiff to the burning ground and there burnt and reduced to ashes. But with the death of this body am I dead? Is the body I? It is silent and inert but I feel the full force of my personality and even the voice of the I within me, apart from it. The body dies but the Spirit that transcends it cannot be touched by death. That means I am the deathless Spirit." All this was not dull thought; it flashed through me vividly as living truth . . .

In this case, a psychodrama imitating death gave rise to an experience of mystical illumination. The encounter with the Self was facilitated by Ramana's not resisting the idea of his imminent death; he let go, gave up. This is reminiscent of some types of NDE. This act of surrender, coupled with the inhibition of normal respiration, may have triggered the experience. Voluntary or involuntary ego-surrender helps. It evokes the latent powers of the Self—the total, objective psyche.

Ego-death. What is that? An invitation to constellate the archetype of death and enlightenment.

An interesting case was brought to my attention by an experienced meditator. Mr. Norman M. of Los Angeles, California, describes himself as professionally trained in Buddhist and Hindu yoga. Mr. M. says that during his eleven years of intensive meditation, he had thousands of psychic experiences: trances, visions, hallucinations, and so forth.

On one occasion, however, he had a "very, very different" experience which "was deeply moving," something unforgettable that stood out above all his notable meditation experiences. He explained how all efforts to reproduce his experience were in vain. Here are details from his written account:

> I lost awareness of my body and my surroundings. All that existed was a vast visual field which appeared dark; suddenly a whirling vortex appeared in this area. It was the deepest, darkest black I have ever seen, circular and whirling. (He included a drawing in his report of a black rotary pattern emanating from a center, imposed on another shade of black in the background, a kind of black mandala.)

> It was 'moving' at incredible speed and 'I' was 'moving' through it. This vortex lasted only a very brief time, and I came out the other end into a bluish turquoise landscape. I cannot adequately describe this scene; it was the most unearthly thing I had ever seen. The blues and turquoise were electric, glowing and self-luminous. I could not pick out any individual structures, though it appeared like a forested area with foliage and waterfalls made of vibrant and glowing colors. I am looking forward and down on this as if I am in the air, hovering in a helicopter. Awareness of my body, my apartment, my 'self,' this world had all completely varnished.

> All that existed was this heavenly sphere. The emotional component was incredible. I no longer existed but only as an awareness. I found this heavenly sphere to be so engrossing and beautiful that I didn't want to come back. I began to feel an ending of the experience. I could not hold on to it and it ended as quickly as it had come. I found myself back in my apartment sitting in my chair.

Mr. M. explained that he was puzzled about the black vortex and other features of the experience until he read Raymond Moody's book, *Life After Life*. What puzzled him was the fact that the experience, so like the prototypical NDE, occurred to him while in perfect health, during meditation, sober and awake.

This suggests a pattern of experience, a recurrent, archetypal psychism, expressed and concretized in different kinds of human experience.

Dreams—The dream is a source of information about this enlightening psychism. In people approaching the end of their lives, Jung observed dreams with rebirth symbolism. From my collection of near-death dreams, consider this.

Less than a year prior to his death, an elderly man dreamt he was climbing a mountain. There were three plateaus to the ascent; at each plateau he stopped—the light and surrounding landscape became brighter, more peaceful and more beautiful. At the top he experienced a wonderful happiness; some men there, who were digging in the earth, told him to go back down by following the path he took to come up. He complied, realizing he had to return something to his wife, a jacket he was holding, the first she gave him fifty years ago.

This resembles an NDE in several ways: the association of light, bliss and beauty with death (the men he understood were digging his grave); reaching a border; and having to turn back because of a link (the jacket) with a loved one. The archetypal overtones of light and bliss on top of a mountain while men nearby are digging his future grave speak loud and clear.

Here is another, curiously similar, example. In this case, a chronically ill woman "gave up," wanted to die and dreamt she went on a journey:

> Upon reaching a mountain I began to climb. As I climbed higher and higher, the great "cloud" that covered everything began to dissolve, and patches of sunshine began to shine through. At last I reached the top and flung myself on to the level ground, whereupon the "sun" suddenly broke out all around and permeated my entire being with healing love and total splendor. It was an indescribable experience of such stark truth that the memory of it seemed to have ingrained itself in my deepest being. I felt the way a person should feel. It was more real than anything I have ever known.[81]

The author goes on to describe herself as if she were flying over meadows of colored flowers and approaching a great golden city where her departed loved ones were waiting. She then remembered leaving her cane at the top of the mountain, which reminded her of her responsibility to her (living) loved ones. With this her super-real dream ended. She felt she had an actual encounter with God and received divine guidance, identifying her experience as a "greatly expanded Jungian archetypal dream."

Morton Kelsey, an Episcopalian priest and student of Jung, wrote the book *Dreams: A Way to Listen to God*. In one story a 75-year-old Anglican priest, sick, anxious and in pain, dreamt he saw his childhood home and other highlights of his life pass in review before him. Then he saw himself sitting in his room; he looked up at the clock on the mantle, which had stopped at 11:00. The mantle changed into a doorway through which a beam of light streamed. Then the old priest rose from his chair and walked through the door into the light. After sharing the dream with his wife, his pain and anxiety vanished, and a week later he fell asleep in his chair and never woke up.

The overall pattern here is similar to the archetypal NDE, and Kelsey cites the dream as an example of numinosity in action. The light is noteworthy, along with the hint of foreknowledge of dying in the chair; also, the panoramic memory and out-of-body experience occur within the dream itself. Finally, it's worth noting how the tunnel-vortex motif is here transformed into a doorway.

It would be easy to multiply examples of dreams with near-death imagery, feelings and aftereffects. Such dream and near-death epiphanies surely stem from the same matrix.

Mythology — The world of myth is the world of collective dreams made public. As such, we might expect to observe in it ample traces of imagery linked to death and enlightenment. An old example will serve us now. Australian aborigine myths of the afterlife contain many motifs of modern NDEs. One tale describes the person beginning the afterdeath journey in darkness, sliding down "hollow grooves" in "a rocky, narrow gorge," entering flames (which scorched bad men), and then coming to clear spaces where the landscape is full of trees, free of undergrowth and the grass is especially green. There in the open space the spirit-traveller is said to meet dead relatives and friends.

They welcome him and take him to a camp where he is dressed and painted, after which there is much shouting and play. The basic motif of enclosure-disclosure, the passage from dark to light, from part to whole is present in this aboriginal myth. So too is the vertical polarity of the ADE for we are told that if the spirit-traveller has been a "greedy and quarrelsome" fellow in life, he will fail to reach the verdant camp of his ancestors.

He is met by an "ugly old man," the archetype of the Shadow, and crows who pick at and knock him about, leaving him scarred and dishevelled. Interestingly, there are no references to anything like a pure being of light.

Mythology and the classics of world literature hint of an archetype of death and enlightenment. ADE motifs run through the deep structure of works like the Epic of Gilgamesh, Dante's *Divine Comedy*, Plato's Allegory of the Cave, the Book of Revelation and Tolstoy's *Death of Ivan Ilych*. Each myth or story reveals a unique perspective on the dialectic of death as an unexpected inroad to enlightenment.

Tolstoy's story explores the fierce denial of death and clinging to one's persona. Ivan Ilych is a judge by profession, accustomed to living by rule and outward shows of rectitude. Meanwhile pleasure, status, and power are his true gods. But his world begins to crumble when he finds himself facing death.

> One by one, the illusions and defences melt away. Pain, loneliness, and his selfish family break him down; his persona, his superficial image of reality, is broken in pieces. For three whole days, during which time did not exist for him, he struggled in that black sack into which he was being thrust by an invisible, resistless force. That very justification of his life held him fast and prevented his moving forward, causing him most torment.

> Suddenly a force struck him in the chest and side, making it still harder to breathe, and he fell through the hole and there at the bottom was light. What had happened to him was like the sensation one sometimes experiences in a railway carriage when one thinks one is going backwards while one is really going forwards.

The logic of enlightenment is strange; transformation takes place at the bottom of a black hole. It was when Ivan's schoolboy son took his hand, kissed it and began to cry that the dying judge let go and fell into the light.

He stepped out of the black hole of himself, saying, "In place of death there was light. So that's what it is!" he suddenly exclaimed aloud. "What joy!"

Mystery and Initiation Rites — Archaic rites of initiation are mainly ritual imitations of death and rebirth. They do in a group setting what Ramana Maharshi did on his own. The same can be said for the mystery rites of Greek and Roman antiquity.

Another impressive example are the ancient Greek Eleusinian Mysteries. The question concerning those august rites, which lasted well over a thousand years, is about the culminating vision. The *epopteia*.

What was the secret of its enlightening power? Ancient testimonials describe the effects: a dramatic reduction of the fear of death, new hope and belief in the reality of an afterlife, and transformation of the quality of their present lives.

Scholars long supposed that a special doctrine was revealed to initiates, persuading them there was a life after death. But Aristotle put this out of court when he wrote that during the rites, celebrants didn't learn anything but were "to be passive" and "to be put into a state" (*pathein kai diatethenai*). The celebrant, in short, was put into an altered state of consciousness. The "learning" was peculiar to that exact altered state of mind.

Some recent ideas may shed light on the riddle of Eleusis. One is psychedelic research. Albert Hofmann, who discovered LSD, argued that the *kykeon*, the ritual drink used in the rites at Eleusis was a potent mind-altering drug, chemically similar to LSD. Drinking the *kykeon* (psychedelic brew) after a nine-day fast would certainly help to bring about the "state" the initiates desired to be in.

Second, look at the archetypal content of the vision. Carl Kerenyi writes that the initiate experienced a beatific vision of the queen of the underworld: Persephone, daughter of Demeter, image of archetypal chthonic force.

The third idea is near-death research, which also features divine light beings that remove the fear of death and touch the soul with enchantment. It is no exaggeration to say that the Mysteries of Eleusis were the gospel, the good news, of pagan antiquity.

Here are the words of the pagan initiate, Cicero: "We have been given a reason," he wrote in his treatise *On the Laws*, "not only to live in joy but to die with better hope."

In a passage from an early Greek writer, Themistios, the connection between near-death and the Mysteries was specifically cited: "The soul (at the point of death) has the same experience as those who are being initiated into great mysteries. . . At first one is struck by a marvellous light, one is received into pure regions and meadows . . .." It looks to me that the inner world of the ancient Mysteries and that of the modern near-death experiencer derive from a common source. We could call it the subliminal psyche of humankind.

The ancient Greeks seem, in fact, to have worked out an effective method for inducing a type of near-death experience. It accounts for the most striking effects of the rite: reduction of the fear of death, deepened hope and expectation of an afterlife, and enhancing the quality of *this* life.

Psychedelics—In settings of modern psychotherapy, entheogens have been used for initiation into the mysteries of death. According to Stanislav Grof and Joan Halifax, some deep psychedelic episodes resemble the near-death experience. Given to the terminally ill (or for that matter to anyone), psychoactive substances like LSD speed up the process of ego-death. The defensive wall is shattered. Near-death effects turn up in drug-induced ego-death states: the life-review, photic phenomena, meetings with supernatural beings. The effect on one's idea of death is powerful:

> Many individuals who had the experience of death and rebirth sometimes accompanied by feelings of cosmic unity independently reported that their attitudes changed toward dying and their concepts of death underwent dramatic changes. Fear of their own physiological demise diminished, they became open to the possibility of consciousness existing after clinical death, and tended to view the process of dying as an adventure in consciousness rather than the ultimate biological disaster. Those of us conducting this research kept witnessing, to our great surprise, a process that bore a striking similarity to mystical initiation . . . [124]

In Charles Garfield's study, people who experimented with mind-altering drugs showed less death-anxiety than non-drug using psychology and theology students, though they were outranked by practiced Zen and Tibetan Buddhist meditators. Drug users looked on the prospect of death as a possible adventure.

The ancient therapist-hierophant worked under more controlled conditions: a group setting, the sanction of common ceremonies, myths and symbols around which psychic energies rallied. Participants were programmed through ritual ablutions, fasting, sacrifices and psychodramas: ways to break down the ego and open to the greater self.

Hyper-analytic modern science has broken asunder what the archetypal vision kept whole.[82] The archetypal vision holds to the unity of mind and heart, intuition and sensation, science and religion, which come apart in the dissociations of modern sensibility. The prevailing medical outlook sees death as terminal, all negative. The archetypal vision, like nature itself, comprehends living and dying as cut from a single cloth. Living is inseparable from dying; the anabolic and catabolic strands are intertwined in every living organism.

UFO revelations — Compared with ancient and primitive societies, modern scientific culture offers few inlets to the rebirthing powers of the collective creative mind. True, the "powers" appear spontaneously in our dreams, NDEs, and elsewhere. If Jung was right, we have also in this age of science been projecting archetypes on the skies in the form of unidentified flying objects (UFOs).[83]

Jung believed that UFO phenomena were signs of the end of the era. "Apparently," he wrote, "they are changes in the constellation of psychic dominants, of the archetypes, or 'gods' as they used to be called, which bring about, or accompany, long-lasting transformations of the collective psyche." The sky epiphanies may, in short, be viewed as psychic byproducts of the near-death experience of modern civilization.

The epilogue to Jung's book on flying saucers dealt with the case of Orfeo Angelucci, a "contactee" who had a close encounter and conversion experience. Based on Jung's account, I found almost every element in the prototypical NDE, along with rarer phenomena such as transcendental music. Orfeo had a series of experiences in which he "saw" lights and apparitions of men and women alleged to be friends from another world. He heard voices and felt he was about to die but also that he had transcended death.

He found himself aboard a UFO that carried him away, saw a white flash of lightning, his whole life in a panorama before him, received teachings, had what Raymond Moody called a "vision of knowledge" and was carried to "heaven" where he saw wondrous landscapes and heard wondrous music. All the motifs of the NDE are present, dressed up in space-age imagery. Lots of powerful metanoid affects, with Orfeo, along with plenty of ego-inflation. It appears that the NDE and certain UFO experiences stem from a common or very similar mental agency.

Could All This Be About a Planetary NDE?

It has been noted how archetypes, being partly images of cosmic forces, analogues linking nature with psyche, may sometimes foreshadow scientific discoveries. Jung said that alchemy prefigured modern chemistry. Alchemy also anticipated developments in modern depth psychology. Physicist Wolfgang Pauli wrote of the influence of archetypal ideas on Kepler's discovery of the three laws of planetary motion, a spinoff from his search for the music of the spheres.

Pauli stresses Kepler's fascination with the archetype of the Trinity and his passion for heliocentrism, an astronomical mandala of the Self. "Because he looks at the sun and the planets with this archetypal image (the Trinity) in the background, he believes with religious fervor in the heliocentric system."[84] Guided by this image and corrected by measurement, he happens on the laws of motion.

We might ask what, if anything, the archetype of death and enlightenment foreshadows? What are these extraordinary images telling us about our place in nature? Do they hint of things we have yet to discover, with or without the tools of science?

The images associate light, a symbol of consciousness, with death. The mind of the deep unconscious repeats in many forms the same message: death is somehow the gateway to greater consciousness, more light, more being. The story goes beyond the bare replication of life and its material goods; it is rather about a transformation in the way we experience life. We could say it is about a new concept of *perception*.

Is there a relation between religion and parapsychology, like the one between astrology and astronomy, or alchemy and chemistry? In each case, the former see in a glass darkly what emerges more clearly in the light of later discoveries. Judging by the past, the new discoveries always surpass initial expectations.

If near-death epiphanies are projections of a higher Self, and if archetypes orient us toward the future, then humanity as a whole may be going through a dark tunnel, at the end of which it will enter a new world of consciousness and panoramic self-understanding. All the motifs of the near-death encounter—borders, landscapes, meetings with the dead, beings of light, crises of decision—all may foreshadow aspects of a wider movement of consciousness to come.

We are led to a disquieting possibility: the counterpart of individual near-death that may be unfolding in history with the near-death of humanity as a whole. Is it a coincidence that just as the scientific intellect is beginning to penetrate the mystery of what may lie beyond the death of the brain the scientific intellect has also created the means to destroy life on earth through nuclear war and/or climate catastrophe?

Part Three: The Transformation

8

THE TRANSFORMATION

Of these I too am now one, a fugitive from the god and a wanderer
who put my trust in raving strife.

PURIFICATIONS
—EMPEDOCLES

A Global Near-Death Experience?

In this chapter I want to discuss the idea of a global near-death experience. Raymond Moody, in his book *Glimpses of Eternity*, describes cases of a dying person drawing people present into his near-death experience. This suggests the possibility of a group near-death experience. Moreover, as noted, being literally near death is not necessary to have the experience. Psychic circumstances – fear, isolation, emergency–may bring it about.

Today global arms trade is the highest it's been since the Cold War. Moreover, a new arms race has begun that promises to be more expensive and more dangerous than ever. The incredible variety of weapons, proliferating today on earth and threatening all life upon it at the moment seem to be holding the reins of history. Fear is growing that the world powers may be on a collision course with catastrophe, which would be the outcome of the hubris of scientific civilization combined with the hubris of mentally and morally unfit leaders of nations with nuclear arsenals.

Jung took the UFO experience to be a sign of the near-death experience of Western civilization, a sign that new psychic constellations were looming on the mental horizon of humankind. In researching my book *The Millennium Myth*, I quickly grew tired of collecting prophecies of doomsday, the Rapture, the arrival of one or another messiah. It recurs on a regular basis; things would seem so bad that endtimes had to be imminent. The doomsayers were always wrong and life would resume.

But something different happened in the 20th century. Scientists with state help figured out how to create atomic weapons that could be used in warfare, weapons that might also destroy civilization, along with life (except for some bugs) on earth. That is the big difference today. We have entered an age when the mythologies of divine retribution in our holy books become realistically imaginable. It is now possible for the fantasies of religious extremists to materialize into bloody tangible reality.

The same religious extremists, wilfully ignorant of science, deny there is a problem with overproduction of CO_2 that has to be dealt with. Ignorance, unbounded greed and moral imbecility are converging forces that put the world at heightened risk of disaster—a disaster many believe we're approaching with increasing speed.

The need to evolve mentally *en masse* has perhaps never before been so great. The prospect of near human extinction from nuclear hostilities followed by starvation and nuclear winter is one possible outcome. The second is the unmistaken arrival of climate catastrophe. The point we need to keep repeating is that these outcomes are inevitable, barring some large-scale and effective revolution of behaviors and values. The status quo is the sure road to the worst outcomes, and the momentum toward disaster is daunting. Reason, politics as usual, democracy itself may not be up to the task.

Is there another possibility? Some barely imaginable, involuntary quantum leap of consciousness may be the only escape route from the general crash of civilization that seems to be approaching.

Wildly accelerating technical prowess has outstripped the default moral sensibility of people everywhere. Threatening forces are unleashed constantly, and we are always reeling from the endless information avalanche. Information, however, is not wisdom. Nor does it make us better human beings.

A lot of knowledge can be a dangerous thing—in our collective unconscious, all the demons of Christian hells and Tibetan bardos are alive and well—but they now have mighty arsenals of military technology to act them out.

In *The Millennium Myth* (1995), I coined the term *technocalypse*—the convergence of technology and the apocalyptic imagination.

"Then the One sitting on the throne spoke, 'Look, I am making the whole of creation new' (Rev. 21:5)." This old dream of a new heaven and earth, of a new humanity look forward to what scientific technology is already doing and what it promises to do.

Technology has revealed a new heaven and earth through modern geology and astronomy, and a new humanity is possible through genetic engineering, though many resist that idea for moral reasons. Modern video and audio technologies connect us in principle to global consciousness and beyond. Bioengineering promises perfection and prolonged life to our bodies, ideas that until the rise of modern science were pure fantasy. The internet swells our possible psychosocial identity, allowing for instant global connectivity by many platforms.

Artificial intelligence extends and surpasses our natural capacities, and some enthusiasts fantasize about human extinction, consoled by the idea of more cooperative robots managing the earth in our place.

In addition to manic expansiveness, there is the dualistic logic of apocalyptic morality that we should worry about. The millennium myth entails that the good guys take the bad guys out. But that could get serious in the age of technocalypse. We have reached a stage of our evolution where it is possible to convert solar physics into a hydrogen bomb that we can point at our enemies and annihilate them, if we decide it is necessary. Of course, our enemies are pointing their bombs at us. Old medieval fantasies of the end of the world now confront us as impending possibilities.

Can technology ward off technocalypse? That sounds hopeful, but my sense is that nothing short of major changes of consciousness are likely to avert the world catastrophe that many see as coming. No amount of clever political jockeying, no inspired diplomatic maneuvers, no unilateral gestures of good will are likely to succeed in stopping the forces in place that are driving us toward a dénouement of the rational materialist conquest of history.

The voice inside is insistent: Nothing short of a new reality principle, a kind of surrealpolitik (to counter the deadly logic of the prevailing realpolitik) is needed to do the job. Who can predict these things with confidence? Nevertheless, the nagging thought persists: without a felt sense of human solidarity in a critical mass of humanity to launch the change, the hands of the doomsday clock sooner or later is going to strike midnight.

We need to feel the spur to an evolutionary imperative. It is our duty to attempt to accelerate—by whatever means we possess, —the creative advance of the consciousness of our race. The choice is between conforming to the lethal truth of the status quo or embracing the truths that serve the necessary inner transformation.

Technology Enables Eschatology

Science may supersede myth, but in military matters, it seems that science is catching up with myth. Old archetypes take on new guises, for example, the myth of knowledge linked to man's downfall. The story is told in Genesis: eating from the tree of knowledge led to expulsion from paradise. The myth appears in Greek tragedy, with Oedipus, for instance, blinded by his passion for insight. The theme runs through modern science fiction, with Dr. Frankenstein paradigmatic of the madness of scientists.

Watching the first atomic bomb explode, Robert Oppenheimer famously recalled words from Hindu mythology: "I am become Death, Shatterer of Worlds." Nuclear technology makes it possible to convert the myth of the destruction of the world into literal reality.

Thus, in the Iranian Zend-Avesta, Ahura Mazda foretells the way the earth will perish and describes the nuclear winter that today's scientists foresee: "Upon the material world the evil winters are about to fall, that shall bring about the fierce, deadly frost," a frost so lethal that grass will grow no more and living things die, as they retreat to the caves and innards of the earth.

The hope for surviving this terminal winter is to build a Vara or enclosure; for outside, it will be a 'miracle' to behold the footprint of a sheep. One wonders if the ancient seers glimpsed in their visions the nuclear winter that would follow a nuclear war.

The creation of man is linked in Greek mythology with the battle of the Olympians and the Titans. The genesis of the world is drenched in imagery of mistrust and violence, of Chronos devouring his young, of Zeus revolting against his father. In the *Theogony*, Hesiod paints this picture of last things before the creation of the new order of humanity:

Then Zeus did not hold back his might any longer, but now immediately his heart was filled with strength and he showed clearly all his force. He came direct from heaven and mount Olympus hurling perpetual lightning, and the bolts with flashes and thunder flew in succession from his stout hand with a dense whirling of holy flame. Earth, the giver of light, roared, everywhere aflame, and on all sides the vast woods crackled loudly with the fire. The whole of the land boiled, and as well the streams of Ocean, and the barren sea. The hot blast engulfed the earth-born Titans and the endless blaze reached the divine aether; the flashing gleam of the thunder and lightning blinded the eyes even of the mighty. Unspeakable heat possessed Chaos.

Today the myth of the destruction of the world by heat and fire is exploding piecemeal into reality, by manmade global warming or the manmade madness of warfare. The Trident was a weapon of mythology—it belonged to Poseidon, the earth-shaker, nemesis of Odysseus—an instrument of godlike destructive power. Back in the '80s it was the name of a gigantic submarine, a monster carrying on a secret, undetectable existence in the sea, capable of destroying 160 cities in the Soviet Union. The waters of the sea, as the myths of old said, are truly the waters of death. The death-bestowing Trident still prowls the oceans of the world. More unnerving is the thought that this "death-bestowing Trident" lives on in the great waters of the unconscious, submerged but poised in ourselves.

The nine nations today with nuclear weapons, already capable of inflicting colossal damage on their enemies, are all busily investing billions in upgrading their nuclear arsenals and other military applications. This may seem insane but there is a logic behind it. Each side is worried that to be one step behind in the hair-trigger world of high speed military technology could be fatal. Opponents must remain in hair-trigger alertness. Falling behind could be fatal. So the upgrading is logical and inevitable, but *all the more* insane. The process goes on strangely out of touch with reality, even though all the moves are made in the name of realism and *realpolitik*.

The global military apparatus engirdling the earth is an artefact of calculating reason. Thermonuclear warheads do not materialize from the demons of the unconscious; they require the organized behavior and collective cooperation of thousands of human beings.

The arsenals of murder are part of well-paid and prestigious corporate life linked to long-range governmental policies, supported by argument and ideology, grounded in what is taken for a coherent moral outlook. The colossal potential to murder and sow destruction is an ordinary, integral feature of modern life, a routine necessity, like smart phones and automobiles.

The global war technology threatens the life of the entire planet, not just humanity. The ecosystem is threatened by destruction of the protective ozone of the atmosphere, which protects us from lethal radiation from the sun. In the aftermath of atomic war, bacteria, viruses and disease-bearing insects will adapt, mutate and multiply into virulent forms. Exposure to radiation will interfere with human immune mechanisms, making survivors susceptible to plagues and epidemics of infectious disease.

Radiation threatens to disrupt the genetic code of the evolutionary process. Pediatrician Helen Caldecott, during the Cold War years, pictured "bands of roving humanoids" that would populate the earth after radioactive assault on reproductive organs. We should mention the nonhuman life forms, vegetation and wildlife, that will suffer from massive doses of lethal fallout, nor of the irreparable damage to the earth's waterways, soil and forests.

Scientific technology has learned how to make all systems of nature serve destructive purposes. The mechanical order is the basis of conventional weaponry. Electronics is mobilized through computer technology for drone warfare and of course the nuclear option is poised for maximum performance. Biological science is pressed to serve biological warfare. Chemistry is there to serve as part of the chemical warfare front. The "conquest" of space falls in line with the military imperative. Atomic power is, of course, the most dramatic example of service to military might.

Although the notion of psychic warfare is shrouded in obscurity, the intent is clear enough. If we could reliably harness psychic power, there is little reason to doubt that attempts would be made to exploit it militarily, for espionage, sabotage and assassination.

A comment from the philosopher Bertrand Russell: "No one can doubt that, unless something very radical is done, scientific man is a doomed species. In the world in which we are living, there is an active and dominant will towards death which has, so far, at every crisis, got the better of sanity."

Russell is right that in a crisis too often we let the will to death overrun sanity. The planet-destroying arsenals are justified by their deterrent uses. Deterrence, however, doesn't always work. And anyway, beyond politics and ideology is something else we have to reckon on: Russell called it the "will to death," or death-instinct, something sinister I call the thanatos conspiracy.

What I mean is an extension of what Edward Thompson described in an essay, "Notes on Exterminism, the Last Stage of Civilization."[85] The nuclear peril is based on addiction to a syndrome of moral, political and economic practices, the inevitable conclusion of a way of life. Thompson wrote that the Bomb creates a "field-of-force that engenders armies, diplomacies and ideologies, which imposes client relationships on lesser powers and exports arms and militarisms to the periphery."

The Bomb draws everything into its orbit; bolstered by a social system, it organizes a vast work force, research and academic centers, special skills and intricate security systems. The profit motive and bureaucratic inertia contribute to the exterminist momentum, besides the ideologies. Technology, unlimited in its possibilities, is driving us to the final stage of civilization, according to Thompson, the conclusion of a long-evolving network of premises.

Materialism as Nihilism

There is a link between the way scientific philosophy evolved in Western civilization and the growing risk of global calamity. Appleyard stressed the inevitability of science, its destabilizing obsession with novelty. Modern science ever since Galileo's physics thinks little of ends, purposes, values. It aspires to ideals of pure objectivity, quantifiable truth, predictability, technological utility and (always in the background) profitability. The human perspective—the internal world of misnamed "secondary" qualities—is bracketed. It is irrelevant to scientific truth. Human identity from here on is in limbo.

About the metaphysical implications of the Galilean revolution in physics, Edwin Burt wrote, "Man begins to appear for the first time in the history of thought as an irrelevant spectator and insignificant effect of the great mathematical system which is the substance of reality."

However, against this nihilistic drift, science may re-assert our identity in the presence of cosmic indifference. Edward Teller, known affectionately as "father of the hydrogen bomb" and inspired believer in its uses, once said that "we would be unfaithful to the tradition of Western civilization if we shied away from what man can accomplish."[86] Teller associated making the hydrogen bomb with fulfilling the duty of Western civilization.

According to this view, we know how important we are by the measure of our capacity to threaten all life on earth. We have become gods of death, destroyers of worlds, as Oppenheimer said when the first nuclear bomb was exploded.

Is there something in the Western way of doing science that got us into the current predicament? One thing may be said. Science evolved in such a way that it came to hold as suspect the reality, the very dignity of what we call feeling, inwardness, subjectivity–indeed, consciousness itself.

The physicalist way of organizing reality desacralizes nature and human society. The world of native lifestyles, customs, beliefs and myths is derided and destroyed. The culture of the computer, fast food, the automobile forms the template for a new world culture, speeded up and gadget-ridden. The lifeways of native traditions seem doomed to extinction, like countless species of other living things on earth. Reductionism *in practice* disdains cultural pluralism as well as it does biological pluralism.

I am not referring to the majority of scientists trying to understand and save the natural world from the ravages of techno-civilization. I am looking at the philosophical underpinnings of the drama that is unfolding before us.

According to reductive materialism: Since creatures of air, sea and land are just complex machines—soulless and unconscious—we may use them to gratify our needs, real or imaginary. And, needless to say, the inanimate, the "environment" is there, at hand, more "raw material," to be exploited for profits that make the rich richer. An aboriginal, an animist, a poet might scruple over exploiting nature on the assumption that it's dead; but a capitalist-materialist would not. Materialism is the philosophy of a dead and deadening universe.

Inevitably, it leads to the triumph of the secular. There is little breathing space for the age-old dimension of the sacred. The sacred signifies something beyond ordinary life. It sets up boundaries; stop here, it proclaims—you may go no further. Some things are off limits; they have transcendent meaning.

This leads to a useful distinction, endorsed by the moral philosopher, I. Kant, between means and ends. Persons are ends, not means; subjects, not just objects. Persons are not to be used as means but respected as ends, inherently valuable; in short, persons' lives matter. They are sacred, we might say.

Reductive science has no sense of the sacred as a dimension of being. As conscious subjects (not as material objects) we may experience life as in some sense sacred. Objects and events are possible openings to another world: the house you live in, your work, your marriage, your solitude, the way you have sex, the way you die. Human life from a sacred perspective is a rite of many passages.

Every juncture, the minor byways and the major turns, offer openings to life-enhancing shocks and surprises. The most negative of events — illness, chaos, death — allow for self-renewal, for reintegration on a higher plane. The sacred universe lives by the law of compensation: if you fast from the senses, you gain gifts of the spirit. If you embrace suffering aright, you court supernatural joy. If you know how to let go, surrender the obvious advantage, something new becomes available.

Modern secular minds have little taste for such talk. No longer a mystery to contemplate, an invitation to explore, the universe becomes an endless puzzle to solve, nature a stupendous source of "raw materials" to be extracted and sold for profit. All the magic is squeezed out of nature and sublimated into the most addictive drug: money. The triumph of the secular leaves behind a world of diminished meanings. Our appearance on earth is the upshot of millennia of accidental mutations. Our life a magnificent freak accident.

The picture is consistent. Death as annihilation mirrors the conception of life as void of meaning. Nullity seeps into our pores and hollows us out. Collapse is the logical endpoint of a dead universe without meaning. Calm down. What's the difference between the living and the dead? Just matter rearranged.

To be fair, our knowledge of the world is vastly richer from the discoveries of natural science. But our inner landscape—the place where we live all the time—has been robbed, reduced, and traduced. The path of transcendence, the highway to the sacred, is prey everywhere to roadblocks. The drones keep growling and shoving a big sign before us: DEAD END. We live in a spiritual wasteland, contaminated by the fallout of unmeaning and the stench of dead gods and rotting ideals.

I am circling around the theme of global near death. There are all kinds of death, subtle and literal, spiritual and physical. In a conflict between two cultures, the one armed with superior technology prevails. Spiritual death by force of arms is common. The cultures of Native America fell before the European musket. The tragedy, the injustice were huge, and reverberate to present times.

The potent blend of materialism and capitalism has been a great success, but for less than one percent of the population. For the rest, it's a period of growing protest, resistance, insecurity and violence with a pervasive sense of dislocation.

In 2015, 65.3 million people, mostly from Syria, Afghanistan and Somalia were forcibly displaced from their homes.

100,000 children, alone and unaccompanied, crossed borders seeking asylum in 78 countries. Children arriving in foreign lands were trapped, mistreated by police and guards, and detained in jail-like facilities. On average, one in twenty people in the Middle East were homeless and displaced.

Ours is becoming the century of refugees and migrants. Millions are stuck in transit from their native lands, living in camps, on boats unable to disembark, on borders between hostile countries. The list of the uprooted could be extended indefinitely— human beings whose traditional way of life, material and spiritual, has been destroyed, or is dying. The uprooters are themselves uprooted; we live as refugees from our own traditions. We are in a sense all refugees because the culture of scientific materialism has displaced the culture of our ancestors.

Animal Apocalypse

It's not only human beings who are suffering from these upheavals. The assault on nonhuman life forms is no less great. Extinction of animal species is today at an all time high. Scientists say that our planet is in the midst of the sixth mass extinction of plants and animals. The rate of extinction is thousands of times faster than what has been established as the normal rate of loss of one to five species per year. There are grim predictions that by mid century 30 to 50 percent of all species will be extinct. All this is due to human causes like global warming, habitat loss, and air and water pollution.

Zoologists say that the appearance of man coincides with the disappearance of many animal species of the Pleistocene era: giant birds such as the teraton of North America, the flightless superswan of Europe, the elephant bird of Madagascar, the dodo of the Islands of Mauritius and the twelve-foot-tall moas of New Zealand. Man is the being that makes other beings disappear: it begins in the mind, in acts of conceptual dismantling, ending outwardly on the plane of life in acts of material annihilation.

Primitive tribesmen, employing newly discovered flint weaponry, descended from Siberia through Alaska and the Americas and devastated, within a thousand years, a fantastic variety of wildlife that once flourished there. The asphalt tar pits of La Brea in Los Angeles, California, preserve traces of many of these prehistoric creatures: huge short-faced bears and coyotes, giant long-necked camels or llama, saber-toothed cats and lions, enormous bison and sloth, mastodons and shaggy, red-haired mammoths, four-hundred pound beavers and other giant herbivores.

It was a foretaste of the carnage to come. Hunting, and related skills, played a role in human evolution. But certain forms of hunting for sport, especially as we find nowadays point to problems in the pathology of human destructiveness. Consider, for instance, the sport of hunting as practiced by certain oil-rich sheiks of the Middle East. The hunters and their guests normally set out in the hot gravel country in air-conditioned Cadillacs.

A fleet of jeeps follows, while planes reconnoiter ahead to spot game. The total hunting envoy of jeeps, Cadillacs and planes is in radio communication. Once game is located, the jeeps herd the animals together until they are within range of the hunters, who rake them down with World War II air-cooled .50 caliber machine guns. Plutocratic hedonism adds to the momentum toward extinction.

Not all the violence committed against wildlife can be ascribed to the pure fun of hunting. A good deal of the killing can be laid up to mundane commercial need. The plight of the whale, the largest creature ever to inhabit the earth, is a case in point. The slaughter of whales has increased in recent years. With the help of huge fleets equipped with sonar, helicopters and explosive harpoons, the Japanese and the Russians have reduced the eight species of these mysterious creatures to near extinction. The Atlantic grey whale is now extinct.

Unsacred scientism has not only depopulated the universe of the supernatural; it is relentlessly diminishing the inhabitants of the natural world. The beings above and those below us in the hierarchy of nature are equally victimized. The thanatos conspiracy is consistent.

The technocratic credo is perhaps best summed up in the words of the ancient Greek Sophist, Protagoras: "Man is the measure of all things." The idea may be flattering to "man," but it has been a curse to the rest of the natural world. If the lakes, rivers, air, hills, valleys and trees that girdle the globe, all the nonhuman inhabitants of Earth, could speak with their own voice, they might say: "No, dear philosopher, the whole earth, the living system of the world, is the measure of all things."

The devastation of the planet's physical body, like the erosion of "archaic" and traditional cultures and the decimation of wildlife, is linked to the rationalist undermining of the sacred sense. People of traditional societies experience the sacred in the natural environment, which in turn shapes their behavior toward it.

The Native American way of life, before the arrival of European settlers, was holistic in outlook. Chief Luther Standing Bear, once an interpreter in Buffalo Bill's Wild West Show, spoke eloquently of the sacred kinship of being, a kinship unknown to modern rationalism. According to Standing Bear, the old people of the Lakota, a western tribe of the Sioux, loved the earth and reclined on the soil "with a feeling of being close to a mothering power."

For most unconscious consumers, the idea of "mother earth" is little more than a quaint metaphor. Natives experienced the soil as a "mothering power," a source of nourishment. A sense of personal kinship defined and imposed limits on his relationship to the earth. Standing Bear continues: "It was good for the skin to touch the earth and the old people liked to remove their moccasins and walk with bare feet on the sacred earth. Their tipis were built upon the earth and their altars were made of earth."

Home was a way of connecting with the earth; the hearth was celebrated as sacred power. The old Indian, Standing Bear says, healed himself with the earth's life-giving forces; when he sat upon the ground, he could "think more deeply and feel more keenly" as well as "see more clearly into the mysteries of life and come closer in kinship to other lives around him." By living in reverent communion with the earth, the Lakota enhanced their psychic sensitivity to the kinship of living forms.

A listening attitude toward nature increased general perceptiveness. It is different with rationalists who like to talk. Too much warm kinship with the earth would be bad business. In line with the credo of Protagoras, man is the measure of value on earth. "Man" is the engineer who, in Bacon's prophetic words, puts nature to the rack. Our common mode of speech with nature is in the imperative mood; the style is to command and appropriate, rarely to listen, an option left to the odd mystic or Romantic poet.

Living in harmony with nature encourages trust between humans and other living creatures. Says Standing Bear:

> Kinship with all creatures of the earth, sky and water, was a real active principle. For the animal and bird world there existed a brotherly

feeling that kept the Lakota safe among them, and so close did some of the Lakota come to their feathered and furry friends that in true brotherhood they spoke a common language.

Native American kinship with the earth enables feelings of oneness with the natural world. Feeling life erodes in denatured society where everywhere is mediated by machines, and there is increasing deafness to the language of living things. The most serious consequence of losing touch with the Earth is explained by Standing Bear:

> The Lakota was wise. He knew that man's heart away from nature became hard: he knew that lack of respect for growing, living things soon led to lack of respect for humans too.

The issue is vital to contemporary life. Since April, 2016, Native Americans have converged at Cannon Ball in protest against building the Dakota Access pipeline, a 3.7 bn project designed for transporting crude oil from North Dakota to a refinery in Illinois. The project threatens to contaminate the water from the Missouri river and infringes on the sacred lands of native peoples.

This is about a spiritual war between mutually alien worldviews and mentalities. In the one, Nature (the mother of all life on Earth) is viewed as raw material to plunder and utilize for the sake of profit, power, and human convenience; in the other, Nature is treated with respect, with awe, and with intuitive rapport.

From a materialist perspective, there are no limits to how we can exploit the natural world; from a sacred perspective, there are limits, constraints and a difference in attitude.

Willingness to risk poisoning our drinking water for profit is not only morally depraved, but points to the suicidal blindness of the dominant worldview. Water, of all things, is essential to life, and already we hear warnings of the coming water wars. This may well be the most fateful consequence of overheating the planet.

"Water is the giver of life in all tribes' prayers," explains Wendsler Nosie Sr., leader of the Apache Stronghold movement. "It is the blood of the world and unifies us all. These teachings go back to the beginning and have been passed from generation to generation, from family to family. They resonate with truth and are unchangeable." The Apache Stronghold movement he leads is an effort to save Oak Flat, an Apache sacred landscape in Arizona.

This seems like a war between those who have all the material power and those who have nothing but spiritual power.

Humans, torn from the mothering power of earth, become hard, insensitive, coldly pragmatic.

The degradation of traditional lifestyles and mythologies, and the exploitation of natural resources, are cut from the same cloth of unsacred scientism. The exploitation of natural resources and of humans stems from the same root: the hardened heart of which Standing Bear spoke, the computational mind detached from living nature.

By reducing nature merely to extended matter, depriving it of personality, of any status as an end or "thou," modern materialism creates a psychic paradigm for aggressive objectivity *toward things in general.* It undermines the imaginative kinship with nature, reducing it all to neuter objects, viewing every aspect of the natural world as potential material for satisfying human needs, real or invented for commercial purposes.

The Suicide of the Spirit

Outlandish threats to life and consciousness became possible with the help of reductive science. Consider, for example, a statement from a distinguished biologist: "Let us try to describe ourselves exactly to each other. We shall find that we can do better then by trying to speak of ourselves as inhabited by a number of pseudo things such as consciousness, mind, experience and the rest of them." Or this from a philosopher: "Contemporary science, in short, does not seem to require the notion of 'experience,' and is getting to the brink of rejecting it, in effect, as 'unreal' or 'non-existent.'" As far as losses linked to unsacred scientism, these remarks say it all. Reducing the human being to a machine completes the building of the nihilist monolith. The work of homogenizing the universe is accomplished.

By contrast, the despised spiritual traditions see the world as many-layered, people as inhabitants of many dimensions of being, sojourners between the worlds of sense and spirit. In the eyes of tradition, a human being is not just a physical object locked in time and space. The Renaissance thinker, Pico della Mirandola, wrote of human existence as a meeting place of many realities. The classic statement is from the *Oration on the Dignity of Man.*

> Taking man, therefore, this creature of indeterminate image, He (God the Creator) set him in the middle of the world and thus spoke to him: 'We have given you, O Adam, no visage proper to yourself, nor any endowment properly your own . . . We have made you a creature neither of heaven nor of earth, neither mortal nor immortal, in order that you may, as the free and proud shaper of your own being, fashion yourself in the form you prefer. It will be in your power to descend to the lower, brutish forms of life; you will be able, through your own decision, to rise again to the superior orders whose life is divine.

Almost akin to a modern conception of evolution, this sees human life as an open-ended process. It invites us to steer the course of our own evolution. Pico formulates the final choice facing us at a turning point in human evolution. We are beings of indeterminate form, yet formers and imagers of our future selves. We may descend to our lower selves (as we frequently do) or rise to a life in tune with our higher potentials (as we occasionally do).

We must be clear about the choice facing humankind. Albert Einstein wrote: "The unleashed power of the atom has changed everything except our ways of thinking. Thus we are drifting toward a catastrophe beyond comparison. We shall require a substantially new manner of thinking, if mankind is to survive."

A substantially new manner of thinking—we should underscore Einstein's words. They suggest that any approach that relies on old formulas for solving the world predicament should be scrapped. A substantially new manner of thinking? Einstein has remarked on the importance of imagination in solving the great scientific problems by stepping outside the box of our usual assumptions.

In Edward Thompson's *Letter to America*, we read: "Nothing less than a world-wide spiritual revulsion against the Satanic Kingdom would give us any chance of bringing the military riders down." The "new manner" needs to be conceived in terms of a spiritual revolution. Einstein and Thompson seem to me right and being right here points to the greatness of the challenge. It is no easy thing to outgrow one's worldview and launch into a revolution of consciousness. Something very jarring needs to happen.

In a short play by Luigi Pirandello, *The Man With A Flower In His Mouth*, a man emerges from a doctor's office with a fatal diagnosis. Possessed by this knowledge of impending death, the world lights up for him, the smallest things swell with significance; he lingers over every detail; the doomed man's awareness changes radically, and he undergoes a brilliant conversion of consciousness.

The question is whether ours is a world with a flower in its mouth. Like the man in Pirandello's play, will our world wake up and see all life in a new enlightened way?

We have been digging around in search of possible resources for changing our worldview, for expanding our consciousness in ways consistent with the survival of our species in a time of technocalypse. We metaphysical malcontents are out hunting for new creative energies, new affective potentials, wider intellectual horizons. If necessity is the mother of invention, we will have to invent new methods for mobilizing our transcendent allies.

Global Near-death and New Consciousness

Analogy between individual and global near-death? In the former, striking changes of consciousness occur. How, then, might we imagine our collective awakening?

Looking for a model in which people were suddenly transformed, became deeply disposed toward peace, we find it among the *hibakusha* of Hiroshima and Nagasaki: these were the victims and survivors of the first atomic attacks. The modern city of Hiroshima has become a symbol of the quest for peace. Scattered around are monuments and bronze tablets that read: "This is our city. This is our prayer. Building peace in this world, O God of evil! Do not come this way again. This place is reserved for those who pray for peace." And on the Peace Park memorial where the names of the A-Bomb dead are inscribed: "Let all souls here rest in peace, for we shall not repeat the evil."

In the aftermath of the 1945 atomic bombings, there remained an outside world. Destruction today would dwarf that of 1945, encompass the whole Northern Hemisphere civilization, possibly the whole biosphere. The monstrous failure of Western civilization will be visible for all (if any) survivors to contemplate.

A nuclear dénouement of Western civilization is a poor model for the road to expanded consciousness. More likely expect a vast contraction of consciousness to follow any such altercation. The chief response of the Japanese, according to Robert Jay Lifton[87] who made a close study of Hiroshima survivors, was a deadening of the sensibility. "I would suggest now," Lifton wrote, "that psychic numbing comes to characterize the entire life-style of the survivor."

Reports on the psychological response to other types of collective catastrophe, like plague and the modern concentration camp, agree with this description: the victim is zombified, anaesthetized.

Collective catastrophe produced marked changes in the reality-sense of survivors. "With such events, so radical is the overturning of the sense of what is 'real'—of what must be psychologically absorbed—that the survivor's mental economy undergoes a permanent alteration, a psychic mutation."

The mutations Lifton describes involve decreased awareness; victims become depersonalized, shut off perception of what is happening to them and act like detached, unfeeling observers.

The psychic mutation described is not the kind that stirs our hope for the future of humanity. The Japanese victims were psychically mutilated, although some of them emerged spiritually transformed. In one case, a woman apparently acquired healing power. She described the encounter with the bomb as "the greatest event in my life." It drove her toward the mystical recesses of her being. "I thought I had come to the extreme point—the very end—and there was absolutely nothing to depend on but religion."

Others emerged from the bomb encounter with a sense of mission. "This sense of a special 'mission' made possible by a 'miracle' was widespread among hibakusha," Lifton writes of someone he interviewed. "Regarding himself as one 'obliged to serve ... in a higher cause he described feeling 'a new source of light, which allowed me to recover myself and surge back ... a call to keep on living.'"

Reports of this type of response suggest that some hibakusha reached levels of consciousness similar to those described in the near-death experience. Perhaps if numbing to outside reality is carried far enough, one would retreat to the archetypal realms. But this was not typical among atomic bomb survivors where the trauma is unimaginable.

There are, moreover, marked differences between the A-bomb survivor and the common near-death survivor. In near-death, vital signs temporarily disappear, but the patient revives. The longer the "clinical" death, the deeper and more powerful the experience. The near-death experiencer is often restored to well-being. This contrasts sharply with A-bomb survivors. Hibakusha are not optimal for modelling higher consciousness.

A clue to the mental world of survivors may lie in "survivalist" publications. Such are for folks who expect the imminent collapse of civilization. They believe, often with religious ardor, in a coming catastrophe:

massive economic breakdown, natural or man-made. Many are urban dwellers anxiously studying techniques for survival in the increasingly elusive "wilderness." Reliance on firearms is the key to preparations for doomsday.

I have an old copy of *A Shooter's Survival Guide*, a publication meant as a guide for doomsday worriers. The cover features a photograph of a well-dressed, middle-aged business executive—with a machine-gun strapped on his back. The caption reads: "White Collar Survival Tactics." The array of "survival" information: articles, ads, editorials, letters on high-powered survival guns, survival knives, methods of making your own survival bullets, setting man-traps, using tear-gas, paralyzers and so forth.

From an article entitled "The Hardcore Survivalists," "The real survivalist," we're told, "has no more trust in police than he does in the rat packs he believes will be coming after his supply of food, water, ammunition and firearms . . . There will be no law other than the law of the jungle. It's a case of 'me against them.'"

If survivalist fantasies reflect the psychic reality of the post-Armageddon populace, it does little to strengthen the dream of a coming higher consciousness. The bardo of the paranoid survivalist is full of wrathful deities ready to spring on us out of every shadow.

Here is how Vico, in *The New Science*, describes the last stages of a culture dying of civil disorder, a culture about to have a near-death experience:

> For such people, like so many beasts, have fallen into the custom of each man thinking only of his own private interests. . . . Thus no matter how great the throng and press of their bodies, they live like wild beasts in a deep solitude of spirit and will, scarcely any two being able to agree since each follows his own pleasure and caprice. By reason of all this, providence decrees that, through obstinate factions and desperate civil wars, they shall turn their cities into forests and forests into dens and lairs of men. In this way, through long centuries of barbarism, rust will consume the misbegotten subtleties of malicious wits that have turned them into beasts made more inhuman by the barbarism of reflection than the first men had been made by the barbarism of sense.

In Vico's scheme, there are two kinds of barbarism: one based on sense, the style of primal humanity; the other based on over-refined intellect, the style of advanced civilization. The old way was frank and open, seen in the savage outbursts of enraged Achilles, grieving the death of his friend, Patroklos. The new way is sly, covert, but "more inhuman." It hides under "soft words and embraces." There is no Achilles to contend with. The maintenance of military power is done calmly, deliberately, under the cloak of soft-spokenness and reasonableness. As we all know, it's essential to the safety and defence of the *American* people. This is the corporate form of subtle barbarism, the system engineered by men Vico called "malicious wits."

Neither hibakusha, nor so-called survivalists, are ideal candidates for a spiritually enlightened world. Call it a nervous tic, but I keep wanting to imagine a new species of transformed beings, inspired, perhaps genetically rewired, by the latent powers of Mind at Large. I imagine a seeding of new consciousness that one day will blossom fully on the stage of history; likely to unfold gradually, haphazardly, a popular uprising of transcendent consciousness, spearheaded perhaps by women who as women share what Vico called a *sensus communis*—a sense of communal identity.

Nuclear cataclysm would be the most drastic stimulus to hasten the evolution of human consciousness. Or we might have a cyber-spawned crash of civilization, caused by enemy hackers or solar flares. The sheer immensity of the disaster would reverberate in the collective psyche and remain there for future generations. Evidence that the old consciousness was radically corrupt would be apparent to all. The lesson will be written in letters brilliant enough for the blind to see: the colossal burn-out of Western civilization.

To wind up this gloomy but possibly promising chapter: the NDE is a clue to a not fully understood system of inner resources. It touches on the deep structure of the human mind, and its elements present a model or template for imagining how major global disruption might trigger mass transformation of consciousness.

The vivid premonition of catastrophe might activate the reordering mechanisms of the deep psyche. At some point a critical mass of humanity confronts its radical angst, suddenly seeing the onset of tremendous danger. This in turn sets into motion the constellation of archetypal images and energies latent within.

The hard part of this speculation: before breakthrough large-scale breakdown seems in some sense to be unavoidable.

9

HIDDEN HELPERS

There are present in every psyche forms which are unconscious but nonetheless active—living dispositions—ideas in the Platonic sense that preform and continually influence our thoughts and feelings and actions.

—C.G. Jung

Granted that life on earth may be facing unprecedented peril. New and deadly dangers are on the increase, and it may be impossible to avoid confronting them. But we don't want to play down hints of a benign intelligence that reveals itself in odd ways, often at critical moments. Remember that Empedocles allows for Philia, the spirit of friendship, to enter the lists of history in competition with Neikia, the god of strife.[88]

How is the picture taking shape? So far we may cite patterns of paranormal and out-of-body experience. These in turn come together as part of the more directed near-death epiphanies. This too seems part of something larger, a psychic configuration that associates rupture, blockage, near death with expansion of consciousness. In fact, as already noted, death and enlightenment resonate together in strange ways.

People have experiences that may be described as helping epiphanies. In the interests of the mythology of transcendence, we can call these helping agents that emerge from our own hidden mental depths.

149

Whatever the source, we should pay attention. They bring good tidings; they encourage, they inspire, they guide and they guard our well-being, often in unexpected fashion.

Humility. Admitting you need help seems to pave the way for the epiphanies. Danger and uncertainty, however, are part of the rescue operations. Circe turned Odysseus' heedless men into swine; but Odysseus, not subject to her spell, made her an ally in his underworld journey. Gilgamesh crossed the sea of death and found the plant of immortality; but he fell asleep and a wily serpent stole it from him.

Myths of Helping Apparitions

Mythology is filled with supernatural entities that intervene in lives and history. All sorts of mediating spirits thought to traffic between heaven and earth have names such as nikes, victories, geniuses, the tutelary agents of antiquity. Some creatures of mythology probably derive from unusual apparitional experiences; the idea of angels, for example, from seeing apparitions of dead relatives.

Angelos, in Greek, "messenger"—appears in Job as servants and troops; in Daniel as visions; in Psalms as ministers and hosts; and in Revelation as spirits. Their functions vary. They announce coming events, as in Chapter 1 of Luke when an angel announced to Mary the conception of Jesus; they worship and attend on God, do his bidding, preside over holy places like the Tree of Life, and protect peoples and individuals. The idea of guardian angels looking over children is widespread.

In Homeric epics, the gods, when they're not hindering are helping struggling heroes. About heroes in the Greek epics, Bruno Snell wrote: "Any augmentation of bodily or spiritual powers is effected from without, above all by the deity." According to Snell, Homer had not yet formed a fully developed concept of the personal will; hence, whenever heroic exertion occurs, it is portrayed through an image of entreating and receiving aid from a god.

But another interpretation is possible. Homer's mythology of helping gods may reflect an understanding of the power of the subconscious will. It seems unlikely that Homer didn't understand that men can exert their wills; but perhaps he knew something that we moderns have forgotten: the hidden depths of the psyche, represented by the spirits or angels we call upon, and that sometimes move us to perform extraordinary feats. For a much needed study of psychospiritual secrets of the late classical Greek philosophers, see the illuminating account of Gregory Shaw.[89]

Harbingers of Intimacy

As the gods protected the heroes in the great epics, so people sought protection under the auspices of the heroes. Nor did the hero cults become extinct with the dying out of paganism. The cult of the Christian saints replaced and transformed the tradition.

Consider a few examples: during crisis and distress, people pray to Saint Jude the Apostle. They invoke Saint Anthony of Padua to help find lost property. Another Saint Anthony, the desert eremite of the fourth century, gave his name to a skin inflammation, erysipelas or Saint Anthony's Fire. Many people were said to be cured of this disease in 1089 by his intercession.

Saint Christopher used to be the patron saint of travellers. Saint Lucy, martyred in Syracuse in the fourth century, succors diseases of the eye. Saint Joseph protects us at the hour of death. Saint Michael the archangel is an ally in the battle against temptation. Saint Joseph of Copertino, levitator *extraordinaire*, looks over students and aviators and anti-capitalists.[90]

The triumph of Christianity, according to historian Peter Brown in his book *Cult of the Saints*, owes much to the rise of the cult of the saint in Latin antiquity. According to Brown, the cult of saints created a sense of intimacy between people and cosmos.

In words of the bishop of Cyrus in the fifth century, the cult of the saints created a ring of "invisible friends" around the Mediterranean world. Theodoret wrote:

> The philosophers and the orators have fallen into oblivion; the masses do not even know the names of the emperors and their generals; but everyone knows the names of the martyrs, better than those of their most intimate friends.

The martyrs astonished the Romans with their unnatural joy in the face of death—so demonstrably potent was their new mythology of death. They defied the gods of the Empire with unheard of courage and serenity. After death, at their graves and shrines they became members of a hierarchy of saints, offering protection and inspiration to embrace and act out the new worldview.

A further note on continuity. The cult of saints was, in a way, a fulfilment of the Platonic cult of Eros. Eros is the protagonist of Plato's *Symposium*—the supreme ally in pagan philosophy, the power that permeates living nature, mediates our humanity and our divine potentiality.

Belief in patron saints, one may argue, helps to liberate the psychic potential latent in believers. Belief is known to enhance psi performance; but trying too hard and being self-obsessed get in the way of psi.

A person misplaces a valuable object; anxious effort to find it can be self-defeating. Instead, relax and offer up a prayer to Saint Anthony – place the task in the hands of an invisible friend who specializes in helping folks find things.

The cult of the Virgin Mary is also about transcendent assistance. In the Marian visions at Fatima and later in the 20th century at Garabandal, Mary—the medium of all graces—appears as intercessor through whom world consciousness may hope to be transformed.

Handing it all over to a "higher" power may be a surprisingly useful strategy. It relieves the petitioner from undue sensations of effort and frees up subliminal ideas to express themselves. She is also freed from feeling personal responsibility for failure or success. In leaving all ego-involvement behind, the petitioner attends to the goal, not the steps for getting there.

According to physicist, Helmut Schmidt,[91] our psi powers work in a goal-oriented fashion. Consider a PK experiment with a random event generator. Placed before one of these machines, all subjects see is a panel of moving lights. They understand nothing of how the machine works. The task is to focus on the goal or outcome—say, lights to move clockwise. One tries to influence the behavior of the machine simply by concentrating, attending to, and imagining the end-state—where you want to be. The thinking is teleological—oriented toward the final outcome. You're in the optative, the let-it-be mood, not the indicative or the imperative. (Note the nuances in the grammar of consciousness.) In Schmidt's experiments, some results were obtained at odds way beyond chance.

Coming back to our prayerful petitioner, she too doesn't proceed with a plan, or a linear strategy. Everything is geared toward finding what is lost and she leaves it to the Saint to bother with *how* to find it. If it works, faith in the power of the Saint is reinforced. If not, the failure is viewed as a test of one's faith. It's a win-win mythology.

So we can understand the durability of religious belief; the more strongly embraced, the more self-confirming a belief will be. To the non-believer, it all seems false and absurd. But to those who "believe" with creative passion and inventiveness, their beliefs will be more important than life itself.

The truth of religious beliefs works according to a logic of creative self-verification. The most powerful construct in this world-old experiment is the one we call God. Belief in God is perhaps the most important parapsychological experiment ever performed in human history. It has been an experiment going on probably since the dawn of human consciousness, and has taken innumerable forms, constantly evolving, an experiment whose future is uncertain and hard to predict.

Apparitions That Changed History

Dreams, visions and psychic appearances in general have played a complex, assorted role in the course of human affairs. In fact, huge changes in history often have their origins in the most fleeting inner, albeit momentous events.

Keeping to early Christianity, consider the Easter Epiphany. It is hard not to assume some kind of postmortem appearance of Jesus, if we hope to make sense of the Christian movement getting off the ground in the first place. The disciples can only have been in despair after the Crucifixion. We know from Peter's three-time denial of Jesus something of the fright of the disciples after the arrest of their Master. How to account for the complete reversal of attitude—the change of a small group of scattered, bewildered, defeated disciples, into the impassioned core of a new religion that would help bring down the Roman empire.

It seems to have been the prolonged appearances of a resurrected Jesus. Belief in the risen Christ is at the heart of Christianity. Paul declares: "And if Christ be not risen, then is our preaching vain, and your faith is also vain" (1 Cor.:14). The ground for this belief was the belief in the conquest of death. The ancient world was ready for this myth of the dying and rising god. Historian Jacob Burckhardt said in *The Age of Constantine*:

> If we seek to realize in brief the true strength of the Christian community at the beginning of the last persecution, we shall find that it lay neither in numbers, nor in a consistent superiority in its member's morality, nor in the excellence of its internal constitution, but in the firm belief in immortality of the soul which permeated each individual

Christian. We shall show presently that later paganism directed all its efforts to the same goal, but by gloomy and labyrinthine paths and without Christianity's triumphant conviction.

According to Burckhardt, Christianity won out in this competition because it "simplified" the problem. But Burckhardt doesn't explain the simplification. Perhaps the pagan initiate had to undergo a specific experience, which was costly, both financially and psychologically. Not everyone could afford the cost of participating in the rites at Eleusis. The new Christian, poor or rich, simply had to embrace with some heart the good news that Jesus was resurrected.

That in some sense Jesus appeared to his disciples after his death is taken for granted even by hard-headed "scientific" historians like Charles Guignebert. Most scholars agree that Peter was the first to whom the Lord appeared. "Where?" asks Guignebert, in his study, *Jesus*. "Probably by the shore of the lake and under conditions favorable to hallucination: in the morning mist or the dazzling blaze of noonday."

But according to Scripture, the Lord appeared to numerous individuals: besides Peter, to James, to the Twelve, to five hundred brethren. It is also clear that these appearances occurred at different times. For Guignebert it's all a complete illusion caused by "contagion". He writes: "Contagion could only fail to be produced if all these men had completely lost their faith or if they possessed a scientific conviction that the appearance of a dead person was an impossibility." This statement is just wild speculation.

As it turns out, psychical research has many reports of apparitions of deceased persons that cannot so easily be dismissed as hallucinations. A scientific study of New Testament writings would take into account the findings of psychical research. An approach to the Resurrection question, which makes use of these findings, may be found in the writings of Michael Perry. Perry, for instance, puts forth (cautiously) what he calls "a telepathic theory of the resurrection appearances."[92]

This is important. Christianity, apart from these first appearances, would never have moved beyond the defeat of the Crucifixion. The Crucifixion of Jesus was followed by a powerful *appearance* of what was claimed to be the resurrected Christ. Surely, this seems like the core attractor of Christianity, the promise that believers can also share in the resurrection, become like the divine son, triumph over bodily death, and go to heaven.

As for accounts of the disappearance of his body in the tomb, and reports that he appeared to his disciples and followers many times, and finally, his ascension into heaven—all this is beyond what historical documentation can tell us.

So the central belief of Christianity is grounded in a mystery. Diarmaid MacCulloch writes: "Nevertheless one can hardly fail to note the extraordinary galvanizing energy of those who spread the story after their experiences of Resurrection and Ascension . . .."[93] Whatever it was that the early Christians experienced, it become part of a vastly influential mythology of transcendence. It became the cornerstone of a new Eleusinian mystery cult, insofar as it enhanced the joy of life and promised a chance of happiness in the afterlife.

Paul's Out-of-Body Prompter

Apparitional experiences played a role in changing death and defeat into a new religious movement that swept across the Graeco-Roman world. The first followers of Jesus gathered in Jerusalem and saw the teachings of the Master as mainly for the "lost sons of Israel." It was Saul-Paul of Tarsis who, after his out-of-body conversion on the road to Damascus, helped found a universal salvation religion. The exclusively Jewish Christians of Jerusalem faded from the scene by 70.

The expansion of Christianity is traceable to Paul and his conversion experience. The similarity of the latter to a near-death experience has been noted;[94] of particular interest is that Paul saw no apparition of Jesus but like modern near-death experiencers, only a powerful light and out-of-body audition. Paul's experience changed world-history.

In 2 Corinthians, he describes his many misadventures: how he was often imprisoned, often whipped to the verge of death, three times beaten with sticks, once stoned, three times shipwrecked and cast adrift on the open sea. A litany of hardships: how he travelled constantly, endured thirst, hunger, cold, sleeplessness, and lack of clothing; how he was in danger from his own people, brigands and pagans. Paul spent a good deal of time hovering in states on the edge of disaster, near death, which, perversely, kept him keenly receptive to the power, the psychic reality, he was attuned to, indeed, driven by.

After recounting his out-of-body experience, how he was "caught up into paradise and heard things which must not and cannot be put into human language" (2 Cor.: 12), he says he was given "a thorn in the flesh" (not clear what it was). The point of it was to prevent him from becoming proud. After pleading to be freed of this "thorn," the Lord declared: "My power is at its best in weakness." The power of the archetypes—of the higher, directing Mind—increases when ego is at low ebb. Best of all when it feels forced to renounce its claim to autonomy.

In *Acts*, 16, Paul is instructed by the Holy Spirit not to preach the word in Asia. However, he has a vision in Troas of a Macedonian who appealed to him thus: "'Come across to Macedonia and help us.' Once we had seen this vision we lost no time in arranging a passage to Macedonia, convinced that God had called us to bring them the Good News."

Thus, as Ernst Benz remarks, it was by means of the directing agency of a dream-vision that Paul "brought Christianity to the soil of Europe."

The Case of Constantine

The conversion of Constantine in the early fourth century was also crucial to early Christianity, and shows that saintliness is not a necessary condition for experiencing helping apparitions. The Roman Emperor, struggling for power with his rival, Maxentius, was opportunistic, calculating and superstitious. In later years, he executed his eldest son Crispus for obscure reasons and his wife, Fausta, for adultery. In part, his "conversion" to Christianity was motivated by the wish to counter the black magic and pagan spells that Maxentius was using against him.

According to Lactantius, the earliest authority, Constantine was given a *caeleste signum* at the Milvian Bridge. He was warned in a dream on the night before battle to draw the monogram of Christ (the two Greek letters chi and rho) on his soldiers' shields. The battle won, the story was confirmed by Eusebius under oath. Further proof of the dream is an inscription by the Senate on the Arch of Constantine dedicated in the year 315. After this episode, Constantine was more favorably disposed to Christianity and issued edicts of toleration, paving the way for the new sect to become the state religion.

At key turning points in the early history of Christianity, helping apparitions played a positive role. First, the resurrection and ascension apparitions, which transformed the death and defeat of the crucifixion into the triumph of the Easter message; then there were Paul's visions which universalized and Europeanized the Good News; and finally, Constantine's vision played a role in converting the political power structure of the Roman Empire to the cause of the new religion.

Helping apparitions, in this large historical context, appear like answers to collective crises. The cycle of pagan culture was at an end;

movements, creeds, mystery religions arose as part of the near-death experience of classical civilization. The Christian expression of the archetype of death and enlightenment (or salvation) struck deep chords in the collective psyche.

Mystics, Saints and Shamans

Sickness and near-death are aspects of shamanic initiation. The traditional initiation ceremony follows the threefold scheme of suffering, death and resurrection. Siberian shamans are described as "dying" as they lie in the yurt for three days without eating or drinking. During a Siberian ceremony of dismemberment, the "candidate remains like a dead man, scarcely breathing, in a solitary place."

Near-death lends itself to receiving helping power. Buryat shamans must be sick for a long time, during which ancestor spirits assail the candidate. "During the operation the future shaman remains inanimate; his face and hands are blue, his heart scarcely beats." This sounds like a near-death experience, as does the Eskimo shaman who contemplates his skeletons and the Australian aborigine who becomes a medicine man by sleeping on graves.

We know of the tunnel imagery in near-death experiences, so it is interesting to learn that caves are part of the initiating imagery of North American shamans. Caves are where they meet their helping dreams and spirits. Inside the cave of the subliminal self, the shaman experiences ecstatic flight, as an OBE, a flying dream, or as levitation. Item for a new mythology of transcendence: entering the cave of near-death puts the candidate in touch with helping powers.

The mythology of future consciousness calls for ideas about practice. How indeed do we break through to the other side of our psyches, the hidden world of high-energy archetypes, of insight and wisdom? There are well-known practices like fasting, drumming, and the use of psychoactive substances. They all break the set; disrupt the sensorimotor circuits. You break through in dreams or visions that occur when you are sick or isolated and resistance is low.

The career of Saint Francis of Assisi began with dreams and visions during sickness. Thomas of Celano wrote how Francis, "worn down by a long illness," was "enticed" by a "nocturnal vision" of glory. It seems that, at first, Francis failed to grasp the meaning of his vision, which consisted of images of military triumph and "a most beautiful bride."

The bride turned out to be Lady Poverty. The warrior imagery was about the battle he would wage against his own mind.

Celano notes the change of attitude in Francis. After the warrior vision, the saint-to-be lost interest in natural beauty. A spiritual incubation had begun. The aesthetic side of his temperament later reappeared when he wrote his Whitmanesque Canticle of Creation. In this early poem of Italian literature, the medieval mind wakes up to the natural world around it. It was signalling the dawn of what later became a *renaissance*.

The modern Franciscan, Padre Pio of Pietrelcina, seems also to have been shaped by a helping apparition with warrior imagery. When the Padre was fifteen, he had a vision just before entering the Capuchin seminary in Marcone while meditating on his vocation. Suddenly, he was robbed of his senses.

He writes about it in the third person to his superiors: "He saw by his side a majestic man of rare beauty shining like the sun. This man took him by the hand and he heard him say: 'Come with me because it is proper that you fight like a courageous warrior.'"

The guide then led him to a spacious plain where two groups of men, good and evil, stood facing each other. A giant emerged in the foreground and young Francesco was to do battle with him. He recoiled in fear but his guide said: "... go forward with courage! I will stay near you and won't allow him to bring you down."

The Evil One, he was told, would return "to the assault to recoup his lost honor," though help would always be forthcoming.

This seems to have been a prophetic vision. Francesco reportedly endured diabolical assaults for much of his life. Many attest to their physical effects. Once, for instance, the young friar's fellow students heard the loud noise of bars banging in his room. In the morning, the iron bars of his window were found twisted. There are photographs as late as 1964 of the Padre's highly visible welts from the alleged attacks.

Perhaps no religious figure of recent times has done more to revive beliefs increasingly viewed, even by religious people, as hangovers from demythologized olden times. Padre Pio, now Saint Pio, is an embarrassment to those who want to see in religion a progressive, rational manifestation of the spirit. The Padre takes us back to a locale in history when mythology was often lived with a surreal intensity.

For example, the guardian angel—a delusion to the rationalist mind – was fully embraced by Padre Pio. In 1912 Padre Agostino of San Marco in Lamis, Padre Pio's confessor, performed an experiment, designed to test Padre Pio's guardian angel.

He wrote letters to Padre Pio in French and Greek (in the Greek script), the Padre knowing neither language. According to Padre Pio, his Guardian Angel translated these letters for him and dictated letters back in French, which may be read in the three volumes of his collected letters. When Padre Pio received these letters, he was at Pietrelcina for medical reasons and under the care of Don Salvatore Panullo; the latter signed a deposition under oath that Padre Pio translated the Greek letters, the translation provided by his guardian angel.

An oddity of the Padre's mental life is worth mentioning. Pio's ecstatic visions were always preceded by diabolical visions, as if the two were in some way inseparable. There is of course the idea that to scale the heights requires that you know the depths. In the eye of eternity the two are one. There may be another message: if we have guardian angels, we must also have problematic devils, which sounds like a balanced psychology.

Shaman, saint, mystic have recourse to helping apparitions. Sometimes the entities announce the onset of a special career in spiritual service; sometimes they appear in a crisis temporarily; sometimes they become permanent allies and collaborators.

The helping powers may be courted, as among native American tribes. They come through sickness, as happened to Black Elk when he was nine, as described in John Neihardt's biography.

Of great interest is the native American vision quest. Unlike the imperial tradition of the Roman Church, native American spirituality is intensely individual.

Lame Deer, a Sioux Medicine Man, tells the story of *hanblechia*, his first vision quest. A boy, he was left for four days and nights on top of a hill, alone and without food or drink, to wait in a pit for a vision.

After some time, the boy heard voices and soared out of his body among what felt like the stars. The voices told him he would be a healer and he had a vision of his great-grandfather, Lame Deer, bleeding from a shot inflicted by a white man's gun. Then he felt a power, or essence, called *nagi* by the Sioux, a kind of inner helping double. He felt it surge through him and fill him with joy. When he came down from the hill after four days and nights, the boy had become a *wicasa wakan*, a medicine man. He took the name of the great grandfather he met in his vision.[95] In an age of spiritual pluralism, the vision quest is an appealing option.

Helping Apparitions in Everyday Life

The Mind at Large we have invoked is a generous democratic spirit. There is evidence that her extraordinary intelligence intervenes in the events of daily life. The "invisible friends" that Theodoret spoke of back when the Roman Empire was falling apart still seem to be in our midst.

An early student of these phenomena, the Edinburgh physician, Samuel Hibbert, in his *Philosophy of Apparitions*,[96] reserved a special chapter for "Apparitions of Good Spirits." Hibbert, an early exponent of medical materialism, was invincible in his opinion that all such apparitions are "spectral illusions . . . nothing more than recollected images of the mind." Even the eyewitness accounts of Saint Teresa's levitations are written off as due to "morbific causes." For students of the near-death experience, it is worth noting that Hibbert, writing in 1824, and reviewing treatises on "spirits" and apparitions that date back to the early 1700s, speaks of the "frequency" and "numerous communications" between dying persons and "benignant spirits." But all these are said to be the "mere phantasies of diseased imagination."

Among them is the case of a Mr. John Gairdner who, in 1717, lay as if dead for two days but revived after he had been sealed in a coffin and was about to be lowered into the grave. Later that evening he "related many strange and amazing things which he had seen in the other world." Based on the known pattern of NDEs, I think we can with reasonable confidence guess what sorts of things Mr. Gairdner "had seen."

Gustave Flournoy's *Spiritism and Psychology*, published in 1910, also contained a special chapter devoted to "beneficent spirits." Flournoy was never quite convinced of the spiritistic hypothesis, though he took the paranormal seriously. He argues with impressive skill that what look like communications from the other side of the tomb are, in all likelihood, the "fiendish by-play of the subliminal mind." This is another way of talking about what nowadays we call superpsi or living agent psi. We have remarked on the difficulties incurred by that view.

Flournoy, apart from his views of survival, was struck by the creative power of what Frederic Myers called the "mythopoetic" or "subliminal mind." Flournoy said that "things happen in the mental life as if we possessed in ourselves an intelligent 'incubator' which continues to hatch out ideas and answer questions which we have confided to its care; a laboratory wisely administered, in which the ingredients placed within it are allowed to simmer and are elaborated into new products, according to our ideas and designs."

The notion of unconscious incubation is apt in some of Flournoy's examples, as, for instance, in the case of the naturalist Agassiz, who solved a problem with fossil fish by clues received in a series of three dreams. In some of Flournoy's examples, however, this hypothesis appears strained, especially in what he calls "anti-suicidal automatisms." He cites the case of a man, about to jump from a window in a fit of suicidal despondency, who was hurled back into his room by a light that appeared between him and the window.

In a similar but more famous case, Benvenuto Cellini was imprisoned in the Castle of San Angelo in Rome. In a damp, dark dungeon, his leg fractured, and overwhelmed by a sense of hopelessness, Cellini contrived to kill himself by striking his head against a wooden device he had propped up. He was about to smash his head when an invisible force seized and threw him several yards away.

The next night, the apparition of a beautiful young man appeared to him: "Let yourself be led by Him," he was instructed, "and do not cease to trust in His power." The prisoner wrote in his Bible words renouncing his intention to commit suicide, rapidly recovered his strength, and was soon released.

More recent studies note the existence of a special category of apparitions with the function of "reassuring" percipients. Celia Green and Charles McCreery, British psychical researchers, wrote: "... there seems to be a distinct class of experiences in which the apparition has the effect of reassuring the percipient at a time when he is undergoing some crisis or situation of stress." Several examples are cited. A woman near to giving birth was awakened during the night by the apparition of a smiling elderly woman, which left her in a state of extraordinary tranquillity. "The feeling I had was one I couldn't forget as long as I lived ..." [97]

An insomniac under great stress was visited by the apparition of a young monk who said: "My child, I will give you a blessing." He laid his hand on her head, and she fell into a sweet, childlike sleep; the woman, not religious, "felt like a different person" in the morning. Another woman (to give one more example from this collection) was worried about her child's health; an apparition of the woman's deceased mother appeared and reassured her that there was nothing wrong with the child. Anxiety evaporated; the doctor's diagnosis was incorrect, and the child was indeed well. The reassuring figures are sometimes familiar and personal, or strangers, or mythical phantoms. They appear when we need them, somehow and from "somewhere."

Zoe Richmond put together a collection of apparitions with evidence of purpose. This type is important for survival researchers, for it shows conscious agency on the part of the entity. In Richmond's collection, the purpose of some of the apparitions was to help.[98]

There is a story of a British General Maisey during a siege in Delhi in 1857. The General described how a voice called after him, causing him to take a sudden turn off the road; just as he left the road, the spot he was at was torn up "by a shower of grapeshot," which would have killed him. Much to the astonishment of Maisey, no one of his fellow soldiers called him. Whether we think of this as resulting from the General's own precognitive talent or the prescience of a friendly spirit, *something* got him to move from the fatal spot.

The General's case is similar to one from my collection. The incident took place in 1967 in Vietnam. A young soldier was stationed in Bien Hoa; during the night, the air-raid siren rang and all personnel had to rush into an underground bunker. Celestino G, the young man in question, didn't go inside the bunker but hid behind a reinforced partition outside the bunker.

While crouching behind the partition, the young soldier heard a voice: "Celestino—come back here!" "What for?" he complained. Celestino didn't move but again he heard a voice call him back into the bunker. This time he got up and entered the bunker, sitting at the first support beam; but once again a voice cried to him to come back. He rose and sat by the second support beam inside the bunker.

"OK?" he asked.

The voice ceased. In the meantime, an Air Force sergeant sat down beside the reinforced partition, and lit a cigarette, at the exact spot where Celestino sat a few moments ago. The next moment, a rocket exploded where the sergeant was sitting, killing sixteen men, every man up to the second support beam. Celestino suffered minor bruises. He later discovered no one had been calling him. The possibility that one of the dead men called him is ruled out, because none of the survivors remember anyone calling Celestino, although they did remember him seeming to carry on a conversation with an invisible person.

If this warning came from Celestino's own precognitive ability, why all the resistance? The voice had to call him three times; after all, if Celestino "knew" subliminally what was coming, why not just move away? In any case, it certainly looks as if some *very* exact information about an essentially incalculable event was involved, for the voice insisted on

Celestino moving back to the second support beam, which was just beyond the rocket's fatal outreach.

Assuming this story is true—I have no reason to doubt it— the "intelligence" behind the voice knew where the rocket would land and precisely how far its kill-power would reach. It somehow knew this before the event actually occurred. It is to my mind a complete mystery how this is possible.

I'll end here with one more example of another precognitive helping apparition. In this case, the apparition stops a person from physically moving and thereby averts a fatal accident. A seventeen-year-old girl approached a red light at an intersection:

> While waiting for the light to turn green, I looked around at some children playing on the sidewalk. I glanced at the light—it had just turned green; I raised my foot from the brake, and pressed the gas pedal. The car slowly started forward. I glanced down to press the cigarette lighter, and as I looked up, my mother, who had been dead since I was five, was standing in front of my car. I had only gone about five feet. I slammed on my brake, and as I did, a tractor trailer ran the red light at about 40 m.p.h., and my mother was gone.

A perfect example of helping apparitions. Again, was the apparition of the mother a projection from the young woman's subliminal self? Or the saving act of a dead mother? Or was it a benign spirit masquerading as her mother? Or something entirely other?

The conclusion, as I take it, is that these phenomena are signs of our extended selves. Our identity seems wider and deeper than common sense would assume. Our lives, it would appear, are entangled in a web of connections whose actual nature is elusive and definitely unknown. This we can incorporate in our nascent mythology of transcendence, a memorandum on our hidden potentials, lost in the cracks of our familiar world.

Madness and High-Minded Hallucinations

Could we learn to tease the hidden helper out of the shadows of madness? According to Wilfred van Dusen,[99] the mad are privy to the archetypal powers of mind; and they sometimes meet the good angels that Swedenborg knew in his visionary journeys. Van Dusen was a psychiatrist for sixteen years at the Mendocino State Hospital in California; he succeeded in getting his patients to share the intimate details of their hallucinations.

He did this by treating the hallucinations as if they were real, and by engaging them in dialogue. On the basis of his conversations, van Dusen discovered two types of hallucination his psychotic patients were having. He also noticed that his observations matched Swedenborg's beliefs about personality types in the afterlife.

Consistency in the types of hallucination was observed. By the way, his patients disliked the term "hallucination." It didn't seem to matter if they were schizophrenics, alcoholics, brain-damaged or senile; the basic pattern was the same. They clearly felt they were in touch with *another* reality. According to van Dusen, all but the most far gone patients could discriminate between their hallucinations and physical reality.

The main finding: patients were either assailed by lower-order voices or helped by higher-order visions. The latter were rarer and comprised only a fifth of the apparitions.

Van Dusen's description of the lower-order entities is striking. "Lower order voices are similar to drunken bums at a bar who like to tease and torment just for the fun of it. They suggest lewd acts and then scold and torment the patient for considering them. They find a weak point of conscience and work on it interminably."

The lower-order hallucinations seek to destroy the patient, to wear and break him down; they do so by talking incessantly, shouting noisily and inanely, distracting their victims with fear and confusion and threatening death. They have no personal identity, though they are quick to fake one. Of crucial importance, they feed on the patient's weaknesses. They are anti-religious and try to interfere with the patients' practices.

In contrast, higher-order hallucinations rarely speak; they appear as light beings and communicate through symbols. They are friendly, supportive and instructive. They are, according to van Dusen, "similar to Jung's archetypes, whereas the lower-order is like the Freudian id." The higher-order entities even explain the function of the lower-order voices to the patients, which is to bring their weaknesses into bold relief.

Van Dusen was convinced that the helping hallucinations "knew" more about religion and mythology than the patients, who very often were poorly educated.

For the most part, these patients fought a losing battle against the lower-order forces—which is why they were in the hospital. The duality of our inner life, the fact that each of us embodies contradictory psychic forces, is vividly displayed by this portrait of madness. Our minds are always at risk of going to war against themselves.

What is interesting from the empirical record is that even those who don't court the higher powers often receive their help. And if we're alert to the possibility, we may discover them in everyday life, often disguised behind coincidences.[100] Now and then in dire scenarios, a higher-order type of entity may emerge and offer a helping hand. We have barely scratched the surface; something is in play that is interested in the upward ascent of Life.

10

EMISSARIES

Ever since the scientific revolution, Western culture has been torn from it mythic roots, alienated from the primordial images of traditional life. There is a widespread need to compensate for those losses, so we have been tracking sources for creating a new mythology of transcendence.

The core concept concerns the transcendent power of mind and consciousness. Our aim has been to marshall empirical materials that suggest two leading ideas: one is that consciousness survives death; the other is that our personal minds are part of, connected and interactive with, a transcendent mind.

The motif of help continues in this chapter, except that now I focus on three types of visionary experiences reported worldwide in modern times: near-death experiences; contactee, abduction, and flying saucer cults; and visions of the Virgin Mary. All, I believe, reflect the return of primordial images buried by science—a life beyond, higher beings come to save us, the return of the goddess.

These configurations have been around for a long time. Marian visions occur throughout Christian history. They began to increase during the late 18th and throughout the 19th nineteenth century—a period bristling with science, skepticism, progress, technology, and revolution – all psychically destabilizing. At yet another level, I believe that visions of Mary compensate for the overbearing patriarchy of the Abrahamic religions.

Despite some early historical signs of activity, modern flying saucer phenomena came into their own in the 1950s and viewed by many to express a reaction to the growing presence of atomic weaponry in world politics. Carl Jung and more recently the Harvard psychiatrist John Mack have interpreted these phenomena as signs of a collective crisis of modern consciousness.

The near-death phenomenon is not new and stories regarding it may be found everywhere in world literature, for example, in Plato's *Republic* and the story of Er's near-death journey. But, with notable irony, it was modern scientific resuscitation technology that made the NDE movement possible. Millions of people in modern times have had this experience, thanks to the technology that brings people back from the brink of death. Millions have had glimpses of something beyond the earthly pale and returned to tell what they saw. The NDE, in fact, is a reaction to near or temporary brain death. This unexpected fact contributes much to a science-based mythology of transcendence.

The Light of Transformation

In each type of experience we find accounts of powerful, transformative light beings or at least light effects; there are prophecies of global cataclysm; and there are visions of a new age of spirit. In the spiritual near-death visions, light beings are often encountered. Moody's "being of light" has become a trope in the new mythology of death. The Coptic Christians who witnessed the Lady in Zeitoun (1968-71) refer to her as the "Mother of Light."

Sometimes this being of light is invested with name and form, but often not. Rather, a quality in the near-death light marks the illumination experience: it is loving, all-embracing, all-forgiving. Anyone acquainted with near-death stories will note the likeness to the Marian experience. Writes John Delaney in *A Woman Clothed With The Sun*, "Without exception, Our Lady's appearances are accompanied by brilliant light—light of an unearthly intensity but which despite its brilliance did not hurt the eyes of those experiencing the vision."[101]

Conchita, in her Garabandal diary, described her visions of a mysterious Lady of Light at age thirteen: "Suddenly, there appeared to me a very beautiful figure that shone brilliantly but did not hurt my eyes at all."[102] Similar accounts of the light are plentiful in NDEs.

As in the near-death experience, the identity of the light being is often unclear. The apparitions begin as clouds or balls of light and then assume a form. At first, the entity was said by the Garabandal children to be Saint Michael. Later, the figure of Mary seemed to crystallize. Lucia, one of the child visionaries of Fatima, describes in her memoirs the Lady as "all of light, more brilliant than the sun dispensing light, clearer and more intense than a crystal cup full of crystalline water penetrated by the rays of the most glaring sun." Yet at first, the Lady announced herself simply as "from Heaven."

In the UFO visions, light beings also appear, in the guise of space brothers and ultradimensional emissaries. They, too, are luminous beings, and the light acts like a living symbol of consciousness. One UFO group believes it communicates with Higher Beings by means of telepathy on a "tensor beam," a kind of mind-light beam with odd spatial properties.

The connection between UFOs and (in particular) the Fatima phenomena was noted by astrophysicist Jacques Vallee. In *The Invisible College*, Vallee explores the links between Marian and UFO visions.

Vallee, like Jung, stressed the psychic side of the UFO phenomenon, playing down the idea of UFOs as machines from outer space. The theological side of Marian visions, as well as the possible "extraterrestrial" factor in UFO visions, are matters on which I suspend judgment. Phenomenology and psychological significance are the concern here, and the archetypal forces that may be acting through the collective unconscious. There are other luminous effects, birds of light that shot across the dome of the Lady that appeared and was photographed in Zeitoun. The Lady's apparition was preceded by a light being who announced himself as an "Angel of Peace."

Vallee links UFOs to some Marian visions; both seem also linked to the near-death experience. With the Fatima phenomenon, we find photons on the rampage, a trick of some pin-wheel meant to stretch the rational mind to breaking point. On the last day in the Fatima cycle of apparitions, October 13, 1917, extraordinary light phenomena were witnessed not only by the three child visionaries but by an estimated 70,000 witnesses, some of them miles from the Cova da Iria.

Many of the witnesses were hostile and skeptical. It had been raining heavily and everybody was soaked—photographs exist of the amazed crowd holding umbrellas in their hands. Shortly after midday, before this vast, mixed multitude, thick gray clouds suddenly parted and rolled away like the curtains of a stage. The sun emerged in a clear blue sky, glowing like a silver disk, unnaturally muted in its brilliance. For a moment, the multitude was enchanted by this oddity in the heavens.

Then the apparent disk began to rotate rapidly—three times, it was said—and blood-red streamers flew from the rim, sending waves of warmth and colorful lights shimmering on the countryside. Suddenly the disk plunged erratically, zigzag, downward; many fell to their knees in terror, believing it was the end. The disk, however, stopped short and rose back into the sky in the same irregular way. When it was all over, many healings were said to have occurred. The sun was back to normal, but the whole countryside, and everybody present, was suddenly dry. As for the movements of the disk, based on eyewitness accounts, it looked like the zigzag "falling leaf" motion of UFOs. Hence the legend of the sun "dancing" at Fatima.

So it seems we have two kinds of light experience, the private and the public. The light that seems to want to raise our consciousness likes to mix up the categories of inner and outer, subjective and objective. Perhaps it means to challenge insular ideas we have of ourselves and of others.

In 1971, Brad Steiger published a book, *The Aquarian Revelations*, which, like the work of Jacques Vallee, documents UFO mediums, individuals who claim to be channelling prophetic information from various Space Intelligences. The likeness to near-death and Marian prophecies is again striking. Light is a central symbol of the UFO Aquarian Revelations.

The archetypal Light permeates "Ox-Ho's" teachings. We hear of a solar government that we must rally around and of a light shield that we can learn to use to protect ourselves in the coming spiritual wars.

Here is a sample of Ox-Ho's Aquarian Revelations, in which the theme is Radiance and Love. The message is virtually identical with that of current near-death visionaries and could easily have come from any one of them:

> Radiance is the giving forth of the Light which expresses Love. Radiance is the beam that shines forth from one who is loved, or who gives love, and is a way of demonstrating in material form the very expression of love itself... in light is love, in love is peace, in peace is brotherhood, in brotherhood is eternal love which shines forth for the radiation of the entire Universe.

And so it goes, anonymous and universal, sounding the ancient themes and clothing them in popular metaphors of space science.

Here, before near-death visionaries, were widely scattered groups that, sensing the threat to life on earth, were using the symbols and imagery of deep near-death experiences.

The NDE, as already suggested, is part of a larger pattern of experience, unfamiliar to orthodox life science and pointing to the possibility of survival. To get at the meaning of UFO, near-death, and Marian visions, it helps to look for the underlying pattern.

Like UFO epiphanies, Marian visions seem, to use Jung's phrase, to signal "the end of an era." The year 1960 indeed marked a period on the threshold of change in the church—e.g., Vatican II, along with many defections or challenges to church authority. The secret Fatima prophecy may have been feared as encouraging even more radical change.

The Ox-Ho "revelation" about Fatima recalls the Russian philosopher, Nicholas Berdyaev, who made a similar point fifty years ago: Communism, rather, the Russians would be the scourge of a false Christianity. The downfall of Western institutions would result from a failure to live by its sworn Christian and democratic ideals, the Russian thinker foretold.

Other Queer Effects

The appearance was accompanied by flashes of light along with thunder-like sounds. In April, 1915, Lucia, Jacinta and Francisco were playing at the entrance to a cave when they heard the rumble of a powerful wind— the latter is, as Vallee notes, "a constant in UFO behavior."

To illustrate the UFO-likeness of events at Fatima: one witness, Maria Carreira, said, during a 1923 inquiry, that she heard "the same buzz when they talked and the same mounting of a rocket at the end." Rumblings and buzzings are also a feature of NDEs. The light appears, the sounds are heard, at the foot of a cave. Caves and grottoes are typical settings for Marian visions.

Cave and tunnel imagery are common in near-death encounters. Lucy, eight years old, was the first link in the chain of Fatima events. While saying the rosary she first envisioned the cloud of light from which the Angel of Peace emerged. Children, anyone in an altered state (dreams being the best example), are more prone than adults to encounter archetypal entities.

Global Catastrophe

All three types of vision project what the facts of military technology and climate change portend today: global catastrophe. Some near-death visionaries, like some UFO seers, foresee Earth convulsing with poleshifts, earthquakes, tidal waves, droughts, and so on; they see a world tottering on the edge of economic collapse and nuclear war. In these prophecies, catastrophe itself is holistic. That is, outer disaster is seen as caused by inner chaos; extreme weather events by moral perversion.

The images of apocalypse also picture postmortem calamity. The Fatima children had a vision of hell, of "lost souls . . . tumbling about constantly in the flames and screaming with terror." This corresponds to the hellish visions reported, infrequently, in NDEs. Images of apocalypse are general and specific, sometimes suggesting precognition. Pointers toward precognition are best illustrated in Marian prophecies.

In 1830, Catherine Labouré was told by Our Lady that "Monseigneur the Archbishop" of Paris would come to grief as part of the political upheaval. Archbishop Darboy was in fact murdered in 1870. So did Archbishop de Quelen twice have to flee for his life during the revolution that erupted shortly after this 1830 vision. Further, Archbishop Affré was shot to death on the barricades in 1848. This particular preview seems to have had multiple confirmations.

At Fatima, several events suggest precognition. The children foretold a "miracle" that would occur on October 17, 1917, at noon; this was confirmed by a spectacular UFO-like display of a disk of light falling to earth in the zigzag pattern of UFOs. The Lady told them that Francisco and Jacinta would die very young (which they did); that another war (the First World War was not yet over) "would begin in the reign of Pius XI"; that it would be heralded by an "unknown light" in the night sky; that the Church would be persecuted; that Russia would spread a godless ideology, fomenting wars and religious persecution; that several nations would be annihilated.

All these but perhaps the last seem to have come true. For example, the prophetic sign of impending war: on the night of January 25, 1938, the sky in Europe and part of North America lit up with a brilliant display of the northern lights. As for the one yet unfulfilled prophecy of nations being annihilated, it would have made little sense to speak of whole nations being annihilated in 1917. In light of possible nuclear wars, it's not hard to imagine the annihilation of whole countries in 2017.

Passport to the Cosmos (1999), by the Pulitzer prize-winning Harvard psychiatrist, John Mack, is a searching discussion of ten years of research with people who claim to have encountered intelligent beings seemingly from another world.

Mack provoked the mainline intellectual establishment when he concluded that the experiences of the 200 or so people he had studied did not fit in any established explanatory schemes. On the other hand, the reported phenomena were baffling, often seeming to float between metaphor and physical fact, dream and reality. Mack felt forced to posit a transcendent form or dimension of reality, from which we filter our fractured consciousness.

Mack's experiencers traffic in symbols of rebirth and transcendence. Going through tunnels toward the light occurs in abduction as well as near-death experiences. The shared imagery point to the same idea of rebirth, breakthrough, transformation. "My findings might require a change," Mack wrote (p.6), "in our view of reality rather than saying that I had found a new psychiatric syndrome whose cause had not yet been established."

This proposal certainly presents a stark reversal of priorities. The psychiatrist—meaning "physician of soul"—would have us recapture the lost soul of our civilization. The dis-ease is not in the patient but in a defective worldview. The "anomaly" is in the everyday habits of our perception, and the only cure is philosophical—the re-enchantment of ontology.

In the dislocations of place, status, wealth, health, etc., people grow numb not knowing who they are, where they are going, who they can trust, or what their purpose is. Besides the millions of refugees and migrants tramping over the face of the earth, are millions of mental refugees and migrants uncertain about where they fit in the world and who they are. Everywhere one hears of crises of identity.

Mack's conclusion was that the experiences he studied were not about physical spaceships or literal extraterrestrials; they were about forging new identities, about initiation into new realities. The experiences are about "transformation, which they attribute to their encounters with an infinite, a creative Source. These experiences often were expressed in the ecstatic language generally associated with mysticism or other experiences of transcendence."

Like Jung, Mack believes UFO contactees and abductees are about spiritual transformation. Transcendence for Mack meant breaking through walls of separation into a wider sphere of existence that touches on the greater mind that modern scientific ideology has discarded as unreal.

A more recent book that reads the "abduction" experience as about initiation into new spiritual reality is called *The Super Natural: A New Vision of the Unexplained* (2016, Tarcher). The authors are novelist Whitley Strieber, author of the abduction classic, *Communion*, and Jeffrey Kripal, a scholar of religion whose many books challenge mainstream scholars of religion. The challenge consists of pointing to the importance of paranormal phenomena as perhaps central to the future of religious studies. The refusal to acknowledge this is based on a rigid conception of what the human mind is and can do. It suggests falling in line with the old dogmas of physicalism.

Kripal explains the title of the book. "With this little provocation, effected by the tiniest and humblest of moves (a single thumb tap on the laptop's space bar), we move beyond both the flatland materialism of scientism (the natural) and the naïve literalisms of certain types of religion, the supernatural." We need, in short, a more comprehensive mythology of transcendence.

As with Mack's book, I cannot cover the wealth of ideas canvassed here. But I will touch on one theme that relates to Marian visions. A recurrent motif in the abduction literature is having sex with aliens, the idea that humans are biologically merging with extraterrestrial visitors. Mack was not inclined to take this literally, and construed this part of the narrative as symbolic of human transformation.

There is a well-worn sci-fi motif, which informs the nightmarishly creepy movie, *Invasion of the Body Snatchers* (1956). Much of the imagery reported along the lines of forced copulation or medically oriented sexual operations on abductees sound anything but erotic or mystical. It engulfs and smothers the human.

Strieber's experience was different. For it describes intimate contact with the divine feminine, he himself ecstatically albeit precariously "lying in the lap of the goddess." In a Christian context, the idea of sexual congress with the divine feminine must be viewed as heretical and blasphemous. Strieber was attacked by fundamentalists for being in league with the devil.

But in Kripal's and Strieber's narrative, what we see celebrates the ritual synthesis of sex and spirituality. Instead of blasphemy, we find a portrait of an incomplete man uniting with his divine feminine: his anima, his shakti, his dakini.

Given the prevailing masculine will to power, wed to capitalism, consumerism, and militarism that is wreaking havoc on our planet, a goddess initiating a man into psycho-sexual bliss seems like a breath of poetic necessity. What if Hitler, Stalin, and Dick Cheney were raped by goddesses? Might they have been humanized and matured by their encounters? Would it have been enough to sublimate their psychopathy into empathy?

The cult of Mary in the Catholic tradition was and remains an outlier to the hyper-masculine Abrahamic religious traditions. In imagining a new mythology of transcendence, a real return of the goddess seems long overdue.[103] It certainly appears like a case of worldviews being out of balance.

Chris Maunder points out in his study of 20th century Marian visions, these manifestations occurred typically when some part of the Catholic populace was threatened existentially.[104] Although Maunder leaves out the story of the Lady of Light appearing so massively to Coptic Christians, but to no avail for as I write, their churches are being bombed and terrorized.

But in spite of the continual setbacks, we still need to move forward toward something beyond established science and religion that makes use of both to serve the interests of Earth and humanity. A great body of forbidden narrative invites us to revise our vision of what is and what may be.

Jeffrey Kripal appreciates that spurts of transcendence are taking place all the time and everywhere. Some of these influxes give rise to cults or movements, some to a more discreet, personal poetics, or some to founding movements, revolutions, even religions.

In the Appendix to *Super Natural*, Kripal makes a move toward founding a movement; and provides a list of wise suggestions for practicing the supreme art form: performing the poetic synthesis of your existence here and now—and with a full palette of possibilities.

Marian Visions and Feminism

The topic of Marian visions raises a special question. They remind us of a problem based on gender, the massive abuse, disrespect, and oppression of women almost everywhere through much of history. The problem is evident in the monotheistic masculinity of the Abrahamic religions.

So, at least at a symbolic level, it was noteworthy when in 1950 Pope Pious XII *ex officio* declared the Assumption of Mary, according to which at the end of her natural life she was taken, body and soul, straight up into Heaven. C.G. Jung later opined in the Book of Job that the Church's declaration was the most significant event since the Reformation. The Reformation, of course, did away with Mary and the Saints (many are women), preferring to stick with an all male personnel in the divinity department.

Jung's view was that the Assumption was a much needed step toward recovering the wholeness of the Western psyche. Moreover, it acknowledged the *de facto* rapport with the Madonna in popular Catholic culture.

Marian visions, according to Jung, are signs of an archetypal awakening of feminine energies and sensibility. More broadly, Jung would say the Marian experience resuscitates the earth goddesses of antiquity. It reconnects modern spiritual sensibilities with the age of Eleusis—the ancient mystery rite designed to evoke visions of Persephone, goddess of the underworld. Under the emperor Valentinian, official Christianity brought to an end the Eleusinian ritual cult in the fifth century. A traditional form of entry into the feminine psyche was closed down.

But there are signs of a return of the repressed in modern Marian visions. In gathering ideas for models of transformation, we have hit on a key issue, the role of the feminine, the notion of a disempowered dimension of the human Self. Deployment of the feminine counterforce offers a way beyond the dichotomies of "right" and "left" toward the politics of a healing center.

The meaning of the various Marian visions is specific and various, depending on where they occur. The comprehensive meaning I want to stress lies in the archetypal awakening of the feminine, a force that, besides what it crucially means for women's rights also touches on the potential of the complete man: the total human Self. Empowering the feminine archetype, emancipating its potential in women and in men, if carried out authentically, would exert a powerful influence on planetary life.

But to be clear, as Marina Warner notes in her study of the myth and cult of the Virgin, *Alone of All Her Sex*, the adulation of disembodied purity degrades women by not respecting their natural sexuality and humanness. In "esoteric" psychology, virginity means androgyny: a quality of wholeness and freedom. It is not something you lose but something you gain, freedom and autonomy. The feminine archetype is complex: nurturing, life-affirming, peace-loving, yes, but also cunning, dangerous, seductive, daring, artistic, sensual, earthy.

Says Karen Rosenberg, "Just when we were beginning to get a sense of the cultural and psychological variety of women's experience, we are told to stop and contemplate the female as harmonious whole."[105] It won't help to project grandiose savior ideals on women.

With all its complexities and contradictions, the archetype links up with the mystery cults of antiquity, Marian visions of modern times and an ever-evolving women's movement. There are real signs of a new psychospiritual power emerging on the global scene. The growing menace to the biosphere ("mother Earth,") born of centuries of man-inspired rapine and aggression, the economic and sexual and religious oppression of women, combined with the availability of global social media, points to the creation of a new and highly active women's movement, for which there are many signs of awakening, of what may be a prelude to the spontaneous self-healing of the species.

So what do we have our sights on? An attempt to redress a dangerous imbalance, awakening the divine Shakti, the neglected consort of Shiva. We've had enough of Neikia, the god of strife, and his face is very ugly; so bring on Philia, whose smile of amity the world yearns for.

Networking Future Consciousness

Is there a global drift to this network of extraordinary experiences? Perhaps to remind us that something terrible is coming, indeed, getting closer, and much faster than anyone predicted? The grim fact is that unless we act, unless we act in concert, climate catastrophe, nuclear war, or both combined will destroy our civilization.

So we are reminded that we have to act, we have to reset our inner compass and change course. We could say that if science this time around is ratifying the coming of endtime, we have a reason to network on future consciousness.

The lights that flash from Mind at Large call us to say farewell to things as they are. They give us glimpses of where we could go and charge us with energy to go there.

UFO and near-death visionaries and seers of the Marian archetype, all are about assisting humanity at large in a great transition, dressed, of course, in whatever mental garb was available at time of seizure. The image that comes through: The species, not just the individual, is on the threshold of near-death. Person and planet are at risk, along with culture and spirit; all hovering "near-death."

The interesting fact is that anyone, regardless of age, locale, gender, culture, intelligence, or standing in society might be the recipient of an NDE, a UFO, or BVM. They seem like intrusions from nowhere, and it's the luck of the draw whether we get to glimpse a brief impression of the transcendent.

Mind at Large as Global Communicator

Suppose that in fact some Big Mind is expressing itself through these psychic manifestations. UFO sightings, like NDEs and BVMs, are a global phenomenon, however sporadic. Except for BVMs (mainly to Catholic kids), they occur to all kinds of people. UFO contactees come from all walks of life, all ages, all countries. The same is true for near-death experiencers.

Marian visions also have a global reach—France, Italy, Portugal, Spain, Lebanon, Egypt, Yugoslavia, Canada and USA. etc.—although they seem mainly confined to Christian (and some Muslim) populations. So what is going on? Why does the figure of the divine feminine keep popping up the popular consciousness? The phrase, *return of the repressed* comes to mind, "Today, the goddess is no longer worshipped. Her shrines are lost in the dust of ages while her statues line the walls of museums. But the law or power of which she was but the personification is unabated in its strength and life-giving potency," wrote Mary Harding in *Woman's Mysteries.*

The spectacular sightings in Zeitoun, photographed and witnessed by multitudes for over two years, is a striking example of the return of the repressed feminine. Zeitoun is a small town outside Cairo, a place where legend says the Holy family stopped while in flight from Herod. One evening in 1968, apparitions of a silent light-form were seen by two Moslem mechanics. Almost immediately the light-form was hailed as Mary. It was the most remarkable display of Marian apparitions in modern times.

Millions of all religious persuasions observed the strange luminous apparitions of Mary and other dovelike aerial light phenomena. The sightings were of unusual duration, sometimes lasting up to six hours. The period in which these frequent and prolonged sightings took place stretched from 1968 to 1971. They were attended by well-documented healings. I have received postcards and photographs of this Lady of Light from an American witness, Pearl Zaki, who witnessed the phenomenon many times.

This democratization of the Marian archetype seems like the result of a long progression. The numbers of witnesses at first were confined to a few children. Since the 19th century, the appearances of the Lady occurred in Paris, 1830, perceived by one young woman; in Salette, 1846, seen by two children; in Lourdes, 1858, one young woman; in Pontmain, 1871, two boys first, then a group of children; in Knock, Ireland, 14 people, mixed population, 1879; in Castelpetroso, 1888, two women, then five hundred witnesses.

This shows the trend. The number and range of percipients is increasing, as is the duration of the experience. At Fatima, appearances were spaced on a monthly basis for six months, longer and more regular appearances than anything in the nineteenth century. In Garabandal and Zeitoun, during the second half of the twentieth century, the duration of the experiences increased significantly again: first, overall, apparitions in a given location recur over a period of years, and, in the spectacular case of Zeitoun, they lasted for hours.

The nineteenth century marked a period of increase of Marian visions, mainly in France, a traditional stronghold of devotion to the Lady, where war between modernism and traditionalism exploded in the French Revolution. Visions of the Madonna again increase in the early twentieth century and then again in the second half of the twentieth century.

Since the threat to life is becoming global, affecting all human populations, we might predict a global apparition, a global experience of the transforming light. Curious that the prophecies of Garabandal speak of just such a thing. According to their predictions, something will appear to inhabitants everywhere on earth. Details are obscure; it is, however, supposed to take place in three stages: a warning, a miracle, and a chastisement. The effect will be tremendous; some will experience profound terror, even death; others, doubtless, rapturous embrace. Its function, in plain words, will be to change our minds, to "convert" us by means of an overpowering vision of supernatural power and splendor.

The global scope of the prophecies may be seen from Conchita's own words. The "miracle" is going to take place *para convertir al mondo entero*—"to convert the whole world." There is also a warning that will precede the miracle. "The warning is a thing that comes directly from God and will be visible throughout the entire world, in whatever place anyone might be."

It will be "like a revelation of our sins and will be seen equally by believers and nonbelievers and people of any religion." It will be "like a purification," "a sort of catastrophe," and "we shall see the consequences of the sins we have committed." The warning will be something "supernatural and will not be explained by science." The miracle will leave a trace, a "sign that will remain forever at the pines . . . that we will be able to photograph, televise and see, but not touch. It will be evident that this is not a thing of this world but from God." The sign will be comparable to "rays of light" but will not be a natural light phenomenon.

Now if none of these bring about a proper change of heart in humankind, we are warned, a chastisement will promptly follow. In June of 1962, Conchita and her co-child visionaries were observed "shrieking in terror," waving their hands, as if to ward off the sight of something horrible. One of them cried out: "Oh! May little children die rather than experience this!"[106]

The child's psyche, Jung has noted, is more open to psychic influence, being less cluttered with memories and concepts. So it's not hard to suppose that this Garabandal nightmare vision was tuning into the nightmares children are nowadays having all over the hellish parts of the planet: places where kids are starving to death, parents and siblings are lost or imprisoned, blown away by war; sick, wounded, driven mad—or elsewhere wiped out by serial killers, mass murderers, religious fanatics. The very young visionaries starting in the 19th century might have been attuned to trends of violence inflicted on children everywhere, regardless of time and space. Perhaps these prophecies are voicing, in their own spiritual dialect, a message of wide import.

Clearly, a similar message is coming from other sources, and the different forms seem rooted in the same process of break down becoming the threshold of breakthrough.

What really lies behind these manifestations? When we consider the prodigies of Fatima—the ability to reduce a crowd of 70,000 to gaping astonishment, to create the illusion of the sun plunging to the earth, to part the clouds, to dry up the rain, to fan the earth with heat and turn a Portuguese countryside into a colorful electric circus—the Garabandal prophecy of a global apparitional experience seems less fantastic. Might we be dealing with a technology originating elsewhere in the universe that operates on us in ways that transcend the constraints of time and space?

Something quite powerful appeared in Fatima to overwhelm the minds of the most hardened and hostile skeptics. Or when we consider the sheer massive publicity of the phenomenon that displayed itself in Zeitoun, again the Garabandal prophecy seems less fantastic. What also comes to mind is another, more recent phenomenon that implies the presence of global mental agency.

But this derives from Hindu religious experience and has been called the miracle of the millennium. On the morning of September 21, 1995, a man in New Delhi dreamt that Lord Ganesha, the Remover of Obstacles, was thirsty for milk. The man woke up and went to the temple with milk that he offered to the elephant-headed god of wisdom. The milk dematerialized on the spot. The action was repeated by others, and the news spread around India and all over the world. For about a day untold numbers of people all over world made milk offerings to statues of Ganesha that dematerialized. The Stock Market in Bombay came to a halt and the country was running out of milk.

That evening I witnessed the phenomenon on CNN. A reporter for the BBC held a spoonful of milk in front of a statue of Ganesha. The camera drew close to the statue and I saw the milk slowly get sucked up into nothing. The milk was not spooned onto the statue; it was held in front of the statue. It was perfectly clear that the milk slowly but decisively disappeared. I will never forget the look of astonishment on the reporter's face.

An Indian philosophy student of mine wrote up an account of his experience. Twice he went on line to get a chance to present milk to Ganesha and watch it dematerialize. Attempts to "scientifically" explain the phenomenon were ludicrous, ranging from "mass hysteria" to some mysterious capillary action and liquid tension gobbledegook that explained nothing. This selective global action of dematerialization is a complete mystery to me; I mention it because it suggests a supernormal action with global outreach. Following this strange day, there was a mass revival of faith among the Hindu population.[107]

Given the increasing lethality index of the world-scene, reflect for a moment on the utility of a global illumination experience: instant panoramic memory, full awareness of the collective consequences of our actions, add chance to taste transcendent joy. That's all it would take, a few timeless moments *outside ourselves.*

It is possible to imagine a transcendent helping intelligence, the friendly side of Mind at Large. Perhaps this benevolent Mind, in a congenial mood, might engineer a spectacular transformative show for the enlightenment of the human race, just like Lucia of Garabandal said back in the 1960s.

Coming back to Earth, we may meditate on the after-effects of these otherworld experiences. Overall, the major effects seem metaphysical—conceptually jolting. The experiences viscerally change one's sense of value, of truth, of reality itself.

This statement from Steiger about UFO contactees could be made about NDE and Marian cases: "Families and friends of the contactee report that he is literally a different and changed person after his alleged experience. Higher intelligence and perception are often mentioned, as well as a seeming increase in ESP or psychic abilities." NDE, UFO and Marian seers all show sharp changes in their spiritual values; they see a new world of love and peace coming. And they somehow acquire a lively sense of a higher, more benign intelligence watching over them.

Among these groups there was an increase of general healing capacity. Psi probably works best when it works to benefit others, and saints, yogis, and mediums mainly use their gifts to benefit others. Thinking about themselves would only distract them from the Transcendent.

Those who have Marian visions are instructed to build new shrines, churches, cathedrals. Visions are turned into stone monuments, and a place is made for others to gather. In time the shrine at Lourdes acquired its own medical staff that decides, according to strict scientific standards, on the status of claimed miracles. That in turn increases the appeal to go on pilgrimages to Lourdes. In short, the vision tends to materialize and grow in history and culture.

In an authenticated miracle, as with Pierre de Rudder's materialized leg bone, you have a phenomenon that defies the general understanding.[108] The late '60s witnessed many reports, some well-documented, of miraculous healings in Zeitoun. Congenital blindness and advanced cancers were said to have been healed from visions of the Mother of Light.[109]

I suspect that nature imposes safety restrictions on our access to this system. Those who have transcended their egos may be *more trusted* with "psychic power."

The Coptic Christians, at the time of the apparitions, were, as a minority, threatened by Moslem and Communist forces. Visions of the Lady of Light helped them to unite with Muslims who revere Mary who is mentioned more often in the Koran than the Bible. As long as the visions lasted, the minority and the majority stood together in peace.

Unfortunately, the less evolved, offshoots of the majority, have recently taken to suicide bombing the Coptic churches of Cairo. On

December 11, 2016, some fanatics lobbed a bomb into St. Peter's Coptic Church, *aimed at* the women and children's side of the Church, exploding and killing 25, wounding 49.

The Zeitoun appearances of the Lady of Light was unable to sustain a pacifying influence. All it offered was the sanction for a new way of being in the world, an alternate sensibility, an indicator of a form of consciousness to explore.

Missionaries and Transformative Forces

One effect on the visionaries is to feel a sense of mission toward others. In a powerful NDE reported by Kenneth Ring, the "Light" told a woman, in these "exact words":

> With the gift you have now received, go forth and tell the masses of people that life after death exists; that you shall all experience my PROFOUND LOVE! Love is the key to the universe; you must all learn to live in peace and harmony with one another on earth while you have the chance. This will be a very difficult task for you, my child, a huge undertaking, but you shall do it. You are loved.[110]

Who or what is this Light? One might think of it as the voice of humanity. In spirit it resembles the Marian message. The idea that spreading the love message will be "very difficult", "a huge undertaking," is similar to the Marian experience. The visionaries at Lourdes, Fatima and Garabandal were forewarned of difficult times and encouraged to prepare for them.

If we're observing the effects of a higher intelligence operation—initiated by the collective mind in response to the looming risks of eco-catastrophe and/or nuclear war—the missionary component makes sense. And the response won't slacken as global tensions and dangers continue to build up.

A mission to change the global mind will need organization, a mass core of people enlisted in the cause, warriors of the rainbow, non-violent worldview-busters. It will also probably require completely new kinds of technology. The NDErs are the newest group of visionaries. Neuroscientist Eben Alexander uses sound technology to achieve altered states conducive to afterlife exploration.

The question then arises: indeed, what sort of practice or technology could we deploy to speed up the much needed collective transformation of consciousness we've been discussing. We may, after all, be running out of time. The eminently sober and informed Noam Chomsky believes that we have entered a new stage of history where the prospect of human extinction must be realistically confronted and considered.

The argument pressed in this book is that a dramatic and broad-based transformation of consciousness is necessary to avert our calamitous future. Neither reason nor impartial scientific judgment are adequate to the task of persuasion. We need to look for new kinds of education that might trigger enlightenment experiences.

This would require the transfer of the world's wealth invested in murder technology to the arts and sciences that serve the flourishing of humanity. There is much to learn here.

The Marian tradition has its spiritual "technologies": the scapular, the miraculous medal, the rosary. All these depend on the intercession of the Virgin, the "mediatrix of all graces." Many extraordinary claims exist, checked out by science, about these psychospiritual technologies. The entity that reportedly spoke to the visionaries of Medjugorge recommended that the populace fast on bread and water every Thursday, as a way of attuning oneself to higher consciousness.

Fasting, practiced for cosmic, not just cosmetic, reasons, is a simple way of disconnecting consciousness from one of its chief mundane fixations.

Probably more enticing than a fast is another time-honored method for creating psychic tension leading to breakthroughs in consciousness and bodily transformation—the method of feeling and manipulating sex energies. The levitations of Teresa Avila and Joseph Copertino are in part products of highly sublimated erotic energies. Kenneth Ring observed the "kundalini" effects triggered by some near-death experiences, kundalini referring to a form of erotically energized consciousness.

One group of UFO contactees, the Order of Melchidezak, tracing itself back to the high priests of the Old Testament, abstained from sexual emissions to obtain spiritual power. The idea has its takes in Tantric and Platonic sex-based practices. The Oneida Community in upstate 19th century New York, led by John Humphrey Noyes, practiced having ecstatic sex without emotional attachment and with male continence.

Noyes believed the Second Coming occurred with the resurrection of Jesus. From that he inferred that we have begun our tenure in paradise and are free to love each other with maximum expansiveness and minimal personal attachment. The community lasted in peace and harmony for almost a half century until some jealous outsiders broke it up, needless to say, in accordance with this or that presumptive law.

The cult of the Virgin may be seen as a type of Tantric yoga.

In Catherine Labouré's vision of 1830, the Blessed Lady was seen standing on a globe with her foot on a green, gold-spotted snake. How to read that? Whoever masters the sexual impulse—the snake under the Lady's foot—can use the world as a footstool. The Virgin is an icon of Catholic tantrism. In the esoteric sense of "virgin," the Lady and the Snake are one, male and female energy fused.

The cult of Mary, esoterically taken, is a quest for sexual wholeness—the natural condition, I would guess, of the angels. In the Gnostic Gospel according to Thomas, we "enter the Kingdom" when we "make the two one, the inner as the outer, the above as the below, and the male and the female into a single one." A powerful image of psychic transformation by discovering the "virgin" within. The goal is psychic rebirth, forming a more integral personality, autonomous and sexually balanced.

These last two chapters are meant to convey the presence of a wider realm of possible experience, surrounding and interpenetrating our everyday world. Hidden helpers turn up in the course of daily life, and recurrent patterns of experience (NDEs, UFOs, BVMs) open windows of possible transcendence. From my experiences and those I have read about and studied closely, I come away with a sense of presence, of being immersed in a world of profound but scarcely awakened potentials.

Coincidentally, after the election of President Trump in 2016, and his cavalier attitude toward atomic weapons, the Union of Concerned Scientists pushed the minute hand closer to midnight on the Doomsday Clock. People are getting nervous. What is to be done? To combat the forces so ready to play games with the death-instinct, we need a discourse on miraculous method. Not René Descartes but Arthur Rimbaud. The new age must begin in fantasy, for the old age is dying of reality.

11

TRUTH IN TRANSFORMATION

The true and the made are convertible.

—Giambattista Vico

Who knows whether the faithfulness of individuals here below to their own over-beliefs may not actually help God in turn to be more effectively faithful to his own tasks.

—William James

We have traced the shadows of a dark future and tried to sketch a brighter template for things to come. A higher, richer and fuller consciousness is part of our human potential; all kinds of strange and stunning matters of fact are there for us to study, muse upon, and practically explore.

The enlarged potential is evident in the experiences of mystic and poet, ascetic and shaman; in vision quests and ancient mysteries; in dreams, in psychedelic, psychotic, and near-death episodes; and in the variety of UFO and abduction experiences, as described by John Mack and more recently by Whitley Strieber and Jeffrey Kripal.

The last chapter covered NDEs, UFOs, and Marian visions. They all suggest that a large scale collective change in human consciousness may be in the offing. What sort of a change? One that would at least broadly support a decent life for our species. That, in my view, would mean the end of war, of consumerism, of rabid intolerance, and of the worship of money and power—for starters. It would mean the emergence of those better angels believed to be waiting patiently within us.

Many in the past looked to prophecy and millenarian fantasies for templates of things to come.[111] Prophecy—more broadly the spirit of protest—is itself often a catalyst for social and even spiritual change. But this can be problematic in the way some Christians see events in the Middle East, and the prospect of the battle at Armageddon, believed to be part of God's plan for the Second Coming. Such views may lead to opposing peacemaking efforts, not wishing to interfere with what is supposed to be the divine plan. Prophecy, in this context, can be dangerously self-verifying, sometimes quite lethal, often fabricating falsehoods that justify racism, land-grabbing, and genocide.

The Poetics of Transformation

Because of the shadow sides of science and religion, many people yearn for a new story, a new picture of reality. People are weary of the old bromides and clichés. There are some like myself who say: We need a modern, democratic story of transcendence that draws upon science *and* religion *and* art, integrating the best of these great branches of human experience, and living the story onward.

Brainwashed by mainstream scientistic materialism, we feel constrained by their ideas of what is possible. Tied to constricted worldviews, we submit to the status quo, however soul-deadening. Faced with more idealistic possibilities, we respond with passive skepticism: "How is any of this possible?" After all, my philosophy teacher told me I was an insignificant dot of protoplasm, lost in a meaningless universe!

As pointed out before, certain facts about the world today are highly disturbing. The nine nations with nuclear weapons are investing heavily in modernizing their weapons' systems, even though they already have are enough to destroy virtually all life on Earth many times over. After the Cold War, Russian and American nuclear weapons' systems are still on hair-trigger alert. It's part of the way we live to be able to threaten our foes with annihilation, just in case one side launches a pre-emptive strike. The idea that peace and our lives depend on such a precarious assumption has the odor of insanity.

The more one registers the facts about the endless military build-up and the extent of the paranoid obsession with guns, power, and weaponry, to my eyes it all starts to look like a conspiracy of the death-instinct working behind the scenes, bringing us closer to the edge, testing the limits of what we can handle—and what we might be able to do about it, if anything.

So it's timely to reflect on the untapped wellsprings of creative power within us, time to meditate on our possible future consciousness. Nor are we seduced by "fake news" or "alternate facts," but we are interested in well-documented accounts of extraordinary human potential.[112]

Problem is that too many truth managers of our culture suffer from metaphysical myopia. It's easy to fall under the spell of a defeatist idea of truth. On the other hand, we run the risk of drowning in seas of information. Which way do we turn? What kind of truth do we need?

There are different kinds of truth. Beyond basic factual truth, there is something else we called saving or healing truth.[113]

All this became more problematic in 2016, the year that the Oxford English Dictionary declared the top new word was *post-truth*, defined as "relating to or denoting circumstances in which objective facts are less influential in shaping public opinion than appeals of emotion and personal belief." In the post-truth world, the soulful constraint, the noble imperative, the respect as well as the feel for the nuances of truth, no longer count.

Imagine two worldviews we have to choose from: *realpolitik* versus *surrealpolitik*. Contrast the word *paranoia* with the word *metanoia*, which means afterthought or conversion to new thought. In the one, the best weaponry is material, the best of the killing technologies—appeals to our fearful nature. In the other, the best weaponry is spiritual, based on rational diplomacy, values, and a sense of the humanity of *others*. The appeal is to the higher so ul-nurtured forces.

We're asked to choose between worldviews: in the one, our minds are conceived as mere shadows of our brains; in the other, our minds use our brains to adapt to and explore the challenges of the world. Now to a key pair of options. In one worldview, life after death is treated as a wish-fulfilling illusion; in the other, it's accepted as a real possibility, grounded in matters of fact.

And finally, we have a contrast in views of human nature: essentially fixed and limited (conservative) or unlimited in evolutionary potential (progressive). So, on the one side we have reductive materialism; on the other a form of spiritualism, with leanings toward panentheism.[114]

This kind of contrast between worldviews raises questions about ideas of truth. Puzzling stuff, to be sure. Moreover, the truth is out there and we are told it will make us free. But what is it? Which is the true or truer perspective on reality? I think that's the wrong question to ask about this kind of truth about a worldview. The question is not, What is the truth? In this case, the question is, What shall I make true? This is a move that hinges on a distinction designed to uncramp our spiritual muscles—if you don't mind my gross metaphor.

Conformist and Transformative Truth

If we hope to transcend the dangerous world we have created, we're going to have to recreate it. For that we need to change our raw perceptions of reality (it can be done) and expand our idea of truth. Now there are different concepts of truth. For example, one I will name *conformist*, the other *transformative*. Both have their uses and both are necessary.

But first: theories of knowledge, dating from Aristotle, define truth as a relation of conformity of subject to object, statement to state of affairs. Truth is about statements. According to the conformist conception of truth, a statement is true when it conforms to a given state of affairs. It is true to say, "The rain is falling on my face," if and only if rain is falling on my face. There is a fact that corresponds with a statement. This is our all-important common-sense idea of truth; without it, everything in ordinary life would promptly unravel, and of course science would be impossible.

On the other hand, we live in a world where from moment to moment we sometimes are forced to improvise and create our own truths. The placebo is our best example of an ongoing experiment in transformative truth. Instead of a statement that conforms to reality, we have a statement, or a belief in the statement, that transforms the reality.

There are many ways that this might come about. For example, take a statement: "God is love." Clearly, this is not a statement to which any obvious state of affairs in the world around us corresponds. Where do we place God in the troubling spectacle of life on earth? But there is another way to view the statement that God is love. We can think of it as *transformative*. Here the truth value lies in the way it helps us act in the world. Seen strictly in the light of conformist truth, we dismiss "God is love" as meaningless. Yet those who believe it is true might be disposed to make it true by sculpting their lives in ways suggesting that

God is indeed love. There is no formula for doing this in a convincing fashion. There is no rule for we in effect create the rule. If enough people act in a way that demonstrates the power of love, it would support the claim that God is love, and transformative truth would have begun to do its job.

Most of us are tyrannized by the mass of conformist truth that by design is imposed on us by those whom Noam Chomsky calls the *Masters of Mankind*.[115] These are the less than one percent of our species who own the wealth of the world and live exclusively for the maintenance of their own class. One can see why the custodians of established truth resist counter-examples to their conformist regime of truth. Self-transformation is risky business, as any one who has challenged conformist truth knows. The creative kind of truth we are disussing must be verified by living it. If it is not lived, it is not true.

Our distinction shows up in varied venues, Hegel's contrast of *Vernuft* and *Verstehen*, for example. There is, according to Hegel, a conflict between reason (*Vernuft*), which is creatively responsive to the living flow of history, and understanding (*Verstehen*), the fixed categories, the frozen conceptions of reality that express partial insights into the past.

We rely on homely, time-honored conformist truth. I expect the weather reporter to distinguish between breezy and a tornado; reliable knowledge is good. But there are also times when a critique of the status quo, of so-called reliable knowledge, is a matter of life and death, times when there's a need to turn everything upside down and do a conceptual overhaul.

This book goes against the reductive grain and argues for an open-ended receptivity to the subliminal depths of the human personality. It questions modes of thought that work in bondage to physicalist and to highlight the outer limits of creative consciousness.

Vico, Truth and Creativity

Modern philosophy was launched by René Descartes, one of the architects of the modern scientific revolution. Critics of Descartes blame him for committing the supreme intellectual sin: dualism, the doctrine that there are two kinds of thing in the world, the mental and the physical. That is not only common sense, but the inability of science to explain consciousness physically strengthens the case for dualism. Dualism is a sin only if you are a devotee of monistic materialism.

Descartes produced a system of thinking that was useful and efficient, in certain definite but limited contexts. The problem is overreach. The Cartesian method has been generalized and used in fields where it doesn't apply and does violence to the subject matter.

According to G. B. Vico (1668-1744), Descartes' *Discourse on Method* was a dangerous, in fact, an ultimately dehumanizing model of education. It was, after all, an attack on the humanities, which deals with extra-Cartesian forms of truth. Descartes has nothing to say about the creative truths of history, philosophy, art or religion, none of which can be mapped in terms of analytic geometry. The Cartesian method does not fit every domain of academic study.[116]

In creative truth, we have to delve into what Vico called the "modifications" of our own minds—in other words, our subliminal mental life. In our mobile, practical world, we are forced to deal with probabilities. What we need to survive, to flourish, is *ingenio*, or ingenuity, and intuition, the ability to assess a complex situation immediately and act spontaneously.

We need skills that transcend analysis and calculation. For Vico, as for Hegel, the founding, the evolution of civilization, depends on creative truth: legal, theological, mystical, artistic, scientific, military, political.

Vico's point is that new societies are founded by works of the imagination, by poets, prophets, and founders whose intellects have not been "rusted" by soul-deadening analysis and reflection.

Vico's critique of Descartes was a critique of the inhumanity and totalitarian power of conformist truth.

Vico's ideas relate to the need for creating something new rather than explaining something old. His chief premise is that *verum* (truth) is something made (*factum*). We create mathematics, for example, by creating the point.[117] The mathematical point doesn't exist in nature; we don't discover it under a rock somewhere. It's a mental creation, which then became an element in constructing mathematics and theoretical physics.

But Vico was mainly interested in the science of humanity. His starting point was not brains or chemical processes but *fantasia*, imagination—the organ that creates human history—laws, religions, mythologies, politics, arts and crafts, customs and languages, and so on and so forth. Imagination was the key to the science of humanity. It follows that if you want to change humanity, you have to change the imagination of humanity.

He devised a model in the *New Science* (1744) of how civil societies are born and die. They begin with a burst of creative imagination; they die with rational self-interest, carried to killing extremes. The inspired ones become the archetypes of a new humanity. In Vico's scheme, as a culture evolves, reason gains the upper hand. Time eventually begins to corrupt consciousness; the common bonds of human society lose their grip. Society, without organic connections, disintegrates. But always from the chaos arise new waves of barbaric poetic power, and a new cycle begins.

In 1709, Vico published *On The Study Methods of Our Time.* Of current significance is this critique of Descartes' famous *Discourse on Method* (1637). It speaks to us because we now find ourselves living in a Cartesian, gadget-dominated universe. Worth noting is a small group of artificial intelligence millenarians. They promise immortality by loading our information selves into a computer chip!

The humanities—the study of history, religion, world literature, music, painting, sculpture, architecture—are dying in American education. Education today is bent almost exclusively toward employment hopes. Mark Edmundson, English lit professor at the University of Virginia, has written a courageous book in defence of ideals, a vanishing species. He begins with a comment on his students: "It is no secret: culture in the West has become progressively more practical, materially oriented, and skeptical. When I look out at my students, about to graduate, I see people who are in the process of choosing a way to make money, a way to succeed, a strategy for getting on in life."[118] He does add that in a few instances they reject the idea of a career devoted to material gain but are at a loss in finding ways to live out their ideals.

A magnetic force orients curricula, slogans, strategies around the American dream, which is to be comfortably, gainfully employed. The traditional four or so years of youthful exploration of ideas, companionship, and learning that was supposed to be part of one's unfettered higher education are missing in this picture.

Vico's critique of the Cartesian method claims that it strips us of our humanity—the place where we live, hopelessly inside our subjectivity. Filtered through this new mathematical and logical method, the depth, color, and almost all of the meaning of the world disappear. Goodbye all! Everything gets reduced to some logical or analytic scheme. The Cartesian mentor would have young people forget about history, literature, mythology, folklore, and religious texts.

There were fanatics of reductive rationalism that Vico saw were invading the schools and infiltrating the soul of the culture. He spoke of them being hyper-argumentative but barren of creative capacity.

Pushed to extremes, he argued, rational egoism destroys the *sensus communis*, without which you can't have human society.

Vico deplored the excesses of logic blunting the student's imagination. "The result is that we raise a youth who is incapable of expressing himself except in a devastatingly arid way; a generation of non-doers who disliking action, sit up in judgement on all matters."[119] We might add that a systematically stunted imagination might do harm by impairing one's capacity to relate to other human beings.

Others have raised questions about the conformist model of truth. For example, Nietzsche's god-hero, Dionysos, embodied the archetype of poetic transformation. The struggle on behalf of creative truth was waged by William James in his famous essay, "The Will to Believe." In particular, he was intrigued by the notion of self-verifying truth, as was the more recent H.H. Price in his book *Belief*, which describes situations where holding a belief is itself a condition for confirming its truth. Belief is a core element in most mythologies of transcendence.

For Cantwell Smith, religious truth is about the individual person. Religions as creeds, as true or false, are destined for extinction, he argued. More than creed or ideology, you must be rooted in a source of piety and good will, in a personal relationship with the Transcendent.

According to Smith, it is dangerous and not pious to suppose that Christianity is true as an abstract system, something "out there" impersonally subsisting, automatically justifying and enhancing our status.

Christianity, for Smith, is not true absolutely, impersonally, statically; rather, it becomes true, if we appropriate and interiorize it, if we live and personalize it from day to day.[120] By this criterion it is hard to think of America as a Christian nation. Although countless citizens try to live their religious beliefs authentically, on balance it is more accurate to speak of the nation as a beacon of pagan materialism, a glittering city on a remote hill, owned by a tiny minority of billionaires.

I want now to focus on a very practical form of creative truth. It is something we have yet to learn. How indeed can we take full advantage of the placebo effect—a definite type of transformative truth. Considerable quantities of evidence prove the healing power of our beliefs and of our imagination, and spectacular examples of this power are on record.[121]

Medical paradigms are gradually absorbing this idea of the creative power of belief. Instead of just being used in drug tests, all efforts should be bent upon learning to exploit the healing potential lying fallow within us. In the long run, the key factor in human health may turn out to be *mental*, and a massive research program on that seems in order.

CUNY psychologist, Gertrude Schmeidler coined the term "sheep-goat effect." A "sheep" believes, expects to do well in a parapsychological test, and does; a "goat" doesn't believe, and gets no effect. Our beliefs in these psychic experiments are often self-fulfilling. They show transformative truth in action. The active, engaged believer-imaginer, in the right environment, is disposed to perform quantum leaps of creative consciousness.

Believers score above chance; disbelievers don't and score below chance. The early Christian church father, Tertullian, must have understood this when he famously pronounced: "I believe because it is absurd." If belief is to prove its creative potential, it must be strong enough to overcome rational doubt. Reason, after all, can trick us as easily as intuition can. None of this entails that we dump our godlike reason; transformative truth becomes dangerous if it is used politically, in corporate advertising, or by religious extremists. For that we need to be sharp observers and careful in the way we reason.

Why do we see the world the way we do? Initial (often largely forgotten) choices are crucial. For example, choice of the kind of data we use to construct our picture of reality. We focus on one set of data and push others into the background—the orthodoxies of science, reports of the mystical life, academic philosophers, Facebook, right wing radio, and so on, ad infinitum.

We favor one hypothesis or another. For one person the evidence for a haunting is dropped as coincidence, the result of an overheated imagination; for another, it's suggestive, worthy of further consideration. Now and then, somebody gets bowled over by a bare fact.

The weight of your response is determined by your prior epistemic commitments. If on principle you ignore psi data or UFO data or "miracle" data, you just won't see anything there, except now and then, as we know, when folks are hit over the head and swept away by something transcendent.

Transformative Psi

The concept of transformative truth has an ally in parapsychology. Believers in psi ("sheep") have more psi experiences and thus confirm their belief in its reality: nonbelievers ("goats") score below chance, which is negative psi, used against themselves. This applies to ordinary life, but even more so to those who believe it possible to move mountains: the saints, yogis, and other adepts of miraculous psi.

An experiment in group psychokinesis, reported in Owen and Sparrow's *Conjuring Up Philip*,[122] touches on the topic of transformative truth. The purpose of the experiment, conducted by a group from the Toronto Society of Psychical Research, was to produce a ghostly apparition through a special group technique.

They made up a story about a mythical personage called Philip. For one year, they meditated on "Philip," aiming to make their fantasy in some way tangible. At first they sat and meditated calmly on their designated figure, rehearsing his tale of love betrayed, of revenge and untimely death—the stuff of many a haunting.

Results at first were poor. But the time spent was not wasted; a sense of solidarity developed among the experimenters. After studying the work of Kenneth Batcheldor and Colin Brookes-Smith, English scientists who worked on the psychology of PK production, the group changed their tactics. Gathered in a circle, as in a Victorian séance, joking and singing, they dropped all self-conscious striving. Meanwhile, still focused on the goal, they tried to merge mentally and surrender to the pathos and imagery of Philip's story.

The new tactic seemed to work, and "Philip" was duly conjured. "He" did not quite make it as an apparition but succeeded in making his presence known physically by sounds of no recognizable frequencies that displayed intelligence and by levitating various physical objects. The results were noted repeatedly by competent observers and were recorded on tape and video.

The implications of this experiment extend the idea of transformative, self-verifying truth. From this experiment, we can form a model showing how the transcendent in nature discloses itself to us. In fact, it probably needs us to actualize its potentiality, which is the point of the William James epigraph above.

Let me generalize a little. Substitute God or any divine entity for "Philip," and normal religious believers for the Toronto group, and we have a basis for an interesting hermeneutic of certain characteristically "religious" phenomena.

The Toronto experiment seems a case of transformative truth. It shows how even a transiently constructed group mind might in various ways alter physical reality. The "Philip" experiment offers a clue to making sense of the collective apparitions of Mary that we have discussed. Given the premise of a greater mind at large, it is hard to avoid the question: Are we, singly or collectively, the subliminal artificers of the spiritual worlds that we inhabit?

Something to Look Forward to

Facing technocalypse, dramatic changes of consciousness seem one way or another to be on their way. If the near-death model is true, we might expect the awakening of new spiritual force. A spectrum of phenomena suggests a potential for development beyond what we can imagine.

There may be a cosmic goal driving us, but we don't know what it is or what our part is. So in the transition we are forced to improvise and write our own script, and put to the test the idea of transformative truth.

The general idea is that the extreme threats coming at us implacably *should* be a great spur to the evolution of human consciousness. The future is menacing but there are also signs of awakening to the great human drama emerging. There are grounds for enormous hope but the grounds are hidden within us.

The final choice is not to accept finality. Choose to believe in a vision of renovation, and we may hasten its coming. Faith in the greatness of the future stems from knowledge of the past, and history teaches that anything can happen. Out of chaos, miracles are born, the way diamonds were created in the violent core of Earth during its birth pangs. Who can guess what new quality of life, what angel of transformation, awaits us in the days to come?

GLOSSARY

To clarify some terms and concepts I use in this book that may not be clear or obvious, the reader might glance below. It's a short list. The glossary is limited to how the terms are used in this book.

Archetype—Referring to types of primordial images, hence archetypal, studied especially by C. G. Jung. People experience these primordial images in dreams, visions, mythologies, psychotic hallucinations and obsessions. The archetypes express the collective experience of the species in the form of symbols of transformation, which are the essence of all phases and aspects of the human life and death cycle.

Archetype of Death and Enlightenment (ADE)—Term used here to identify an archetypal constellation of images around the idea of death as an opening to transcendent consciousness. The near-death experience is the great empirical find of a group of American researchers during the last quarter of the 20th century, and it perfectly illustrates the ADE in a deeply dramatic form. But you find the ADE all over the place, as descriptive of mystical and shamanic practice and conversion, as a figure in great literature, or as an element of creativity in the arts. Whatever it is, it represents a stinging paradox: Enlightenment via death.

Consciousness: The mystery of mysteries. That without which there is nothing. Best understood ostensively. Next time you wake up from dreamless sleep, look around for a second. The difference between dreamless sleep and what happens when you wake up and notice the sun breaking through the drawn shades—the difference is consciousness. Two points about the way the term is used here. The first almost everybody agrees with. Consciousness escapes all physicalist explanatory nets. Consciousness is its own thing, a substance; it's related to the brain but not reducible to, or identical, with the brain; it uses the brain as a transmitter, diffractor, or concentration of consciousness. The second point is that consciousness has, beyond the personal perspective, a transpersonal dimension. In other words, we are more deeply intertwined with the wider world at a deep level of our mental life.

Empirical—This term derives from a Greek word means experience. In modern scientific circles, the term too often is reserved exclusively for sense-based, measurable experience. Dreams and other mental experiences are not sense-based or measurable, but they are nonetheless empirical; they are experiences, private and subjective, but ultimately that is where we all live every second of our existence.

Evolution, evolutionary—we inhabit a changing universe, and that seems to be true for the entirety of nature, down to our bodies, and every atom of our body, as well as our societies, as Vico saw, and the stream of consciousness that is our mental life. The fundamental fact of reality as process already implies an evolutionary perspective. Darwinian ideas about evolution are another question.

Mind—the fundamental term. Mental events occur below the threshold of awareness, without consciousness; but every conscious event is a mental event. Consciousness is a property of minds. In dreamless, nonconscious sleep, mind carries on, often busily, creatively. But we can infer that only when we are conscious, and in that sense consciousness is fundamental.

Mind at Large—Since there are no physical parts of mind, no spatial or temporal boundaries, mind itself must be numerically one, as Irwin Schroedinger, inspired by the Upanishads, said. If so, then our minds are part of one great mind and we might speak of "mind at large," a phrase borrowed from Aldous Huxley. As minds we are all at some level part of the one mind, but each of us filters the one mind through our embodied personalities, embedded in different cultures.

Myth—a term with contradictory connotations. A false story, like the myth of the fountain of youth or the story believed by early immigrants coming to America that the streets were paved with gold. But myth (*mythos*, a Greek word) also refers to stories of gods and heroes, creation stories, adventure stories and spiritual stories. This kind of myth speaks to heart and imagination, articulating the great human truths about life and death. Myth is at war with itself and needs us to straighten it out.

Mythology—Study of stories around a particular subject, sifting the meaning and wisdom, using science and hermeneutics, and whatever it takes to tell a story and bring it to life. I use the expression mythology of transcendence to include all references to the idea of transcendence, scientific, oneiric, mythical, medical, historical, experimental, and whatever we meet.

Physicalism and materialism—terms for reductive, monistic metaphysical stances—here viewed as indefensible in the full light of human experience, which is mediated by our bodies, but not reducible to them.

Psi—This little word covers a giant realm of human experience. Psi is the first letter of the Greek word *psyche*. In psychical research and parapsychology, psi refers to the two sides of paranormal phenomena: extrasensory perception (ESP) and psychokinesis (PK).

Subliminal Self—our total psychical identity and potential, supraliminal and subliminal. This may be one of Myers' most fruitful concepts for understanding the genesis of a host of religious ideas.

Technocalypse—I introduced this term in my book, *The Millennium Myth* (1995). Defined as marking a period when the apocalyptic imagination and modern technology converge. The idea is hopeful and terrifying. The prophets talk about transforming nature, about lion and lamb lying down together, about the perfection of humanity. That's the hopeful part, technology in service to the flourishing of humanity. But there is also a terrifying part. The primitive apocalyptic imagination is pure in its hatred of the Other. When that attitude begins to merge with nuclear weaponry and biochemical warfare and surveillance technology, we enter the supreme danger zone called technocalypse.

Transpersonal—there are important features of human experience that have roots outside one's personal purview. Experiences with archetypal elements (often through dreams or artistic effort:), any influence we think has a telepathic or psychokinetic source would count as *transpersonal*. The truth is that we are clueless with regard to the boundaries of our transpersonal minds. A general rule of thumb might be this: always leave room for visits from strangers.

Transcend—Literally, from the Latin, to climb over or across. The term can be used widely to describe getting over any hurdle. More often my use is sharper and defined in terms of mind transcending body or anything physical.

Transcendent—rising above the constraints of ordinary physical reality.

The Transcendent—very occasionally, I will capitalize the noun form if the context fits.

REFERENCES

1. *Soulmaking: Uncommon Paths to Self-Understanding* (1997) Hampton Roads.

2. Dossey, L.: *One Mind*. Hay House. 2013.

3. Sorokin, P. *The Crisis of Our Age*. New York: Dutton, 1941.

4. Myers, F. W. H. *Human Personality and its Survival of Bodily Death*. London and New York: Longmans, Green, 1903. (2 Vols.)

5. Murphy, G. *Three Papers on the Survival Problem*. New York: American Society for Psychical Research, 1945.

6. Beloff, J. *The Existence of Mind*. New York: Citadel Press, 1962.

7. Randall, J. *Parapsychology and the Nature of Life*. New York: Harper & Row, 1975.

8. Smith, J. M. *Evolution Now*. San Francisco: Freeman, 1982.

9. Eliade, M. Yoga: *Immortality and Freedom*. New York: Bollingen, 1958.

10. Von Bertalanffy, L. *Problems of Life*. New York: Harper Torchbooks, 1960.

11. Da Ripabottoni, A. *Padre Pio da Pietrelcina*. Foggia: Centro Culturale Francescano Convento, 1974.

12. Bergson, H. *Creative Evolution*. New York: Random House, 1944.

13. Hardy, A. *The Living Stream*. New York: Harper & Row, 1965.

14. Sidgwick, H. and Committee. *Report on the census of hallucinations*. Proceedings of the Society for Psychical Research (1894).

[15] Bozzano, E. *Dei Fenomeni di Telecinesia in Rapporto con Eventi di Morte.* Verona: Casa Editrice Europa, 1948.

[16] For a detailed study of this mystic whose life was unique in the abundance and variety of psychophysical marvels, see Grosso, M. (2016) *The Man Who Could Fly: St. Joseph of Copertino and the Mystery of Levitation.*

[17] Caycedo, A. India of Yogis. Delhi: National Publishing House, 1966.

[18] Eliade, M. *The Two and the One.* New York: Harper Torchbooks, 1965.

[19] Rao, R. Theories of psi. In *Advances in Parapsychological Research* 2, op. cit.

[20] Honorton, C. Psi and internal attention states. In Wolman, op. cit. and Braud, W. G. Psi conducive conditions: explorations and interpretations. In *Psi and States of Awareness.* New York: Parapsychology Foundation, 1977.

[21] See chapters 3 and 4 in *Beyond Physicalism* (ed. E.E. Kelly, 2015), one that covers the history, the other the neurobiology of the transmission view of the mind-brain relationship, the idea that the brain does not create but transmit consciousness.

[22] Palmer, J. Extrasensory perception: research findings. In Krippner, S., ed. Advances in Parapsychological Research 2. New York: Plenum, 1978

[23] Evans-Wentz, W. Y. *The Tibetan Book of the Dead.* New York: Oxford University Press, 1960.

[24] Osis, K. and E. Haraldsson. *At The Hour of Death.* New York: Avon Books, 1977.

[25] Greyson, B. Organic brain dysfunction and near-death experiences. Presented at the American Psychiatric Association 135th Annual Meeting, Toronto, 1982.

[26] Cruz, J. C. *The Incorruptibles.* Rockford, 111.: Tan Books, 1977.

[27] Thurston, H. *The Physical Phenomena of Mysticism.* London: Bums Oates, 1952.

[28] See Craig S. Keener, (2011) *Miracles: The Credibility of the New Testament Accounts.* Baker Academic. (Two volumes). Covers contemporary accounts of phenomena that were reported in the ancient Gospel stories.

[29] See Lowith, K. *Meaning in History.* Chicago: University of Chicago Press, 1958.

[30] Cohn, N. *The Pursuit of the Millennium.* New York: Oxford University Press, 1981.

[31] Marcuse, H. *Eros and Civilization.* Boston: Beacon Press, 1966.

[32] See my book, *The Millennium Myth*, pp. 261-283.

[33] Unamuno, M. *Tragic Sense of Life.* New York: Dover, 1954.

[34] See *The Jefferson Bible: The Life and Morals of Jesus of Nazareth*. Ed. Forrest Church. Boston: Beacon Press, 1989.

[35] Rank, O. *The Double*. New York: Meridian, 1979.

[36] Harrington, A. *The Immortalist*. Millbrae, Cal.: Celestial Arts, 1977.

[37] Ed. .E.E. Kelly, *Irreducible Mind*, (2007); Braude, S. *Immortal Remains*, (2003).

[38] Becker, E. *The Denial of Death*. New York: The Free Press, 1973.

[39] Goodman, L. *Death and the Creative Life*. New York: Springer, 1981.

[40] Arendt, H. *Between Past and Future*. New York: Viking Press, 1961.

[41] See Alvarado's "Out-of-body Experiences, 183-218, in *Varieties of Anomalous Experience*, 2000, Eds: Cardena, Jay Lynn, Krippner.

[42] Sheils, D. A cross-cultural study of beliefs in out-of-body experiences. *Journal of the Society for Psychical Research* 49 (1978).

[43] Mead, G. R. S. *The Doctrine of the Subtle Body in Western Tradition*. Wheaton, 111.: Quest, 1967.

[44] Brookes-Smith, C. Recent research in psychokinesis. In Pearce- Higgins, J. D. and G. S. Whitby. *Life, Death & Psychical Research*. London: Rider, 1973.

[45] Ullman, M. and S. Krippner. (with Vaughan, A.) *Dream Telepathy*. New York: Macmillan, 1973.

[46] Bullough, E. Psychical distance. *British Journal of Psychology*. Vol. 5 (1915).

[47] Kant, I. *Critique of Judgment*. New York: Hafner, 1961

[48] Marcuse, H. Art as a form of reality. In *On the Future of Art*. New York: Viking Press, 1971.

[49] Rao, R. Theories of psi. In *Advances in Parapsychological Research* 2, op. cit.

[50] Rhode, I. *Psyche*. (2 vols.) New York: Harper Torchbooks, 1966.

[51] Jung, C. G. *Memories, Dreams, Reflections*. New York: Random House, 1961.

[52] Orage, A. R. *Consciousness*. New York: Samuel Weiser, 1978.

[53] Hardy, A. *The Living Stream*. New York: Harper & Row, 1965.

[54] Scheler, M. *Man's Place in Nature*. Boston: Beacon Press, 1961.

[55] Another rich source book on the contemporary near-death phenomenon is *The Self Does Not Die: Verified Paranormal Phenomena From Near-Death Experiences*. Titus Rivus, Anny Dirven, Rudolf Smit. 2016, IANDS Publicstions.

[56] Osis, K. and E. Haraldsson. *At The Hour of Death*. New York: Avon Books, 1977.

57 Bozzano, E. Apparitions of deceased persons at deathbeds. The Annals of Psychical Research (1906).

58 Hyslop, H. Psychical Research and the Resurrection. Boston: Small, Maynard, 1908.

59 Barrett, W. F. Deathbed Visions. London: Methuen, 1926.

60 Ring, K. *Life at Death*. New York: Coward, McCann & Geoghegan, 1980.

61 Lundahl, C. *A Collection of Near-Death Research Readings*. Chicago: Nelson-Hall, 1982.

62 Kohr, R. Near-death experience and its relationship to psi and various altered states. *Theta* 10 (1982).

63 Greyson, B. Increase in psychic and psi-related phenomena following near-death experiences. *Theta* (1983).

64 Ring, K. *Heading Toward Omega*. New York: William Morrow, 1984.

65 See their joint effort, *The Interpretation of Nature and Psyche*, 1955.

66 David Lindorff, *Pauli and Jung*, 2009, Quest Books.

67 See, for instance, Eben Alexander, *Proof of Heaven*; Jill Bolt Taylor, *My Stroke of Insight* (2006); Marjorie Hinds Woolacott, *Infinite Awareness: The Awakening of a Scientific Mind* (2015).

68 Proceedings, Vol. XXXVI, pp. 517-524.

69 Stevenson, I. *Twenty Cases Suggestive of Reincarnation*. Charlottesville: University Press of Virginia, 1974.

70 This idea is found throughout Jung's work, but a good place to look is *Modern Man In Search of a Soul* and the essay "The Undiscovered Self", in Vol. 10, *Civilization in Transition* (247-305).

71 Jung, C. G. *The Archetypes of the Collective Unconscious*. Princeton, N. J.: Princeton University Press, 1971

72 See Edward Robinson, *The Original Vision: A Study of the Religious Experience of Childhood*. 1977, Oxford.

73 See chapter 5 in my *Frontiers of the Soul* (1992).

74 Osis, K. and E. Haraldsson. *At The Hour of Death*. New York: Avon Books, 1977.

75 Atwater, P. M. H. *Coming Back*. Vital Signs 1, 4 (1981).

76 Ring, K. *Life at Death*. New York: Coward, McCann & Geoghegan, 1980.

77 In this chapter, I capitalize Self to identify it as Jung's objective psyche. See, for example, Jung, (Aion, 1959, Bollingen, p.5) ". . . the personality as a total phenomenon does not coincide with the ego, that is, with the conscious personality, but forms an entity that has to be distinguished from the ego."

[78] Eliade, M. *The Two and the One*. New York: Harper Torchbooks, 1965.

[79] See discussions *(where)* of Harrington and Becker.

[80] Noyes, R. Dying and mystical consciousness. *Journal of Thanatology* 1 (1971).

[81] Skaar, M. My personal encounters with death. *Vital Signs* 2, 1 (1982).

[82] See Appleyard, discussed above, whose explication of this downward arc toward psychic disintegration is compelling.

[83] The possible physical realities associated with these sky phenomena are not the issue here; their psychology is our concern.

[84] Pauli, W. The influence of archetypal ideas on the scientific theories of Kepler. In C. G. Jung and W. Pauli. *The Interpretation of Nature and the Psyche*. London: Routledge and Kegan Paul, 1955.

[85] Thompson, E. P. Notes on exterminism, the last stage of civilization. *New Left Review* 121 (1980)

[86] Thompson, ibid.

[87] Lifton, R. J. *Death in Life: Survivors of Hiroshima*. New York: Random House, 1967.

[88] See The Presocratic Philosophers, Kirk & Raven, 1957, pp. 320-361.

[89] Shaw, G. (1995) *Theurgy and the Soul*. Pennsylvania State University Press.

[90] For details see my *Wings of Ecstasy* (2017)

[91] Schmidt, H. Psychokinesis. In Mitchell, E. D. and J. White. *Psychic Exploration*: A Challenge For Science. New York: Putnam's, 1974.

[92] Perry, M. *The Resurrection of Man*. London: Mowbrays, 1975.

[93] *Christianity*: *The First Three Thousand Years*, Viking, 2009, p.95.

[94] Grosso, M. (1992) *Frontiers of the Soul*. Quest Books. Ch.5.

[95] Lame Deer and R. Erdoes. *Lame Deer Seeker of Visions*. New York: Simon and Schuster, 1972.

[96] Published in 1824 and reprinted by Arno Press in 1975.

[97] Green, C. and C. McCreery. *Apparitions*. New York: St. Martin's Press, 1975.

[98] Richmond, Z. *Evidence of Purpose*. London: G. Bell, 1938.

[99] Van Dusen, W. *The Presence of Other Worlds*. New York: Harper & Row, 1974.

[100] See Bernard Beitman's mind-opening study, *Connecting With Coincidence*. 2015

[101] Delaney, J. J., ed. *A Woman Clothed With Sun*. New York: Image Books, 1961.

[102] Pelletier, J. A. *Our Lady Comes to Garabandal*. Worcester, Mass.: Assumption Publication, 1971.

[103] See Whitmont, *The Return of the Goddess*; and Stern, *Flight From Women*.

[104] Maunder, C. *Our Lady of the Nations*: Apparitions of Mary in 20th Century Catholic Europe. Oxford University Press.

[105] Rosenberg, K. Peacemakers and soldier girls. *The Nation* (April 14, 1984).

[106] Ibid. Pelletier

[107] There is enough about this on the internet for readers to decide for themselves about the phenomenon. To my mind, the alleged "scientific" explanation is totally worthless.

[108] Rogo, D. S. *Miracles*. New York: Dial Press, 1982.

[109] Tadros, M. B. *Forty Miracles of the Lady Virgin*. Cairo: Coptic Orthodox Church, 1976.

[110] Ring, K. *Heading Toward Omega*. New York: William Morrow, 1984

[111] See my *Millennium Myth* (1995), which shows how persistent is the dream of a grand climax of history and the recreation of the world and humanity.

[112] See the Commentary on future consciousness and the concept of supernature in *Wings of Ecstasy*, in press.

[113] The medieval thinkers emphasized the notion of saving or spiritual truth. See, for example, Bonaventure's Reduction of the Arts To Theology, p.27. 1955. St Bonaventure University, NY.

[114] See Michael Murphy's essay on panentheism in Beyond Physicalism.

[115] Chomsky, N. *Masters of Mankind: Essays and Lectures*, 1969-2013. Haymarrket Books. 2014.

[116] See Vico, G. *On the Study Methods of our Time*. New York: Bobbs-Merrill, 1965.

[117] Vico, G. *On the Most Ancient Wisdom of the Italians*. Cornell University Press (Trans. L.M. Palmer), 1988.

[118] Edmundson, M. *Self and Soul: A Defense of Ideals*. Harvard University Press, 2015.

[119] G. Vico, *On the Study Methods of Our Time*, p. xxiii.

[120] Smith, W. C. *The Meaning and End of Religion*. New York: Harper & Row, 1978.

[121] See Alexis Carrel's *The Voyage to Lourdes* (1950) for the author's eyewitness account of a complete, rapid healing of a patient on threshold of death, a healing due to intense faith and expectation.

[122] Owen, I. M. and M. Sparrow. *Conjuring Up Philip*. New York: Pocket Books, 1977.

Paperbacks also available from
White Crow Books

Jesus of Nazareth with Simon Parke—*Conversations with Jesus of Nazareth*
ISBN 978-1-907661-41-9

Thomas à Kempis with Simon Parke—*The Imitation of Christ*
ISBN 978-1-907661-58-7

Julian of Norwich with Simon Parke—*Revelations of Divine Love*
ISBN 978-1-907661-88-4

Allan Kardec—*The Spirits Book*
ISBN 978-1-907355-98-1

Allan Kardec—*The Book on Mediums*
ISBN 978-1-907661-75-4

Emanuel Swedenborg—*Heaven and Hell*
ISBN 978-1-907661-55-6

P.D. Ouspensky—*Tertium Organum: The Third Canon of Thought*
ISBN 978-1-907661-47-1

Dwight Goddard—*A Buddhist Bible*
ISBN 978-1-907661-44-0

Michael Tymn—*The Afterlife Revealed*
ISBN 978-1-970661-90-7

Michael Tymn—*Transcending the Titanic: Beyond Death's Door*
ISBN 978-1-908733-02-3

Guy L. Playfair—*If This Be Magic*
ISBN 978-1-907661-84-6

Guy L. Playfair—*The Flying Cow*
ISBN 978-1-907661-94-5

Guy L. Playfair —*This House is Haunted*
ISBN 978-1-907661-78-5

Carl Wickland, M.D.—*Thirty Years Among the Dead*
ISBN 978-1-907661-72-3

John E. Mack—*Passport to the Cosmos*
ISBN 978-1-907661-81-5

Peter & Elizabeth Fenwick—*The Truth in the Light*
ISBN 978-1-908733-08-5

Erlendur Haraldsson—*Modern Miracles*
ISBN 978-1-908733-25-2

Erlendur Haraldsson—*At the Hour of Death*
ISBN 978-1-908733-27-6

Erlendur Haraldsson—*The Departed Among the Living*
ISBN 978-1-908733-29-0

Brian Inglis—*Science and Parascience*
ISBN 978-1-908733-18-4

Brian Inglis—*Natural and Supernatural: A History of the Paranormal*
ISBN 978-1-908733-20-7

Ernest Holmes—*The Science of Mind*
ISBN 978-1-908733-10-8

Victor & Wendy Zammit —*A Lawyer Presents the Evidence For the Afterlife*
ISBN 978-1-908733-22-1

Casper S. Yost—*Patience Worth: A Psychic Mystery*
ISBN 978-1-908733-06-1

William Usborne Moore—*Glimpses of the Next State*
ISBN 978-1-907661-01-3

William Usborne Moore—*The Voices*
ISBN 978-1-908733-04-7

John W. White—*The Highest State of Consciousness*
ISBN 978-1-908733-31-3

Stafford Betty—*The Imprisoned Splendor*
ISBN 978-1-907661-98-3

Paul Pearsall, Ph.D. —*Super Joy*
ISBN 978-1-908733-16-0

All titles available as eBooks, and selected titles available in Hardback and Audiobook formats from www.whitecrowbooks.com

Lightning Source UK Ltd.
Milton Keynes UK
UKHW040806140319
339132UK00001B/156/P